D0069737

Inspiriting Influences

GENDER AND CULTURE

Carolyn G. Heilbrun and Nancy K. Miller, EDITORS

GENDER AND CULTURE

A SERIES OF COLUMBIA UNIVERSITY PRESS

Edited by Carolyn C. Heilbrun and Nancy K. Miller

Michael Awkward

INSPIRITING INFLUENCES

Tradition, Revision, and Afro-American Women's Novels

COLUMBIA UNIVERSITY PRESS · NEW YORK

An earlier version of chapter 1 appeared in *Studies in Black American Literature III: Black Feminist Criticism and Critical Theory*, edited by Joe Weixlmann and Houston A. Baker, Jr. (Greenwood, FL: Penkevill, 1988); a portion of chapter 2 appeared as "Roadblocks and Relatives: Critical Revision in Toni Morrison's *The Bluest Eye*" in *Critical Essays on Toni Morrison*, edited by Nellie McKay (Boston: G. K. Hall, 1988). Permission to use these materials is gratefully acknowledged.

Columbia University Press
New York   Oxford
Copyright © 1989 Columbia University Press
All rights reserved

Library of Congress Cataloging-in-Publication Data
Awkward, Michael.
Inspiriting influences: tradition, revision, and Afro-American
women's novels/Michael Awkward.
p.   cm. — (Gender and culture)
Bibliography: p.
Includes index.
ISBN 0-231-06806-9
1. American fiction—Afro-American authors—History and criticism.
2. American fiction—Women authors—History and criticism.
3. American fiction—20th century—History and criticism.
4. Women and literature—United States—History—20th century.
5. Afro-American women—Intellectual life.
6. Afro-American women in literature.
7. Influence (Literary, artistic, etc.)
8. Intertextuality.
I. Title. II. Series.
PS153.N5A94   1989
813'.5'099287—dc19   88-33290
CIP

Printed in the United States of America
Casebound editions of Columbia University Press books are Smyth-sewn and printed on permanent and durable acid-free paper

C10 9 8 7 6 5 4 3 2

In loving memory of my mother, Anna Marie Awkward (1929–1986), who, in her inimitable way, taught me that life is no crystal stair, and insisted, despite this daunting fact, that I keep climbing.

Contents

Acknowledgments

MANY PEOPLE have contributed, in ways I can only begin to hint at here, to the completion of this book. For their various contributions, I thank, first of all, members of the faculty of the University of Pennsylvania, where this project began, especially Peter Conn, Betsy Erkkila, Phyllis Rackin, John Roberts, and Wendy Steiner. Also, I want to thank Celeste Langan, Claire Satlof, and Thomas Yingling, whose friendship and interest in my project proved invaluable during some quite difficult stages. I thank my family—including my sisters Carol and Deborah, my brother Eric, my mother, Anna, my aunts, Mrs. Grace Tyler and Mrs. Peggy McCalla, my nephews and nieces—for loving me unconditionally and for keeping me sane. Also, I want to thank my in-laws, John and Edna Rich, for welcoming me into the clan.

I offer thanks to the University of Michigan, in particular the Center of Afroamerican and African Studies and its tireless leaders, Lemuel Johnson and Walter Allen, for providing financial support that greatly assisted my efforts to complete revisions of the manuscript. I thank Mary Bretlik for transferring the typewritten manuscript onto a computer file that made revisions much more manageable, if not necessarily easier, and Shalane Sheley, who spent hours educating me about computer word processing. Thanks also to my research assistants, Rosemarie Gooden and Charita Ford, for their efforts on my behalf.

At Columbia University Press, I owe a special debt to its Executive Editor, Jennifer Crewe, for her continued faith, and to Nancy K. Miller, co-general editor of the Gender and Culture series, who offered quite useful suggestions for improving this project at a particularly crucial time.

There are three people whose love and support I want especially to acknowledge here: my friend and mentor at the University of Pennsylvania, Houston A. Baker, Jr., who read numerous drafts of the manuscript with an unfailingly sharp and critical eye, and whose continued encouragement has been, in a word, inspiriting; Elizabeth

Kerwin, who made me read Gloria Naylor and Alice Walker, and who challenged me to think more deeply than I ever had about questions essential to my work and life; and Lauren Michelle Rich, my "kissin'-friend," confidant, my best and most exacting reader, who has believed in this project and in me at times when such faith surely did not seem warranted.

Inspiriting Influences

Introduction

"Mah Tongue is in Mah Friend's Mouf": Toward An Intertextual Reading of Afro-American Women's Novels

So in the beginning of this was a woman . . .

Zora Neale Hurston
Their Eyes Were Watching God

Obviously we will have to learn to read the Afro-American literary tradition in new ways, for continuing in the old way is impossible. In the past ten or fifteen years the crucial task of reconstruction has been carried on by a number of scholars whose work has made it possible to document black women as artists, as intellectuals, as symbol makers. The continuities of this tradition, as Hortense Spillers tells us, are broken and sporadic, but the knitting together of these fragments has begun.

Mary Helen Washington
"Introduction," *Invented Lives*

[A]ll readers, male and female alike, must be taught first to recognize the existence of a significant body of writing by women in America and, second, they must be encouraged to learn how to read it within its own unique and informing contexts of meaning and symbol. Re-visionary rereading, *if you will.*

Annette Kolodny
"Map for Rereading"

NTOZAKE SHANGE'S moving and provocative feminist choreopoem, *for colored girls who have considered suicide when the rainbow is enuf,* begins with what is perhaps the dominant image in the recent creative and critical writing of Afro-American women: the struggle to make articulate a heretofore repressed and silenced black female's story and voice. Against a backdrop of patently stereotypic misreadings of black women ("are we ghouls?/children of horror?/the joke?/ . . . are we animals? have we gone crazy?"),[1] Shange's woman in brown plaintively cries out for accurate, revelatory representations of Afro-American women's lives:

> somebody/anybody
> sing a black girl's song
> bring her out
> to know herself
> to know you . . .
> sing her song of life
> she's been dead so long
> closed in silence so long
> she doesn't know the sound
> of her own voice
> her infinite beauty . . .
> sing her sighs
> sing the song of her possibilities
> sing a righteous gospel
> the makin of a melody
> let her be born
> let her be born
> & handled warmly (2-3)

The remarkable recent outpouring of sophisticated, compelling literary works by Afro-American women writers suggests the almost life-sustaining urgency felt by black females to "sing a black girl's song." If the early 1970s Afro-American woman reader, confronted by a literary canon overwhelmingly male in its focus and authorship, was unfamiliar with "the sound/of her own voice," she most certainly has achieved (re)birth and warm handling in recent texts by such novelists as Paule Marshall, Toni Morrison, Alice Walker, Toni Cade Bambara, Sherley Anne Williams, Gloria Naylor, and Terry McMillan. Indeed, the last decade alone has witnessed the arrival of such a remarkably sophisticated body of black female expressivity that the criticism devoted to its explication has only begun to analyze in full and illuminating ways the discursive power of Afro-American women's literature. That important work has, however, indeed begun; as Mary Helen Washington has asserted, black feminist criticism at the present time can be said to "represent an effort to piece together those 'broken and sporadic' continuities that constitute black women's literary tradition."[2]

The most influential early efforts to connect the disparate pieces of an Afro-American woman's expressive tradition are found in Alice Walker's "In Search of Our Mothers' Gardens," an essay which profiles her own (and, by extension, contemporary black women writers') artistic genealogy. Walker credits black female folk artists, ancestral figures whose creativity found expression in such forms as quilting and gardening, as having "handed on [to contemporary Afro-American female writers] the creative spark."[3] Such ancestral figures, whom Walker refers to as "our mothers and grandmothers" (240), serve as important artistic precursors because of their daring and willful expression of their artistic sensibilities in the face of the obstacles of racism and sexism that had seen other black women "driven to a numb and bleeding madness by the springs of creativity in them for which there was no release" (233). These Afro-American female precursorial figures, in short, "kept alive," in previously undervalued, nonliterary, everyday use artistic forms, "the vibrant, creative spirit that the [contemporary] black woman [writer] has inherited" (239).

Walker's concern with black female genealogical connections is shared by Barbara Smith's "Towards a Black Feminist Criticism." Unlike Walker, however, whose primary focus in the aforementioned essay is the establishment of artistic connections with black female folk artisans (including her own oratorically and horticulturally skilled mother), Smith's specific concern is textual manifestation of the Afro-American woman's creative spirit, is *literary* ancestry. She insists that an essential feature of black feminist criticism must be a delineation of an Afro-American woman's literary tradition. Smith asserts:

> Black women writers constitute an identifiable literary tradition. . . . [T]heirs [is] a verifiable historical tradition that parallels in time the tradition of Black men and white women writing in this country. . . . [T]hematically, stylistically, aesthetically, and conceptually Black women writers manifest common approaches to the act of creating literature as a direct result of the specific political, social, and economic experience they have been obliged to share.[4]

For Smith, the Afro-American woman's literary tradition results from its writers' common "cultural experience" as gendered and racial outsiders in a patriarchal white American society. It is this common experience which explains, for Smith, the thematic and formal similarities between texts in the black female tradition and "results in a miraculously rich coalescing of form and content and also takes their writing far beyond the confines of white/male literary structures" (174).

As the following pages demonstrate, this study, which is an intertextual analysis of four novels in the Afro-American woman's tradition—Zora Neale Hurston's *Their Eyes Were Watching God*, Toni

Morrison's *The Bluest Eye,* Gloria Naylor's *The Women of Brewster Place,*
and Alice Walker's *The Color Purple*—is influenced in several ways by
the formulations in Smith's groundbreaking essay. I am not, however, fully in accord with her assertions about the conditions which
shape the Afro-American woman's literary tradition. I believe that
the textual affinities between black women's works generally exist
not simply as the result of a common sexual and racial oppression,
but, rather, most frequently occur as a function of black women writers' conscious acts of refiguration and revision of the earlier canonical texts.[5] In this respect, my views are closer to those of Henry Louis
Gates, Jr., who has argued about the Afro-American literary tradition
generally: "It is clear that black writers read and critique other black
texts as an act of rhetorical self-definition. Our literary tradition exists because of these precisely chartable formal literary relationships,
relationships of signifying."[6]

Such acts of authorial self-definition are necessary first steps for a
female aspiring to become a writer in what has historically been as
overwhelmingly male—and sometimes virulently misogynist—an
expressive tradition as the Afro-American literary canon. The novice
Afro-American female writer, seeking to participate in a tradition which
had until recently offered women very little in the way of accurate
representation or authorial canonization, could struggle to become a
writer "only by actively seeking a female precursor," as Sandra Gilbert and Susan Gubar—in a deft revision of Harold Bloom's
theories of male literary influence—have argued, "who . . .
proves by example that a revolt against patriarchal literary authority
is possible"[7]

In order to comprehend the contours of the black female literary
tradition where the "chartable formal literary relationships" of which
Gates speaks is concerned, it is helpful to distinguish at this point the
nature of intertextuality in the Afro-American women's novels on which
this study focuses from that which exists between male-authored canonical works. For theories which successfully describe the frequently
competitive act of writing the male self into the male canon fail to
provide adequate models for descriptions of black female literary
relationships.

Certainly the most widely known theories of canonical influence
are Harold Bloom's psychoanalytically informed studies of what he
designates "the anxiety of influence." Bloom elaborates a complex
system of Freudian defense mechanisms to describe a literary manifestation of what the Afro-American critic James Snead believes is a
general mainstream Western culture's resistance to repetition. Ac-

cording to Snead, a philosophically progress-oriented Western hegemonic culture "resists all non-progressive views [and] . . . develops," frequently by imposing, by means of willful acts of self-deception, "a character of progression and improvement onto . . . often non-progressing" phenomena.[8] For Snead, then, mainstream Western culture views repetition as a phenomenon that must be mediated in the name of progress.

Snead's discussion of a (white) Western cultural resistance to overt manifestations of repetition offers a fruitful means of understanding what Bloom describes as the problematic nature of the repetition and revision of cultural signs, codes, and figures by successive generations of Western white male poets bent on absorbing their precursors and establishing their own "non-repetitive" priority. Western culture's insistence on improvement, its intolerance in the face of nonprogressive repetition, forces writers such as the poets with whom Bloom is primarily concerned to employ various defense mechanisms in order to create what the culturally informed reader and critic will accept as "strong" texts. According to Bloom, "Strong poetry is strong by virtue of a kind of textual usurpation."[9] Such usurpation is essential for Western male writers who, in order to create strong, culturally informed work, must, through definable revisionary ratios, revolt against their literary "fathers."

It is not coincidental that Bloom's "influenced" writers are all male. For if intertextuality—by which I mean a paradigmatic system of explicit or implied repetition of, or allusion to, signs, codes, or figures within a cultural form such as the novel—is problematic in the (predominantly white male) Western literary tradition, such problems must, I believe, be seen as the function of what psychoanalytic paradigms have demonstrated is the competitive nature of male identity formation. Indeed, it is possible to characterize this psychodrama of Euro-American male artistic maturation as, in the words of the feminist critic Judith Kegan Gardiner, the novice "boy" writer's attempt to "become a separate, autonomous individual, like his [literary] father."[10]

A general emphasis on male gender identity as a means of explaining an anxiety of literary influence seems quite appropriate, for Bloom's paradigm of violent verbal revision accurately describes not only white male-authored poetic texts, but is also useful in an analysis of canonical literary works by Afro-American men. Indeed, two black critics, Gates and Robert Stepto, see a revisionist tendency in the Afro-American canon that leads to oedipal linguistic battles in which black (predominantly male) writers attempt strenuously to overthrow the

theories of Black life and fiction held by their precursors, striving
always to establish their own priority. Gates, for example, discusses
the parodic intertextual—or, *signifying*, to use the Afro-American vernacular term that describes ritualistic verbal jousting—relationship
between Richard Wright's *Native Son* and Ralph Ellison's *Invisible
Man:*

> Ellison in his fictions signifies upon Wright by parodying Wright's
> literary structures through repetition and difference. . . . The
> play of language . . . starts with the titles: Wright's *Native Son*
> and *Black Boy*, connoting race, self and presence, Ellison tropes
> with *Invisible Man*, invisibility an ironic response, of absence, to
> the would-be presence of "blacks" and "natives". . . . Wright's
> reacting protagonist, voiceless to the last, Ellison signifies upon
> with a nameless protagonist. Ellison's protagonist is nothing but
> voice, since it is he who shapes, edits, and narrates his own
> tale . . . (293)

According to Gates, the goal of what he defines as cultural signifying is a criticism by Ellison of Wright's use of naturalism as both
a literary and a life-interpretive device. Gates asserts:

> By explicitly repeating and reversing key figures of Wright's fic-
> tion, . . . Ellison exposed Wright's naturalism as merely a
> hardened conventional representation of "the Negro problem,"
> and perhaps part of "the Negro problem" itself. . . . Ellison re-
> corded a new way of seeing and defined both a new manner of
> representation and its relation to the concept of presence. (294)

Ellison's signifying, then, like the revisionary gestures delineated
by Bloom, is considered by Gates progress-oriented. Implicit in the
discussion adduced by Gates is his assumption that Ellison strives
for not only a "new way of seeing" and representing Afro-American
life, but a *better* way. Ellison is, thus, defined as clearing imaginative
space for himself and his novel by attempting to negate, through intertextual signifying, the accuracy and importance of Wright's
achievement.

The intertextual relationship between Afro-American women's novels differs markedly from the Western male systems of canonical repetition and revision. While male texts in the Afro-American canon follow a traditionally Western male pattern of textual competition,
women's novels seem to form a more harmonious system, characterized aptly by Alice Walker's almost obsessive efforts to "save" Zora
Neale Hurston's texts and personal history from obscurity, efforts

which include a search for and placing of a tombstone upon the precursor's unmarked grave. Indeed, Walker's textual relationship with Hurston lends quite compelling support to Gilbert and Gubar's claims concerning female literary influence. When, for example, Walker speaks about becoming "aware of my need of Zora Neale Hurston's work some time before I knew her work existed" (83) and discusses her temporarily debilitating fear of being met by the type of condemnatory, largely masculinist responses to which Hurston's life and corpus had previously been subjected, it is possible to perceive of Walker's act as a self-conscious search for a rebellious and successful Afro-American female literary precursor. That is to say, Hurston provides for the younger writer not only specific models of what Walker has termed "womanist" figurations of Afro-American life, but, as importantly, an immensely talented example who "proves," in Gilbert and Gubar's words, "that revolt against patriarchal literary authority is possible" (49). According to Gilbert and Gubar, "The woman writer . . . searches for a female model not because she wants dutifully to comply with male definitions of her 'femininity' but because she must legitimize her own rebellious endeavors" (50).

Judith Gardiner's assertions that the differences between male and female identity "traits have far-reaching consequences for the distinctive nature of writing by women" (183), then, seem, where the Afro-American literary tradition is concerned, quite accurate. Unlike the novice black male writer concerned with usurping his black male precursor, the Afro-American woman writer attempts to establish with her female predecessor the type of positive symbiotic merger which, according to Gardiner, Nancy Chodorow, and others, characterizes the patterns of female identity formation. Thus, while the male, socialized to believe that independence and autonomy are signs of maturity's achievement, sees writing as yet another area in which he must attempt to establish his priority over male parental figures, the female, who has been taught to "develop capacities for nurturance, dependence, and empathy" (182) in her relationship with her mother, views the creation of fiction as an occasion for cooperative textual interactions with maternal figures.[11]

The sense of legitimacy which Hurston provides for Walker or, for that matter, Hurston and especially Toni Morrison provide for Gloria Naylor, results from what Gilbert and Gubar call "unique bonds that link women in what we might call the secret sisterhood of their literary subculture" (51). It is this sense of bonding, of energetic explorations for and embrasure of black female precursorial figures, which distinguishes the Afro-American women's novels that are explored in the following chapters from competitive black male intertextual relations. Instead of an anxiety of influence, in other words, this study argues that these novels constitute a textual system characterized by what I call "inspiriting influences." Even when the younger female writer presents perspectives that are apparently critical of or antithetical to those of the precursor—Gloria Naylor's deconstruction of *The Bluest Eye*'s narrative strategies, Alice Walker's delineations of the achievement of (comm)unity in response to its ultimately quite dubious possibilities in *Their Eyes Were Watching God*—such perspectives are offered as supplemental to, and made possible by, the precursor's courageous example. In these novels, it is clear that, as Gilbert and Gubar argue about nineteenth-century white female influence, the black female precursor represents not "a threatening force to be denied or killed" (49), but a literary forebear whose texts are celebrated even as they are revised, praised for their insights even when these insights are deemed inadequate to describe more contemporary manifestations of Afro-American women's peculiar challenges in a racist and sexist society.

In addition to non-expropriating refigurations of precursorial texts, the system of Afro-American women's novels with which I am concerned here is revisionary in its adaptations of the Western genre of the novel to reflect Black cultural imperatives. Mikhail Bakhtin's discussion of the necessity of discursive appropriation serves as a means of situating the revisionary impulses which Afro-Americanist scholars have argued are generally operative in Afro-American expressive culture. Bakhtin asserts:

> Language . . . becomes "one's own" only when the speaker populates it with his own intention, his own accent, when he appropriates the word, adapting it to his own semantic and expressive intention. Prior to this moment of appropriation, the word does not exist in a neutral and impersonal language, . . . but rather it exists in other people's mouths, in other people's contexts, serving other people's intentions: it is from there that one must take the word, and make it one's own.[12]

Following my own appropriative, afrocentric impulses, I refer to this revisionary tendency in Afro-American culture as *denigration*. While the verb "denigrate" is taken by the vast majority of English speakers to mean, as *The American Heritage Dictionary* states, "To belittle or calumniate the character or reputation of; defame,"[13] my employment of the word suggests an attempt to infuse it with my "own semantic and expressive intention" by returning to the latinate word ("from *denigrare*, to blacken: *de-*, completely + *nigrare*, blacken, from *niger*, black" (352)) its original, non-pejorative meaning. It is clear that the same virulently racist perspectives that allowed whites to figure blacks as evil and other both during and after American slavery motivated the connotative transformation of the word "denigrate."

I use *denigrate* in this study to describe the remarkable appropriative impulses extant in many areas of Afro-American expressive culture, including the black women's novel. By *denigration*, I mean here precisely those appropriative acts by Afro-Americans which have successfully transformed, by the addition of black expressive cultural features, Western cultural and expressive systems to the extent that they reflect, in black "mouths" and "contexts," what we might call (in Bakhtinian terms) Afro-American "intention" and "accent."

Toni Morrison's comments about her own work suggest how Afro-Americans *denigrate* Western verbal systems. She says in "Rootedness: The Ancestor as Foundation":

> There are things that I try to incorporate into my fiction that are directly and deliberately related to what I regard as the major characteristics of Black art . . .
>
> I don't regard Black literature as simply books written by Black people, or simply as literature written about Black people, or simply as literature that uses a certain mode of language. . . . There is something very special and identifiable about it.[14]

Two of the elements of Black art Morrison utilizes in her fiction are a "participatory relationship between the artist or the speaker and the audience" (341) and a formal employment of a chorus in the narrative events or content (and, in the case of *The Bluest Eye*, the narrative strategies or form) of her texts. Using these features that are dominant in systems of Black expressivity such as music and religion, Morrison "incorporates into that traditional genre the novel, unorthodox novelistic characteristics—so that it is, in my view, Black, because it uses the characteristics of Black art" (342). In addition to establishing intertextual relationships with other Afro-American expressive systems, Morrison *denigrates* the genre of the novel by infusing it with the spirit and specific elements of an Afro-American cultural perspective.

The *denigrative* potential of Afro-American expressive systems plainly suggests that Black culture has survived its barbaric transportation to the West and manages to express its communal beliefs through

Western cultural systems that are philosophically opposed to such beliefs. It survives in a language system in which blackness is negative, absence and evil in a formal *denigration* (Black English) which adds to the English language system Black "meaning, nuance, tone and gesture."[15] It survives in a religious system (Black Religion)— despite the fact that white slaveowners justified the inhumanity of their institution by means of self-serving "interpretations" of this religion's scriptures—to which blacks have added elements of West African religions such as spiritual possession and antiphonal (call-and-response) preacher-congregation verbal interaction. And it survives in a Western literary system, the novel, as a function of the kind of generic adaptations referred to by Morrison.

Afro-American linguist Geneva Smitherman's discussion of the traditional African world view suggests the specific patterns to which the merging of opposites such as Black cultural elements and Western religious, verbal, and artistic systems should conform. She says that in Black culture,

> there is a fundamental unity between the spiritual and the material aspects of nature . . . [in which] the spiritual domain assumes priority.
>
> The universe is hierarchical in nature. . . . Though the universe is hierarchical, all modes of existence are necessary for the sustenance of its balance and rhythm. . . . Thus we have a paradigm for the way in which "opposites" function. That is, "opposites" constitute interdependent, interacting forces which are necessary for producing a given reality. (75)

Blacks in America have united Western "material" or systems with Black expressive elements to create Afro-American systems in their forms recognizably Western, but dominated by Black cultural "spirit" or essence.

This *denigration*, this infusion of Black cultural "spirit" into Western "matter" which alters that matter in essential ways, occurs quite interestingly in the novels that the following chapters explore. Earlier I alluded to Morrison's statement that the use of a chorus in her work is one of the ways in which she incorporates into her fiction major characteristics of Black expressivity. The "chorus" in *The Bluest Eye*—which Morrison states is the first-person narrator of the novel, Claudia—in fact plays an integral part in the structure of the novel itself. Because Morrison wants both a presence which empathizes with the novel's tragic protagonist, Pecola Breedlove, and a narrative scope capable of delineating the past of its adult characters, she employs two narrators in *The Bluest Eye:* Claudia, Pecola's contemporary, who narrates the story of both Pecola's and her own experiences, and an omniscient narrator who relates the incidents in the novel of which Claudia is unaware. The result is the intricately woven text which contains, in addition to two narrators, two prologues, four sections— "Fall," "Winter," "Spring," and "Summer"—each of which is subdivided into three chapters, of which Claudia narrates the first and the omniscient narrator the following two. Not only, then, can appropriative acts add "unorthodox novelistic characteristics" to a novel's content, but they can also help dictate the "unconventional" narration and structures of Black texts.

Literary critics have observed a general authorial fascination with intricate structure (the "matter") in Afro-American novels, and have attempted to account for its presence. Raymond Hedin's "The Structuring of Emotion in Black American Fiction" offers a case in point, suggesting a link between Afro-American novelists' manipulations of structure and strategic attempts to encode in their texts a racial anger that is a function of oppression in America. Hedin argues that Morrison's narrative strategy in *The Bluest Eye* is a means for the author to call attention to her own personal anger:

> In Toni Morrison's *The Bluest Eye* . . . the central character, Pecola Breedlove, is too vulnerable and uncomprehending to be angry at what happens to her. It is Morrison who is angry, and the careful form of the novel intensifies rather than deflects the reader's sense of that anger.[16]

While some implicit relationship may exist in Afro-American texts between structure and anger (the existence of verbal indirection in such Black verbal behaviors as signifying and spirituals suggests that blacks do encode anger), a more convincing interpretation of the cultural codes employed in Morrison's novel insists that other cultural phenomena account for *The Bluest Eye*'s structural complexity. Hedin correctly observes the eventual fate of the protagonist—"she can achieve peace only by retreating into schizophrenia" (50)—but he fails to draw any connection between Pecola's psychological splitting into two voices and the double-voiced narration of the novel. We could read the lonely, isolated girl's schizophrenia in the ways that Morrison's comments about her novel suggest—that is, as Pecola's desperate manufacturing of a "chorus" to respond to what, in her insanity, she believes to be "The bluest eyes in the whole world."[17] But the dual voices of narrator and protagonist are also, in fact, coded intertexts of W. E. B. Du Bois' discussion of a Black "double con-

sciousness" in *The Souls of Black Folk*. Morrison's narrative is most
adeptly described in accordance with Du Bois' formulations. Du Bois'
much-quoted statement reads:

> It is a peculiar sensation, this double consciousness, this sense of
> always looking at one's self through the eyes of [whites]. . . . One
> ever feels his twoness,—an American, a Negro; two souls, two
> thoughts, two unreconciled strivings; two warring ideals in one
> dark body, whose dogged strength alone keeps it from being torn
> asunder.
>
> The history of the American Negro is the history of this strife,—
> this longing . . . to merge his double self into a better and truer
> self. In this merging he wishes neither of the older selves to be
> lost. He would not Africanize America. . . . He would not bleach
> his Negro soul in a flood of white Americanism. . . . He simply
> wishes to make it possible for a man to be both a Negro and an
> American.[18]

According to Du Bois, it is the merging of the binary opposites
"spirit" and "matter" for which the Afro-American strives. Morrison's double-voiced narration in *The Bluest Eye* encodes not the anger
of the author as Hedin argues, but her employment and refiguration
of this Black cultural code. Pecola's means of achieving peace—double voicedness—is Morrison's means, through the complexity of her
narrative structure, of positioning her novel in relationship to other
Afro-American texts that explicitly explore *structural* means of merging two almost antithetical "selves." *The Bluest Eye* resonates in the
company of Du Bois' *Souls* and Zora Neale Hurston's *Their Eyes Were
Watching God*.

Indeed, while Morrison's novel is an intertext of a number of works
(Du Bois and Ellison come immediately to mind), its primary precursor is *Their Eyes Were Watching God*. In fact, Hurston's work is
positioned vis-à-vis contemporary Afro-American women's novels as
what Michel Foucault calls an "initiator of discursive practices."[19]
Hurston's novel not only refigures the dual consciousness code defined by Du Bois, but also delineates strategies that lead to a unity
between the "selves" of its protagonist. Foucault says of discursive
initiators: their "distinctive contribution . . . is that they produced
not only their own work, but the possibilities and the rules of formation of other texts" (131).

The following study suggests that Hurston's position as initiator of
an Afro-American woman's tradition in novels can be seen in subsequent Afro-American women writers' refigurations of Hurston's

complex delineation of black female unity in *Their Eyes Were Watching God* in their novels' content and form. Hurston's thematic focus and narrative strategies are consistent with her refiguration of Du Bois' double consciousness code in the content of her novel and represent most elaborately her response to the formulations of the esteemed black male writer and her *denigration* of the genre of the novel.

Janie's double consciousness results from her husband Joe Starks' insistence on her silent subservience. She is able to merge her dual selves, her "inside" and "outside," only through an immersion in the wisdom of Black culture. While the text confirms unquestionably that Janie has gained a cultural voice and is quite capable of narrating her story, such a narration, despite Janie's announcement to Pheoby that she will tell her own tale, does not occur in the text. As I will discuss more fully in chapter 1, Janie refrains from such narration because of the same cultural imperatives that allow her to feel no compulsion to tell her story to the females who contemptuously see her return to Eatonville in the novel's initial scene. Janie is uninterested in her personal narration of her tale: she trusts her friend Pheoby to narrate it accurately for her. She says to Pheoby: "You can tell 'em what Ah says if you wants to. Dat's just de same as me 'cause *mah tongue is in mah friend's mouf.*"[20] What is important to Janie is not individual textual control, but that the narrator of her story be a "friend" upon whom she can "depend . . . for a good thought" (19). Just as Janie gives Pheoby permission to tell her story to the town's hostile female community, she allows the text's omniscient narrator—whose sensitive rendering of Janie's tale makes it apparent that she shares Janie's afrocentric and feminist inclinations—to tell her Afro-American feminist story to a potentially hostile reading public.

The figure of a common (female) tongue, of a shared Afro-American woman's authorial voice, serves as an appropriate metaphor not only for Janie and Pheoby's cooperative textual relationship, but also for the Afro-American women novelists' textual system which is explored in this study. The following chapters examine the status of Hurston's *Their Eyes Were Watching God* as initiator of discursive practices in order to demonstrate some of the significant ways in which this novel has influenced contemporary Afro-American women novelists. This study, then, seeks to demonstrate, with reference to a small segment of the Afro-American woman's literary corpus, the accuracy of Barbara Smith's claim that "Black women writers constitute an identifiable literary tradition." *Their Eyes Were Watching God, The Bluest Eye, The Women of Brewster Place,* and *The Color Purple* certainly all represent important texts in any assessment of that tradition. Taken together, they form, in their complex figurations of self-division, a cooperative system of textual sharing, each portraying, by means of double-voiced strategies of narration, Afro-American female protagonists' efforts to end delibitating psychological disjunction (or double consciousness) and isolation from the larger black community. The four novels upon which I focus here delineate, in other words, a common Afro-American woman's quest for (psychic and narrative) unity and community (or what I refer to as (comm)unity).

What follows in these pages is one black male's contribution to the immensely important project which Mary Helen Washington describes, in one of the epigraphs to this Introduction, as "the knitting together" of the "continuities" of the Afro-American woman's literary tradition. My perceptions of the tradition's continuities are informed not only by an emerging black feminist criticism, but also by advances in contemporary critical theory and in the study of Afro-American expressive culture that have been coterminous with black feminist criticism's development. It is my hope that the convergence of and interplay between such perspectives provide an interpretive tapestry adequate to the explication of the aesthetically complex and ideologically challenging novels of Afro-American women.

1

"The Inaudible Voice Of It All": Silence, Voice, and Action in *Their Eyes Were Watching God*

> . . . *if we look at it squarely, the Negro is a very original being. While he lives and moves in the midst of a white civilisation, everything that he touches is re-interpreted for his own use. He has modified the language, mode of food preparation, practice of medicine, and most certainly the religion of his new country, just as he adapted to suit himself the Sheik hair-cut made famous by Rudolph Valentino.*

> Zora Neale Hurston
> "Characteristics of Negro Expression"

> *There is enough self-love in that one book* [Their Eyes Were Watching God]*—love of community, culture, traditions— to restore a world. Or create a new one.*

> Alice Walker
> "On Refusing To Be Humbled By Second Place"

DESPITE THE varying ideological persuasions of its authors, recent criticism of Zora Neale Hurston's *Their Eyes Were Watching God* has been almost unanimous in its assumption that Janie Crawford achieves a powerful and independent cultural voice as a result of her experiences. Critics also agree that Janie's achievement of voice is, unquestionably, a key factor in her eventual self-possession. Barbara Johnson, for example, argues that "Janie's increasing ability to speak grows out of her ability not to mix inside with outside."[1] In a similar vein, Cheryl Wall suggests that "Janie's self-discovery depends on her learning to manipulate language. Her success is announced in the novel's prologue when, as a friend listens in rapt attention, Janie begins to tell her own story."[2] A third example of the conflation of achieved voice and studied self-possession is offered by Missy Dehn Kubitschek, who believes that Janie "discovers her own soul only through the art of storytelling, thus intimating the artist's responsibility to, and dependence on, the larger community."[3]

Though essays focused on Janie's storytelling as a key to her self-definition are richly suggestive, such essays uniformly fail to acknowledge that despite an undeniable emphasis in the novel on the importance of the protagonist's achievement of voice, she does not seem at all enamored of her oratorical skills when she makes her final return to Eatonville. When Pheoby tells her that the female porch sitters are discussing her return and suggests that she " 'better make haste and tell 'em 'bout you and Tea Cake,' " Janie answers: " 'Ah don't mean to bother wid tellin' 'em nothin', Pheoby. 'Tain't worth de trouble.' "[4] She, thus, seems uninterested in becoming a public spokesperson sharing the wisdom of hard-won cultural experience with the group. Later, when she has completed a private narration of her story to Pheoby, she clarifies her perspective on the porch sitters who have "got me up in they mouth":

> Let 'em consolate theyselves wid talk. 'Course, talkin' don't amount tuh a hill uh beans when yuh can't do nothin' else. And listenin' tuh dat kind uh talk is jus' lak openin' yo' mouth and lettin' de moon shine down yo' throat. (285)

While Janie's statement expresses impatience at being the topic of town gossip, the very extremity of her view of "talkin' " and "tellin' " suggested by the statement seems inconsistent for the character presented in the novel. Not only does Janie appear to dislike the obvious malevolence of the porch critics, she also seems to issue a general condemnation of verbal performances that are not (and *cannot be*) supported by appropriate action. In other words, she claims to dislike talk for talk's sake.

Earlier in her life, however, Janie very much enjoyed listening to such talk. The narrative tells us:

> When the people sat around on the porch [of the store] and passed around the pictures of their thoughts for the others to look at and see, it was nice. The fact that the thought pictures were always crayon enlargements of life made it even nicer [for Janie] to listen to. (81)

Clearly, Janie has not always desired that words be complemented by action. In fact, for the greater part of her life, she wishes no such correspondence, for verbal exaggeration made the store porch expressivity "even nicer to listen to." For example, Janie enjoys Sam and Lige's ongoing argument that "was a contest in hyperbole and carried on for no other reason" (99). She also responds enthusiastically to Jim and Dave's "acting out courtship" of Daisy (105). Ap-

parently, then, her views with respect to unauthenticated (i.e., by action) voice are altered radically when, after Tea Cake's death, she
returns to Eatonville.

Perhaps the best evidence of her transformed perspective is the narration of Hurston's novel. First introduced by an omniscient narrator,
Janie insists that she will serve in the role of storyteller in order to
relate to Pheoby the important incidents of her life. These incidents
will include, apparently, not only her sojourn with Tea Cake during
the preceding year and a half, but also enough information about her
entire history to provide Pheoby, a "kissin'-friend" (19) of twenty years,
with "de understandin' to go 'long wid" her depiction of her life with
Tea Cake. In a text which concentrates so intensely on the question
of Janie's establishment of a powerful black cultural voice, one feels
that such a concentration should be complemented by action. Janie,
indeed, should narrate her own story in the novel. Because she expresses such a strong perspective on action and voice and, yet, fails
to emerge as the exclusive—or even the primary—narrator of her
story, *Their Eyes Were Watching God* seems flawed (as numerous critics whom I will later cite have claimed) in ways that diminish the
overall effectiveness of Hurston's novel.

In the discussion that follows, I shall attempt to show that Hurston's narrative strategies demonstrate not a failure of the novelist's
art, but her stunning success in *denigrating* the genre of the novel. To
show how the author accomplishes her task, it is necessary first to
discuss narrative events in *Their Eyes Were Watching God*. In the novel,
there exists an observable tension between saying (words) and doing
(acting upon those words)—between voice and action. The tension
between the two is most clearly represented in the philosophies of
life, or "texts," of the three most influential figures in Janie's development: Nanny, Joe Starks, and Vergible "Tea Cake" Woods.

II

IN ITS introduction of the young Janie, *Their Eyes Were Watching God*
makes the reader acutely aware of the protagonist's spirituality. This
spirituality is evident in the edenic scene in which she discovers her
sexuality. The language of the scene insists that she literally has been
summoned by nature:

> It had called her to come and gaze on a mystery. From barren
> stem to glistening leaf-buds; from the leaf-buds to snowy virgin-
> ity of bloom. It stirred her tremendously. How? Why? It was like

a flute song forgotten in another existence and remembered again.
What? How? Why? *This singing she heard had nothing to do with
her ears . . .*

   She was stretched on her back beneath the pear tree soaking
in the alto chant of the visiting bees, the gold of the sun and the
panting breath of the breeze when the *inaudible voice of it all*
came to her. She saw a dust-bearing bee sink into the sanctum
of a bloom; the thousand sister-calyxes arch to meet the love embrace and the ecstatic shiver of the tree from root to tiniest branch
creaming in every blossom and frothing with delight. *So this was
a marriage! She had been summoned to behold a revelation.* Then
Janie felt a pain remorseless sweet that left her limp and languid.
(23-24, my emphasis)

This scene has been viewed in the criticism of the novel as Janie's
sexual awakening.[5] What interests me most about this scene, however, is a physically active nature's role as Janie's instructor, especially the manner in which this instructor communicates its "text"
to her. Nature's text is not limited strictly to the sensual. To be sure,
the passage cited does describe, beautifully, the reproductive activities of natural entities. But to decode fully the densely figurative language of the scene, it is necessary to concentrate on nature's *mode* of
communication. This "inaudible voice"—that which makes a young
Janie's experience comprehensible—is the function not of sounds (the
text clearly indicates that the intelligible voice she experiences "had
nothing to do with her ears"), but, rather, of *actions*. In fact, Hurston's depiction of the natural world suggests what appears to be her
view of an organic, precultural, prelinguistic relationship between voice
and action. Before man established complex symbolic systems of
sounds, the passage suggests, action possessed a generative relationship to interpretable messages or to what the novel's narrative labels
an "inaudible voice." The type of relationship between voice and action designated is inconceivable in a spoken-language dominated human community, for such communities rely on sounds (and written
representations of these sounds) to encode and convey interpretable
meaning. The designated relationship is even more improbable in Afro-
American culture which was created during a period when the actions of the vast majority of its inhabitants were controlled and commercially exploited by white slaveowners. During the formation of
Afro-American culture, then, action represented for blacks the anti-
pode of their will and their "voice"—a voice encoded and audible in
secular songs and spirituals that have survived to express Afro-American resistance to the institution of slavery.

Janie's natural education offers an example of a relation between voice and action that is quite different than what exists in her own culture. Because she observed this precultural phenomenon, Janie is likened to the first human before the creation of his mate. Adam is the original connector of signifieds and signifiers. As Genesis informs us, "whatsoever Adam called every living creature, that was the name thereof" (2:19). By interpreting the significance of God's creation of Eve from one of his ribs, moreover, Adam defines the parameters of ideal human coupling or marriage. He says of the newly created Eve:

> This is now bone of my bones, and flesh of my flesh: she shall be called Woman, because she was taken out of Man.
> Therefore shall a man leave his father and his mother and shall cleave unto his wife: and they shall be one flesh. (2:23-24)

Adam's act is, in a semiotic sense, the first act in the creation of culture. He assigns symbolic designations to animals, to females, and to abstract concepts such as marriage.

While Janie does not herself create names, she is able in her ahistorical backyard to observe what God originally intended marriage to be. After such observation, she searches the yard for a being she can hold in an "ecstatic" "love embrace." As the text suggests, she is "seeking confirmation of the voice and vision" of nature she has experienced. Such confirmation, however, eludes her within the yard's boundaries. She envisions herself as Adam—a signal creation without a mate. While she is "looking, waiting, breathing short with impatience," she observes a being she can passionately embrace:

> Through pollinated air she saw a glorious being coming up the road. In her former blindness she had known him as shiftless Johnny Taylor, tall and lean. That was before the golden dust of pollen had beglamored his rags and her eyes. (25)

Clearly, Janie's "pollinated" perception of Johnny Taylor is faulty. She views him in a manner that is inconsistent with her knowledge of his character. In her intense desire for a mate, Johnny becomes for Janie a man without a history. But while the elements of her garden—bees, flowers, trees—may be ahistorical, human beings cannot be.

What Hurston sets in opposition in the garden scene, then, are two images of Janie: (1) prelapsarian, precultural human being, and (2) prophet in a fallen world summoned to behold a "revelation." The language describing the protagonist's sexual awakening intentionally recalls the first chapter of Genesis, but this implicit reference is ultimately undercut. For the text makes it abundantly clear that the world outside Janie's yard is not a new one, nor is it an ahistorical one. And Janie—despite her intimate knowledge of the original conception of marriage and the precultural relationship between voice and action—is not the first human. The novel suggests, in fact, that the postures of priority and originality are inappropriate in an obviously fallen world.

In "Characteristics of Negro Expression," Hurston writes:

> It is obvious that to get back to original sources is much too difficult for any group to claim very much as a certainty. What we really mean by originality is the modification of ideas. The most ardent admirer of the great Shakespeare cannot claim first source even for him. It is his treatment of the borrowed material.[6]

While Afro-Americans as a group cannot "get back to original sources" in order to reestablish culturally the primary relationship between voice and action, Janie, in her role as summoned prophet, is still able to observe this original association.

For Hurston, culture can be viewed as an adaptation of the principles of nature for social purposes. Such adaptations are apparent in Afro-Americans' conflations of the primary relationship between voice and action. In the essay cited above, Hurston says of the Afro-American's modification of the English language:

> [The Afro-American's] very words are action words. His interpretation of the English language is in terms of pictures. One act described in terms of another. Hence the rich metaphor and simile. . . . Frequently the Negro, even with detached words in his vocabulary—not evolved in him but transplanted on his tongue by contact—must add action to it to make it do. So we have 'chop-axe,' 'sitting-chair,' 'cook-pot' and the like because the speaker has in mind the picture of the object in use. Action. Everything illustrated. So we can say the white man thinks in a written language and the Negro thinks in hieroglyphics.[7]

According to Hurston, Afro-American vernacular discourse conflates the properties of voice and action to produce "action words." This conflation is an attempt on the part of Afro-Americans to "add action" to words such as "chair" which are detached from their function (and, in Hurston's conception, their "pictures") and appear, consequently, completely arbitrary designations. The word "chair," for example, does not suggest what the thing does, but is simply the term that speakers of the English language have agreed to employ when referring to (as Hurston puts it) "that-which-we-squat-on." Afro-

American vernacular discourse, then, attempts to display, as in the case of the seemingly redundant compound word "sitting-chair," the original relation between arbitrary signifier (acoustic image or "voice") and "picture" and/or function (action).

The relationship between voice and action that exists in Black vernacular discourse differs, in interesting ways, from what Hurston presents as their primary, precultural relation. In Janie's backyard experience, the action of natural entities produces (inaudible) voice, and furthermore, the protagonist is herself able to connect the signifier "marriage" to its original design (and is, because of her knowledge, unable to be satisfied in her "unnatural" marriages to her first two husbands). In its precultural manifestation, then, voice exists as a means of categorizing action. In Afro-American vernacular discourse, on the other hand, the properties of action (cook-pot, chop-axe) are added to apparently disconnected, arbitrary signifiers in an attempt to re-connect voice (that is, what an object *is called*) and action (what an object *is* or *does*). So, while voice performed a precultural function of categorizing action, we find in Afro-American vernacular an attempt to reconnect acoustic image to the object's function, to eliminate, if you will, the arbitrariness of the signifier.

Afro-American culture is not able to reestablish the primary relationship between voice and action. Despite its best efforts, humanity cannot, as Hurston insists in "Characteristics of Negro Expression," return to origins. What human beings do instead of leading "original" lives is to develop theories (or what I will call hereafter "texts") of life that promise opportunities for fruitful living. If we apply Hurston's dictum to such texts, we know that they consist not of new ideas, but of modifications of previously conceptualized thoughts. The most poignant examples of such modifications in *Their Eyes Were Watching God* are the verbal acts of the Eatonville community as a whole which suggest that this community privileges voice over action, and the strategically prepared and articulated texts that others—particularly her grandmother Nanny and her second husband Joe Starks—impose upon Janie.

III

MARIA TAI Wolff's essay on *Their Eyes Were Watching God* persuasively argues that Janie's oppression is a function initially of the passivity with which she acquiesces to the roles or texts imposed upon her by others.[8] Nanny's insistence that her granddaughter marry is the first such imposition. After viewing Janie's "lacerating" kiss of Johnny Taylor, Nanny forces her to wed Logan Killicks, a middle-aged widower whose affluence includes an "often-mentioned sixty acres" of land (38). To ensure Janie's adherence to her instructions, Nanny slaps her violently and informs her of her belief that "De nigger woman is de mule uh de world" (29). As a result of her own slave experiences, Nanny has developed a rhetoric and a pattern of living that she deems appropriate for all Afro-American women. However, she herself has been unable to realize her own goals or to share her text. Her actions, in other words, have not allowed for an expression of voice. She tells Janie:

> Ah wanted to preach a great sermon about colored women sittin' on high, but they wasn't no pulpit for me. Freedom found me wid a baby daughter in mah arms, so Ah said Ah'd take a broom and a cook-pot and throw up a highway through de wilderness for her. She would expound what Ah felt. But somehow she got lost offa de highway and next thing Ah knowed here you was in de world. So whilst Ah was tendin' you of nights Ah said Ah'd save de text for you. Ah been waitin' a long time, Janie, but nothin' Ah been through ain't too much if you just take a stand on high ground lak Ah dreamed. (31-32)

Nanny's is a text of voluntary inactivity and of "classing off" from the masses of Afro-Americans. Having survived an enslavement in which both her labor and sexuality were controlled by a white male owner, Nanny wants black women to share the leisure of their more affluent white counterparts. While her sacrifices do enable Janie's physical escape from "de white folks' yard" (37), Nanny's text evidences her unfortunate failure to liberate herself psychologically from the influence of whites. For her text is derived from the experiences of a white, southern aristocratic society in which womanhood is viewed as a docile condition and women themselves are regarded as attractive possessions.

Until she shares her text with Janie, it had gone unspoken. Her failure to articulate what she terms "a great sermon" results, as Houston Baker argues, from her inability to achieve for herself a location "on high" from which to deliver her text. Baker writes:

> She [Nanny] feels that the achievement of a "pulpit" from which to deliver such a sermon is co-extensive with the would-be preacher's obtaining actual status on high. In a sense, Nanny conflates the securing of property with effective expression. Hav-

ing been denied a say in her own fate because she was *property*, she assumes that *only* property enables expression.[9]

Nanny's perceptions, unfortunately, also deny Janie a say in her own fate.

When Janie pleads not to be forced to marry a man whose image symbolizes death for her—"He look like some old skull head in de grave yard" (28)—Nanny refuses to relent, asserting that marriage is strictly an economic arrangement: "Tain't Logan Killicks Ah wants you to have, baby, it's protection" (30). Such protection is not solely financial, to be sure. Marrying Janie to Killicks will shield her from the sexual advances of "trashy . . . breath-and-britches" men like Johnny Taylor (27). But marriage, in Nanny's economically pragmatic sense of the word, does not guarantee freedom from physical abuse. Rather, it simply limits such abuse to the province of one's own household.

When Janie approaches her grandmother for advice after her marriage to Killicks, Nanny assumes that the advice sought will concern either pregnancy or physical abuse. Janie assures her in unequivocal terms that she is not pregnant. Nanny immediately inquires: "You and Logan been fussin'? Lawd, Ah know dat grass-gut, liver-lipted nigger ain't done took and beat mah baby already!" (40) Nanny's "already" suggests her belief that such abuse is inevitable in marriage. Marriage, then, does not offer protection from physical abuse, as Janie's later beatings at the hands of Starks and Tea Cake suggest. Rather, it simply provides a social context that mitigates, in some respects, the effects of such mistreatment.

Nanny's text, however, is based on a reading of the Afro-American experience that Hurston's novel fails to support. For the narration of *Their Eyes Were Watching God* insists that for Janie: "The vision of Logan Killicks was desecrating the pear tree" (28). Nanny's "vision"—her appearance as well as her perspective on life—also profanes the image of the pear tree. The physical description of Nanny offered just after she witnesses Janie's first kiss associates her with death:

> Nanny's head and face looked like the standing roots of some old tree that had been torn away by storm. Foundation of ancient power that no longer mattered. The cooling palma christi leaves that Janie had bound about her grandma's head with a white rag had wilted down and become part and parcel of the woman. (26)

Nanny's degradation during slavery had, like a powerful storm, separated her from the type of natural view of existence witnessed in the pear tree trope. She seems to be a poison that destroys what is natural. Her experiences as a slave have effectively severed her ties to her people and her culture. She believes that Afro-Americans generally are also rootless. She tells her granddaughter: "You know, honey, us colored folks is branches without roots and that makes things come round in queer ways" (31).

The critic Lillie Howard, who offers a particularly sympathetic reading of Nanny, argues that at this point in the narrative, "Nanny's vision is clearer than Janie's." In addition, Howard insists that:

> Nanny's only flaw is that she wants to keep the romantic Janie from finding out about living for herself. . . . What Janie "comes to find out," though she never admits it in the novel, is that her grandmother . . . had seen farther than she had after all. Life is not a pear tree in bloom. For "colored folks", it's more like "branches without roots that make things come round in queer ways."[10]

While Hurston's narration displays a sensitivity to the causes of Nanny's domination of Janie, Howard mistakenly equates such sensitivity with condonement. By associating Nanny figuratively with death, the text makes it abundantly clear that her refusal to permit Janie the freedom to "find . . . out about living for herself" is not, as Howard insists, a minor flaw. Rather, it is a serious error that has disastrous results.

Hurston was undeniably critical of Afro-Americans who allowed the obvious difficulty of being black in a predominantly white society to hinder their efforts to lead fulfilling lives. In an essay entitled "How It Feels To Be Colored Me," she wrote:

> I AM NOT tragically colored. There is no great sorrow dammed up in my soul, nor lurking behind my eyes. I do not mind at all. I do not belong to the sobbing school of Negrohood who hold that nature somehow has given them a low-down dirty deal and whose feelings are all hurt about it.[11]

It would appear that Nanny—her positive qualities notwithstanding—is "tragically colored." Hers is a condition that *Their Eyes Were Watching God* suggests is akin to death. She forces Janie to live according to principles of an "ancient" text in which her granddaughter has little faith. Nanny insists that her granddaughter will eventually grow to love Killicks. But because Janie cares little for the social respectability her marriage is supposed to provide, she is never able to appreciate Killicks or his putative wealth. Compared to the active pollination that Janie witnesses in nature, Killicks and his property signify only absence and death: "It was a *lonesome* place like a *stump* in the middle of the woods where *nobody* had ever been. The house was *absent* of flavor, too. But anyhow Janie went on inside to wait for love to begin" (39, my emphasis).

Predictably, her patience remains unrewarded. Sixty acres and two mules—almost twice the amount promised by Reconstruction—do not encourage Janie. And after Nanny's death, she feels betrayed: "The familiar people and things had failed her so she hung over the gate and looked up the road towards way off. She knew now that marriage did not make love. Janie's first dream was dead, so she became a woman" (44). After this realization, Janie leaves Killicks for Joe Starks, "a cityfied, stylish dressed man" (46) who insists that "he would be a big ruler of things [in the all-black town of Eatonville] with her reaping the benefits" (50).

In many respects, Starks' text closely resembles Nanny's insofar as it includes a place on high for Janie. During their brief courtship, Starks promises Janie a leisurely existence. When she informs him that her first husband has "gone tuh buy a mule fuh me tuh plow," he says:

> You behind a plow! You ain't got no mo' business wid uh plow than uh hog is got wid uh holiday! . . . A pretty doll baby lak you is made to sit on de front porch and rock and fan yo'self and eat p'taters dat other folks plant just special for you. (49)

Starks persuades Janie to abandon Killicks by promising to show her "what it was to be treated lak a lady" (50). When she hesitates, he tells her reassuringly: "leave de s'posing and everything else to me" (50). After Killicks orders her to "come help me move dis manure pile befo' de sun gits hot" (52), she makes her way to Starks who, she quickly learns, desires quite literally to make decisions for her. When they reach Eatonville and Starks begins to implement the capitalist economic concepts he had learned while working for successful white businessmen, the townspeople organize a party to welcome the newly elected mayor and his wife to their town. One of the men calls for "uh few words uh encouragement from Mrs. Mayor Starks" (69). Joe summarily interjects: "Thank you fuh yo' compliments, but mah wife don't know nothin' 'bout no speech makin'. Ah never married her for nothin' lak dat. She's uh woman and her place is in de home" (69).

Starks has chosen for Janie a psychologically and physically limited role—that of "wife"—which does not include public speaking.

In a community whose dominant social doctrines insist that "good" women are pliable possessions—a position reflected in the statement of another townsman who thanks Starks for providing Eatonville with "yo' beloved wife, yo' store, yo' land" (67)—Janie's exhibition of an independent voice would necessarily undermine Starks' authority. Cheryl Wall comments: "Joe assigns her the role of "Mrs. Mayor Starks'. She must hold herself apart from the townspeople, conduct herself according to the requirements of his position. Under no circumstances must she speak in public" (386).

While Starks' text is sophisticated and socially updated, his plans for Janie are not dissimilar to Nanny's. Nanny lacks a pulpit and the leisure to deliver her sermon to a larger community; her sole audience is Janie whom she, in effect, physically subdues to secure her attention. Starks, however, is able to implement, on a larger social scale, the principles of his capitalist text. Eatonville becomes the personification of his vision. Starks—Mayor, postmaster, storekeeper— is in Eatonville *the big voice* and literally its only figure of authority. He is not only a "big voice," however, but is an extremely effective executor of that voice. More than anybody else in *Their Eyes Were Watching God*, Starks is characterized by an ability to coordinate voice and action. His accomplishment of a big voice is, in fact, a function of deeds. This conflation nominally recalls the primary relationship between voice and action. But Starks perverts that relation by executing a self-oriented text that denies others self-determined action and voice.

Janie eventually recognizes the immutability of Starks' text and the utter impossibility of achieving satisfactory pollination in a marriage where her status is that of a voiceless, obedient servant. As when Starks insists that she is devoid of oratorical skills, his dominance takes "the bloom off of" the relationship (70). No more capable than the other townspeople of physically resisting the commands of her husband, Janie, who once believed in the necessity of coordinating thought or "inaudible voice" and appropriate action, detaches herself psychologically from the role that Starks imposes upon her.

When Afro-Americans—both during and after slavery—have been powerless to resist the commands of those who have been institutionally more powerful, they have, in the words of Paul Laurence Dunbar's best known poem, assumed a grinning, lying mask. This response to an inescapable oppression is reflected in the lines of a famous blues: "Got one mind for white folks to see/'Nother for what I know is me." Janie's defensive self-division after Starks violently slaps her results from a similar feeling of powerlessness. She:

. . . stood where he left her for unmeasured time and thought. She stood there until something fell off the shelf inside her. Then she went inside there to see what it was. It was her image of Jody tumbling down and shattered. But looking at it she saw that it never was the flesh and blood figure of her dreams. Just something she had grabbed up to drape her dreams over. In a way she turned her back upon the image where it lay and looked further. She had no blossomy openings dusting pollen over her man, neither any glistening young fruit where the petals used to be. She found that she had a host of thoughts she had never expressed to him, and numerous emotions she had never let Jody know about. Things packed up and put away in parts of her heart where he could never find them. She was saving up feelings for some man she had never known. She had an inside and an outside now and suddenly she knew how not to mix them. (112-13)

Janie's experiences have informed her, painfully, that it is dangerous to correlate observable (outside) action and inaudible (inside) voice in a situation where cooperation and true pollination are absent.

This is a striking passage, one which exhibits Hurston's masterful control of language as well as her ability imaginatively to encode the black cultural trope of double consciousness. Barbara Johnson's essay "Metaphor, Metonymy and Voice in *Their Eyes Were Watching God*" offers a provocative explication of the passage's figurative language:

just after the slap, Janie is standing, thinking, until something "fell off the shelf inside her." Janie's "inside" is here represented as a store that she goes in to inspect. . . . [H]ere we find an internalization of the outer: Janie's inner self resembles a store. The material for this metaphor is drawn from the narrative world of contiguity: the store is the place where Joe has set himself up as lord, master, and proprietor. But here Jody's image is broken, and reveals itself never to have been a metaphor but only a metonymy of Janie's dream: "looking at it she saw that it never was the flesh and blood figure of her dreams. Just something she had grabbed up to drape her dreams over." (211-12)

Johnson's reading of this key scene in Hurston's novel brilliantly decodes the compelling images employed to signify the beginnings of Janie's self-conscious self-division.

Johnson's reading, limited as it is to the figurative, fails, however, to identify an equally important historical significance for Hurston's scene. Starks is able to "set himself up as lord, master, and proprietor" everywhere in Eatonville, and not just in his general store. His power in Eatonville approximates the white man's almost total institutional control of America. In Eatonville at least, if nowhere else in America, a black man is "de ruler of everything." Hurston's figurative representation of Janie's inside as Starks' store wherein the mayor's image is "broken" signals Janie's very Afro-American refusal of an oppressor's proprietorship.

Hurston's concern, then, is not just tropological, but also historical. Starks' capitalist text is derived from theories that whites used to justify the commodification of blacks. Just as whites justified their "peculiar institution" and subsequent others that purposely oppressed Afro-Americans through theories of black cognitive and (ironically) moral inferiority, so, too, Starks justifies his virtual enslavement of Janie. He insists that she can "see ten things and don't understand one" (111). By escaping psychologically, if not physically, from Starks' influence and denial of her humanity, Janie follows in the tradition of tens of millions of Afro-Americans who, though powerless to end their servitude, nonetheless exhibited undeniable courage by employing a type of silent revolution.

Janie's self-division results from her erudition in the principles of lying sessions and mock courtships. These verbal rituals suggest to her that there need not be a correspondence between thought, or "inaudible voice," and action. Her self-division protects her very essence from her second husband's potentially debilitating physical and verbal abuse. In effect, what results from her discovery of a necessity for self-division is a rediscovery of nature. Her new knowledge enables what might be thought of as her psychological reincarnation:

> . . . one day she sat and watched the shadow of herself going about tending store and prostrating itself before Jody, while all the time she herself sat under a shady tree with the wind blowing through her hair and her clothes. Somebody near about making summertime out of lonesomeness. (119)

By establishing—if only imaginatively—her former relationship with nature, she confirms the possibility of determining her own fate—of composing, that is to say, her own text. Her "inside" will wait under a shady tree for a man better suited than Starks to serve as her beeman.

Self-division follows from impulses like those that prompt long-suffering black Christians to divorce themselves emotionally from the degradations of their daily experiences. These Christians believe that their earthly misery will be redeemed in Heaven.[12] And the necessity for self-division forces Afro-Americans to regard putatively irreconcilable opposites such as spirit and matter as impermeable categories. As I suggested in the Introduction, the most enduring discussion of the nature and inherent dangers of Afro-American self-division is W.E.B. Du Bois' much-quoted formulations of the "peculiar sensation" that he terms "double consciousness." Du Bois' portrait of the Afro-American psychological state has for the most part been accepted as an accurate representation of the difficulties of simultaneous membership in antithetical cultures. But the establishment of Du Boisian double consciousness as a major code in systems of Black expressivity has not—especially in the last thirty years—insulated his formulations from critical and creative revisions in Afro-American letters.

Henry Louis Gates, for example, argues that our comprehension of Ralph Ellison's *Invisible Man* is contingent upon our recognition of the ways in which Ellison is signifying on Du Bois' ideas. Such signifying, for Gates, is readily observable in the epilogue to Ellison's text which reads: "Now I know men are different and that all life is divided and that only in division is there true health."[13] For Ellison, according to Gates, double consciousness is not strictly an Afro-American phenomenon, but, rather, a human one; it is neither a source nor a sign of psychological maladjustment, but a signal of "true health."

Gates further argues that Ishmael Reed's *Mumbo Jumbo* and his poem "Dualism: in ralph ellison's invisible man" signify on both Du Bois and Ellison's revision. Gates suggests that Reed's poem is an especially clear signification:

> i am outside of
> history. i wish
> i had some peanuts, it
> looks hungry there in
> its cage.
>
> I am inside of
> history. its
> hungrier than i
> thot.[14]

Gates argues that "Dualism":

> parodies, profoundly, both the figure of the black as outsider [which Ellison uses] and the figure of the divided self. For, as he [Reed] tells us, even these are only tropes, figures of speech, rhe-

torical constructs like "double-consciousness," and not some preordained reality or thing. To read these figures literally, Reed tells us, is to be duped by figuration.[15]

Gates accurately interprets the refiguration of Du Bois' formulations in subsequent texts. Whether he is correct in suggesting that double consciousness, or, for that matter, the status of the Afro-American as outsider in American society, are strictly figurative constructs, however, is another matter.[16] He refers to *Their Eyes Were Watching God* as "a paradigmatic signifying text" (290). Before either Ellison's or Reed's refigurations of Du Bois, Hurston's text explores— both in its content and, as I will discuss later, in its narration—the accuracy and applicability to Afro-American life of what Gates terms Du Bois' "rhetorical construct."

Such exploration by Hurston's novel becomes apparent when we recognize the historical implications of a self-division motivated by an elaborate attempt on Starks' part to break Janie's spirit and thus guarantee a "submission" that he vows "he'd keep on fighting [for] until he felt he had it" (111). Starks, whose carriage reminds Janie and Eatonville's other citizens of that of an affluent white man, builds in the black town "a gloaty, sparkly white" house that made "the rest of the town look . . . like servant's quarters surrounding the "big house" (75). He has complete control over the town's economic institutions. His demeanor, the "bow-down command in his face" and his manipulation of his constituency, stir a particularly identifiable form of resentment in the Eatonville community: "They had murmured hotly about slavery being over" (75). Starks, then, not only brings to Eatonville the capitalistic philosophies of his former white employers. In addition, he effectively establishes himself in this black community as their replacement. Consequently, his desire for Janie's submission seems intended as more than merely chauvinistic. Rather, his striving for complete control is meant to suggest the abusive efforts of white slaveowners to beat blacks into submission. Because his oppressive tactics are not simply rhetorical constructs, one doubts that Hurston intended Janie's self-division in the face of Starks' brutality as simply a rhetorical figure.

Hurston does differ from Du Bois in her perception of Afro-American self-division. For Du Bois, double consciousness, a state that causes the Afro-American to feel as though she has "two warring ideals in one dark body," leads necessarily to a form of psychic pain. Hurston, however, associates the assumption that blackness and pain are necessarily correlated with a mindset that she designates "tragically colored." As I discussed earlier, she describes the tragically colored as members of "the sobbing school of Negrohood who hold that nature [by cursing them with black skins] somehow has given them a low-down dirty deal." In "How It Feels To Be Colored Me," she also asserts, obviously with Du Bois in mind: "I have no separate feelings about being an American citizen and colored."[17] By establishing historical referents (Starks as abusive oppressor) and figurative constructs (Janie's inside as store), Hurston is then able to suggest that double consciousness is not as problematic a state as Du Bois insisted. Before we can correctly comprehend the novelist's perspective, however, it is imperative to identify first the shortcomings of previous readings of Janie's division into inside and outside.

IV

BARBARA JOHNSON'S reading of Janie's self-division typifies the recent, discourse-oriented interpretations of *The Eyes Were Watching God*. She argues that the protagonist's duality engenders a

> power of voice . . . [that] grows not out of her identity but out of her division into inside and outside. Knowing how not to mix them is knowing that articulate language requires the co-presence of two distinct poles, not their collapse into one-ness. . . . Far from being an expression of Janie's new whole-ness or identity as a character, Janie's increasing ability to speak grows out of her ability not to mix inside with outside, not to pretend that there is no difference, but to assume and articulate the incompatible forces involved in her own division. (212)

Janie does assert herself verbally just after recognizing the possibilities of self-division. Overhearing the typically sexist conversation of several men, including her husband, she asserts boldly that these men incorrectly perceive the cognitive abilities of women. She says: "Sometimes God gets familiar wid us womenfolk and talks his inside business" (117). However, her remark is addressed specifically to men who are her acknowledged social inferiors. Predictably, Starks is annoyed by Janie's assertive display of voice and reestablishes his dominance by forcing her into servile voicelessness: "You gettin' too moufy, Janie. . . . Go fetch me de checker-board *and* de checkers" (117). Starks' response displays his dominance and suggests his belief that Janie's cognitive deficiencies are so profound that she needs to be reminded to bring both board and checkers. Beyond this unpharacteristic remark, she asserts no power of voice for a period of at least eleven years.[18] During this period, despite Johnson's insistence on an empowering self-division, Janie does not verbally challenge Starks. The text informs us: "No matter what Jody did, *she said nothing*" (118, my emphasis).

Obviously, then, Janie's self-division alone does not account for her eventual exhibition of a powerful voice. If Janie's deconstruction was as empowering as Johnson argues, then she would not have endured eleven subsequent years in which "she received all things with the stolidness of the earth which soaks up urine and perfume with the same indifference" (119). No, Janie's verbal assertiveness occurs, in part, because she reads clear signs of Starks' physical deterioration. She recognizes that:

> Joe wasn't so young as he used to be. There was already some-thing dead about him. He didn't rear back in his knees any longer. . . . His prosperous-looking belly that used to thrust out so pugnaciously and intimidate folks, sagged like a load sus-pended from his loins . . . (119-20)

Her observations help her to summon the courage to respond to Starks' continual verbal assault. He strives to maintain control by diverting attention from his own decline: "he began to talk about her age all the time, as if he didn't want her to stay young while he grew old" (120). This deflective maneuver is ineffective, however, precisely because it does not correspond to objective reality: quite simply, he looks old, while Janie does not. For the first time in their relationship, Starks is unable to create a sense of harmony between words and reality:

> If he thought to deceive her, he was wrong. For the first time she could see a man's head naked of its skull. Saw the cunning thoughts race in and out through the caves and promontories of his mind long before they darted out of the tunnel of his mouth. (120)

Despite her recognition of Starks' motives, Janie has no conscious plans to assert a power of voice. Rather, she resolves to wait patiently for her husband's impending death as her release from tyranny: "She saw he was hurting inside so she let it pass without talking. She just measured a little time for him and set it aside to wait" (120). John-son's contention that "Janie's increasing ability to speak grows out of her ability not to mix inside with outside," when considered in the context of Hurston's text, seems inaccurate. Though aware both of her own and of her tormentor's self-division, Janie clearly chooses to maintain silence until Starks' death.

Ultimately, however, she is unable to keep her vow of silence. On one occasion, while being upbraided by her husband for another exhibition of ineptness as a store clerk, Janie is told by an increasingly abusive Starks: "Don't stand dere rollin' yo' pop eyes at me wid yo' rump hangin' nearly to yo' knees!" (121). This is a fairly typical remark from Starks, and one to which Janie would not have responded, all things being equal. What is not equal on this occasion, however, is the rationale for Starks' degradation (deflective self-aggrandizement) and the reaction of the townspeople:

> A big laugh started off in the store but people got to thinking and stopped. It was funny if you looked at it right quick, but it got pitiful if you thought about it awhile. It was like somebody snatched off part of a woman's clothes while she wasn't looking and the streets were crowded. (121)

I will later discuss the importance of audience in Afro-American expressivity. For the moment, however, it will suffice to say that audience reaction is effectively determinative in a black speaker's delivery of his or her message. Because Starks has violated an audience's sense of what constitutes an appropriate playing of "the dozens," he loses the allegiance of the townspeople who, up to this point, have never openly disagreed with him. This audience's reaction, by contrast, prompts Janie—who had been referred to earlier by one of the townspeople as a "'born orator'" who can "put jus' de right words tuh our thoughts" (92)—to challenge her husband. She says:

> Naw, Ah ain't no young gal no mo' but den Ah ain't no old woman neither. Ah reckon Ah looks mah age too. But Ah'm uh woman every inch of me, and Ah know it. Dat's uh whole lot more'n *you* kin say. *You big-bellies round here and put out a lot of brag, but 'tain't nothing' to it but yo' big voice.* Humph! Talkin' 'bout me lookin' old! When you pull down yo' britches, you look lak de change uh life. (122-23, emphasis added)

What has distinguished Starks from his constituency has been his ability to authenticate his voice. He is no speaker of exaggerated thought pictures. He, in fact, does what he says he will do. When, for example, he informs Janie of his realization of the necessity for a street lamp on the town's main street, he resolves quickly to fill this need: "The very next day with money out of his pocket he sent off to Sears,

Roebuck and Company for the street lamp" (71). Like the God of the
Old Testament, Starks (whose favorite expression is "I god") virtually
wills light into existence with the power of his voice (and wallet). His
power to actualize his voice contrasts directly with the mock courtships and crayon enlargements of a speaking community unable, or
unwilling, to authenticate its voice through action.

In fact, the Mayor's power over the townspeople is a direct function
of his authenticating skills. Janie's exposure of his shortcomings destroys his claims to superiority because his charges of aging are revealed, devastatingly, as his own defects. His words are revealed as
self-protective lies. Consequently, he loses his status as Eatonville's
"big voice" and becomes but another of the thought picture makers
who cannot back up his big talk:

> Janie had robbed him of his illusion of irresistible maleness that
> all men cherished, which was terrible. . . . [S]he had cast down
> his empty armor before men and they had laughed, and would
> keep on laughing. When he paraded his possessions hereafter, they
> would not consider the two together. They'd look with envy at
> the things and pity the man that owned them. . . . Good-for-
> nothing's like Dave and Lum and Jim wouldn't change places
> with him. For what can excuse a man in the eyes of other men
> for lack of strength? Raggedy-behind squirts of sixteen and sev-
> enteen would be giving him their merciless pity out of their eyes
> while their mouths said something humble. (123-24)

Soon after his wife's devastating and assertive display of independent
voice, Starks dies. Henry Louis Gates has argued that Janie's voice
is largely responsible for Starks' ultimate demise: "Janie 'kills' her
husband, rhetorically" (290).

After his death, Janie feels compelled to maintain her self-division.
But since she has been liberated from Starks' dominance, her self-
division serves as both reinforcement for her essence and amnion that
protects her while she undergoes rebirth. The amniotic nature of her
self-division is observable in the text's description of her sensibility
during Starks' funeral. She:

> starched and ironed her face and came set in the funeral behind
> a veil. It was like a wall of stone and steel. The funeral was going
> on outside. All things concerning death and burial were said and
> done. Finish. End. Nevermore. Darkness. . . . Weeping and
> wailing outside. Inside the expensive black folds were resurrec-

tion and life. She did not reach outside for anything, nor did the things of death disturb her calm. She sent her face to Joe's funeral, and herself went rollicking with the springtime across the world. (136-37)

An essential feature of this "resurrection" is Janie's ability to correctly interpret her past. Maria Wolff suggests that Janie grows to understand the consequences of living in accord with the texts of Nanny and Starks by doing "a series of 're-readings' of her past" (31). These re-readings, shared with the reader in her autobiographical conversations with Pheoby, consist, in the main, of remarks in rejection of the capitalistic orientation of both Starks' and Nanny's texts. A more self-reliant Janie, approaching rebirth and free from the influences of the texts of others, rejects suitors' advances as well as standards of community decorum for mayors' wives. She tells Pheoby: "Ah jus' loves dis freedom" (143). Having emancipated herself from the influences of others, she is free to "think new thoughts" and live in accord with her own interpretations of life. She is free, in other words, to create her own text.

Recent critics of *Their Eyes Were Watching God*, reacting to what they deem the limited (and in some cases sexist) readings of Hurston's novel as a romance, have argued that what the author is most interested in chronicling is Janie's search for and achievement of an autonomous, self-defined identity and voice. Already I have discussed Barbara Johnson's views on the relationship between self-division and identity. In addition, Robert Stepto suggests that "Janie seek freedom, selfhood, voice and 'living.'"[19] And in the reading that seems most dedicated to undermining the view that *Their Eyes Were Watching God* is simply a love story, Missy Dehn Kubitschek criticizes interpretations that fail to "recognize in Janie the independence and strength of the archetypal quester" (109).

Certainly, freedom from the exceedingly restrictive texts by which Starks and Nanny virtually imprison her allows Janie an opportunity to develop an autonomous identity. The novel insists, however, that Janie does not immediately take advantage of her freedom. To be sure, Hurston's protagonist takes several crucial steps in freedom's direction—symbolically liberating herself from Starks' influence by burning the head rags he has forced her to wear and gently rejecting the advances of her respectable, honorable suitors whom she knows are mere replicas of previous husbands. But she takes no greater steps than these toward a self-determined identity before she meets Tea Cake. Rather, she waits passively. The text informs us: "She was just

basking in freedom for the most part without the need of thought"
(143).

Their Eyes Were Watching God does not support contemporary readings which argue that Janie and Tea Cake are coequal voices in their
relationship.[20] It is clear that Tea Cake differs significantly from Starks
in his view of the role of women, or, more specifically, of Janie in
marriage. That he teaches Janie to hunt or play checkers and encourages her to come to work *with*—as opposed to *for*—him in the
muck of the Florida Everglades signals his difference from Starks where
woman's proper place is concerned. However, his difference should
not necessarily be taken as evidence that he holds a late-twentieth-
century, liberated male's attitude toward women. For, in a number
of instances, he, too, exhibits traditionally sexist behavior that undermines a reader's ability to interpret his character in a wholly positive way. And Janie's passive acceptance of Tea Cake's sometimes
aggressively sexist behavior calls into question the degree to which
she actually desires a relationship of equality.

The first suggestion of a gender-determined imbalance in Janie's
third marriage appears in her explanation to Pheoby—again, in the
text of the novel and not in its frame—of the nature of her relationship. She justifies her plan to sell Starks' store in the following way:

> . . . Tea Cake ain't no Jody Starks, and if he tried tuh be [and
> managed the store], it would be uh complete flommuck. . . . So
> us is goin' off somewhere and *start all over in Tea Cake's way.* Dis
> ain't no business proposition, and no race after property and ti-
> tles. Dis is uh love game. *Ah done lived Grandma's way, now Ah
> means tuh live mine.* (171, my emphasis)

Janie's statement explicitly contrasts the manner of living for which
she is preparing to the life that Nanny desired for her and the existence that Joe Starks—the novel's preeminent procurer of "property
and titles"—forced upon her. Additionally, she seems to suggest that
Tea Cake's and her own "ways" are identical. The remainder of the
text, however, provides little evidence to support this suggestion.

Already we have seen that Janie is neglectful in establishing a personal text after her husband's death. This fact might suggest that an
excessively sheltered Janie, though she has undergone undeniably
momentous psychological alteration, has entered a relationship with
Tea Cake with scarcely a firmer sense of true identity than she possessed when she married Starks. Indeed, her subsequent discussion
suggests that she has very few genuinely personal interests. It is Tea
Cake who instructs the older Janie, teaching her "de maiden language

all over" (173), as well as informing her of what clothes she should wear and where they should live. Granted, I may be minimizing the import of narrative acts meant to suggest Tea Cake's positive influence in Janie's acquisition of self-esteem. The novel, however, seems to lend weight to my analysis of Tea Cake.

In fact, Janie's third husband's own words, particularly after he uses his skills as "one uh de best gamblers God ever made" (187) to replace money that he has squandered, give the reader a sense of Tea Cake's perspective. He tells Janie: "Put dat two hundred back wid de rest, Janie. . . . Ah no need no assistance tuh help me feed mah woman. From now on, you gointuh eat whatever mah money can buy yuh and wear de same. When Ah ain't got nothin' you don't get nothin.'" (191) It is difficult to interpret these lines as anything other than unabashed sexism. Nor is it possible to view Janie's response to Tea Cake's statement—her meek "Dat's all right wid me" (191)—as more than assent to such attitudes. And her assent would seem to provide cogent evidence against an interpretation of her as a wholly liberated, self-defined, independent woman—a status that many critics argue for her at this point in her development. Quite clearly, Tea Cake—in this instance and countless others during the remainder of the narrative—is a traditionally domineering male. Janie, despite scores of interpretations to the contrary, is here a submissive woman, suppressing her will to fit the needs of an exceedingly charming, but nonetheless frequently domineering, husband.

The fact that Tea Cake allows Janie greater freedom than did Starks might be seen primarily as a function of his class identification. Starks, as Cheryl Wall argues, borrows his "criteria for success from the white world" of the Southern aristocrat which considered an idle, helpless woman as the ultimate complement to the financially successful man's social status (385). Tea Cake, on the other hand, is in Wall's view "so thoroughly immune to the influence of white American society that he does not even desire [this society's] external manifestations of power, money, and position" (388). His immunity prevents him from "classing Janie off." It does not, however, preclude his exhibition of other forms of undeniably sexist behavior.

The foregoing analysis of Tea Cake's and Janie's relationship places greater emphasis on the imperfections of their union than almost any reading of *Their Eyes Were Watching God* with which I am familiar. Interpreters of the novel have tended almost uniformly to gloss over such deficiencies. Wall is a rare exception; she attempts to explain Tea Cake's sexism as a result of Hurston's desire to portray him realistically:

Even Tea Cake, strongly idealized character though he is, has had difficulty accepting Janie's full participation in their life together. Zora Hurston knew that Tea Cake, a son of the folk culture, would have inherited its negative attitudes toward women. She knew besides that female autonomy cannot be granted by men, it must be demanded by women. Janie gains her autonomy only when she insists upon it. Under pressure, Tea Cake occasionally falls back on the prerogatives of his sex. . . . In the main, though, Tea Cake transcends his chauvinistic attitudes of the group. He largely keeps his pledge to Janie that she "partake wid everything." (388)

But even this reading, while it is much closer to the text Hurston has written, de-emphasizes Tea Cake's flaws, referring to them as "occasional . . . fall[ings] back on the prerogatives of his sex." This tendency in the criticism to mitigate the seriousness of Tea Cake's baleful behavior is even more clearly observable in interpretations of the narrative incidents on the muck that involve Nunkie and Mrs. Turner's brother.

These characters on the muck represent serious threats to Janie's and Tea Cake's marriage—Nunkie because of her interest in and unsubtle pursuit of Tea Cake, and Mrs. Turner's brother because of his sister's stated desire (a statement made to Janie and overheard by Tea Cake) to play matchmaker and homebreaker. Kubitschek discusses these events as functions of the fact that Janie:

no longer wants compassion or protection from violence. Admitting the depth and intensity of her feelings, she is willing to use physical violence to combat the threat of Nunkie. Similarly, she accepts Tea Cake's violent protest over Mrs. Turner's brother without flinching, for these are not, like the earlier experiences [Nanny's and Starks' slaps], examples of violence used to enforce an action or behavior, but violence used to make another person aware. (112)

Kubischek can only speculate about whether Janie's acceptance of Tea Cake's beating was unflinching because the text—and I believe strategically—fails to provide Janie's reaction to the incident. Surely, though, Kubitschek distorts the text here. For while Janie is indeed "willing to use physical violence" on Nunkie—a willingness which, in part, might accurately be termed cautionary—she also physically assaults Tea Cake. This assault occurs in the privacy of their home and is witnessed by no one; it is meant, not to caution potential rivals about the strength of Janie's love for Tea Cake, as Kubitschek argues, but, rather, as an expression of Janie's angry suspicion that Tea Cake has been unfaithful and to caution *him* against the continuance of the suspected behavior.

A short time later, Tea Cake, in response to what he perceives as the threat of Mrs. Turner's brother, publicly beats Janie. Despite the various justifications of this beating in the criticism surrounding *Their Eyes Were Watching God*, the act is one of unmotivated violence. Janie has clearly done nothing to warrant it. The act is made even more problematic by Tea Cake's statement to the townspeople afterwards. He insists that he is the dominant figure in his marriage: "Janie is wherever Ah wants her tuh be" (219). What is most telling, however, is Janie's failure to reinforce Tea Cake's and the community's positive reading of the beating.

She says nothing at all in the entire chapter in which the beating occurs. Her silence recalls her quiet response to Starks' psychological and physical abuse, and suggests—voicelessly but powerfully—her disapproval of her third husband's method of dealing with the threat of an apparently unspectacular rival for whom Hurston does not even bother to provide a name. This is the only chapter in the entire novel where Janie makes no appearance whatsoever. Her silence and absence signal, I think, an application of the strategic self-division that she had employed in her second marriage. She withdraws when Tea Cake beats her into a voiceless absence. She no more accepts his abuse "without flinching" than she accepts Starks' mistreatment. Rather, her silence indicates that she employs what has been her only means of protest throughout much of the text of the novel.

Despite his instances of mistreatment, though, Tea Cake provides an environment in which Janie improves her self-image. Most importantly, he teaches Janie how to play, how, in both senses of the phrase, to enjoy herself. What initially attracts Janie to Tea Cake is his invitation to play checkers, an invitation that both surprises and delights: "Somebody wanted her to play. Somebody thought it natural for her to play" (146). In fact, his life is characterized by a hedonism that encompasses every imaginable aspect of existence. During their courtship, he says to Janie:

> Ah betcha you don't never go tuh de lookin' glass and enjoy yo' eyes yo'self. You let other folks git all de enjoyment out of 'em 'thout takin' in any of it yo'self. . . . You'se got de world in uh jug and make out you don't know it. But Ah'm glad tuh be de one tuh tell yuh. (157)

Tea Cake indeed does "tell" Janie about her positive qualities and teach her how to enjoy them. The feature of his interaction most often praised by critics is his willingness to aid in Janie's redefinition. As Maria Wolff suggests, Tea Cake "becomes a mirror for her" (31); he not only allows her to see her physical and spiritual beauty, but also shows her how to enjoy such reflections. This willingness, especially when contrasted to the degradation she suffers at the hands of Starks, endears Tea Cake immeasurably to both Janie and to sympathetic readers. He, thus, shares with the thought picture makers of Eatonville the attraction to play and verbal drama. The novel emphasizes that "He was always laughing and full of fun" (197). This playfulness is exhibited in instances from the games he and Janie play during courtship to his "romping" with Janie while picking beans in the Everglades. He responds to almost every situation in which he is involved as play or, perhaps more to the point, as a setting for dramatic performance.

While Eatonville's other thought picture makers play strictly for amusement, however, Tea Cake is able to effect significant changes by means of his drama. In addition to aiding Janie, he uses his dramatic abilities to help remove an avowed hater of blacks from the Everglades. In an elaborate drama, Tea Cake provokes a battle between several of his friends while in Mrs. Turner's diner, pretending all the while to serve as peacemaker. He tells his quarreling friends: "Looka heah, y'all, don't come in heah and raise no disturbance in de place. Mis' Turner is too nice uh woman fuh dat. In fact, she's more nicer than anybody else on de muck" (223). Mrs. Turner's diner is destroyed during the ensuing battle, and she decides to leave the muck and return "tuh Miami where folks is civilized" (226).

There are occasions, however, when his attraction to play and drama proves problematic for his marriage. One of these instances is his decision to enjoy himself by spending Janie's two hundred dollars. With this money he buys dinner for a large group of strangers and pays women whom he deems unattractive not to attend his party. When he returns home, he fails to comprehend the nature of his wife's concern about his absence. Observing Janie's dejection upon his return, he is able to understand that she might have feared that he had stolen her money and deserted her. But he never understands that his irresponsible failure to inform Janie of his whereabouts produced anxiety.

Furthermore, his "brainstorm" to counter the threat of Mrs. Turner's brother by beating Janie seems motivated by his dramatic affinities:

> When Mrs. Turner's brother came and she brought him over to
> be introduced [to Janie], Tea Cake had a brainstorm. Before the
> week was over he had whipped Janie. Not because her behavior
> justified his jealousy, but it relieved that awful fear inside him.
> Being able to whip her reassured him in possession. No brutal
> beating at all. He just slapped her around to show he was boss.
> (218)

This beating is performance par excellence. It is intended to exhibit
to others the extent of his authority over Janie. Wendy McCredie suggests that Tea Cake means for his beating "to protect [Janie] from
Mrs. Turner's brother."[21] Kubitschek, as I discussed earlier, argues
that Janie "accepts Tea Cake's violent protest over Mrs. Turner's
brother without flinching" because Janie understands that in this instance Tea Cake's "violence [is] used to make another person aware"
(112). The text, however, fails to substantiate either of these readings.
Tea Cake's issuance of threats to his putative rival subsequent to his
beating Janie reflects his awareness that his abuse of his wife has not
performed the service of deterring his interest. His beating—as the
narrative says—"relieved that awful fear inside him" and "reas-
sured" him and the townspeople that "he was boss."

Tea Cake's attraction to the dramatic, his ability, as Maria Wolff
points out, to create a "text . . . out of 'everything'" (31), while it is
unquestionably beneficial in some respects, is sometimes injurious.
The most explicit example in which his approach to life is clearly
inappropriate and disruptive is an event where human presence can
exert no control—a destructive natural phenomenon. As a hurricane
approaches, he is warned on a number of occasions to leave the muck.
He decides, however —for both himself and Janie—to remain in place.
It seems characteristic that as the storm approaches, Tea Cake is
playing a "show-off" game of dice (233). Later, when he, Janie, and
Motorboat are convinced of the reality of the hurricane and attempt
to escape its fury, Janie suggests that they remain in their house, advice that Tea Cake quickly rejects. But when the storm causes Lake
Okechobee to overflow, Motorboat insists that they wait in the large
abandoned house to which they have fled. Tea Cake refuses, and he
and Janie are left to battle the storm's destructive force. Faced with
this menace, Tea Cake continually makes incorrect decisions. His her-
oism in rescuing Janie from a rabid dog is undermined by the defec-
tive judgment that has, in fact, put Janie in the way of such danger.
Further, it is after Janie is out of the reach of the dog that Tea Cake
arrives to defend his wife:

The dog raced down the back-bone of the cow to the attack and
Janie screamed and slipped far back on the tail of the cow, just
out of reach of the dog's angry jaws. He wanted to plunge in after
her but dreaded the water, somehow. Tea Cake rose out of the
water at the cow's rump and seized the dog by the neck. (245-
246)

Later, when they have survived the hurricane, a rested Tea Cake,
impatient for adventure, decides to survey the damage done to West
Palm Beach. Janie cautions him against going outside:

What dey want you tuh help do, you aint' gointuh like it. Dey's
grabbin all de menfolk dey kin git dey hands on and makin' 'em
help bury de dead. Dey claims dey after de unemployed, but dey
ain't being too particular about whether you'se employed or not.
You stay in dis house. De Red Cross is doin' all dat kin be done
otherwise fuh de sick and de 'fllicted. (250)

Janie's voice has no effect. Ignoring his wife's warning, Tea Cake goes
out and soon afterward is forced by well-armed white men to join a
work force involved in a segregated burial of the dead.

After this experience, he and Janie return to the Everglades where
the rabies he had contracted from the mad dog's bite begins to affect
his judgment further. But even during advanced stages of his illness,
he is still able to charm Janie with his words:

You's uh lil girl baby all de time. God made it so you spent yo'
ole age first wid somebody else, and saved up yo' girl days to
spend wid me . . .

Everytime Ah see ah patch uh roses uh somethin' over sportin'
theyselves makin' out they pretty, Ah tell 'em "Ah want yuh tuh
see mah Janie sometime." You must let de flowers see yuh sometimes, heah, Janie. (268)

At this point, however, his actions do not complement his words. Just
after he delivers his charming suggestion that Janie exhibit her beauty
to a patch of egotistical roses, she "felt the pistol under [his] pil-
low. . . . Never had Tea Cake slept with a pistol under his head before" (268). His subsequent actions, then, like Joe Starks' during his
lingering physical deterioration, fail to authenticate his voice.

It seems to me that close attention to his continual display of faulty
judgment serves to invalidate currently popular views of Tea Cake as
an unquestionably heroic figure whose misdeeds are either situation-
ally or culturally justifiable. His deficiencies during and after the

hurricane suggest that other decisions that he makes (for example, slapping Janie because of the threat of Mrs. Turner's brother) are meant to be viewed as inappropriate.

I do not, however, share Lloyd Brown's position that Janie's positive memories of Tea Cake result from what Hurston designates in the beginning of her novel as a uniquely feminine ability to alter reality—in other words, to make the dream the truth. Brown's position, because it differs so radically from the popular critical view of Tea Cake, deserves to be quoted at length:

> Janie's memories of him do not simply transcend his death but also his manifest limitations. She is able to pull in the horizons (of her dream-ideal) around her immediate reality only by remembering what she does not want to forget about Tea Cake and by forgetting whatever she does not want to remember. And the single most important thing that she chooses to forget is the fact that Tea Cake was as brutally possessive and insensitive as Killicks and Starks had been.
>
> . . . Consequently when she kills him in self-defense her act emphasizes the ambiguous nature of their relationship and her memory; and in destroying the mad-dog Tea Cake she cherishes the bee-man Tea Cake who "could never be dead" because he came closer than any other to fulfilling her dreams. This kind of memory is therefore as self-defensive as the act which ends Tea Cake's life. It attempts to transcend the ultimate disillusionment of Janie's life—the discovery that there is really no bee-man . . . —by preserving *selected* images of her dead lover. And this is how she finally makes her dreams truth, cherishing them with a persistence which becomes a heroic affirmation of her spiritual energy and imaginative power, but which, in the very process emphasizes the limitations of her life and her men.[22]

Brown misreads several features of the novel in order to support his contention that the major goal of the work is to explore and delineate a uniquely feminine method of manipulating reality. He insists, for example, that Tea Cake "regularly" beat Janie (44), a reading that Hurston's text clearly does not confirm. Also, his claim that Tea Cake's "declaration that Janie is only what he wants her to be . . . echoes a similar manifesto by Joe" (44) ignores the novel's emphasis on the importance of Tea Cake's instructing Janie in self-appreciation. Despite his misreadings of Hurston's novel, though, his perspective adds a stark contrast to the general universe of critical discourse. It is a contrast tied unmistakably to what the novel's "pro-

logue"—if it is appropriate to call it that—introduces as a major
theme: the difference between men's and women's reactions to fate.
While, in Hurston's much-discussed formulations, "the life of men"
is characterized by a "resignation" to the whims of fate, women are
much more (psychologically) active in attempting to attain their
dreams. Hurston writes that, for women, "The dream is the truth.
Then they act and do things accordingly" (9).

To be sure, the Tea Cake whom Hurston presents has many wonderful qualities. Adventurous, charming, loving, and possessing a
wonderful oratorical gift, he merits the devotion of Janie as well as
the praise of critics. But he also possesses major character flaws that
even the most laudatory comment cannot erase. His text of dramatic
play does not go uncriticized in the novel, even though it has received
virtually no censure from the novel's critics.

V

IN THE foreground analysis of *Their Eyes Were Watching God*, I have
attempted to demonstrate that the effectiveness of the texts of Nanny,
Joe Starks, and Tea Cake depends on each character's success in coordinating voice and action. For these characters, major difficulties—
including death—arise from or are signalled by an inability to bol-
ster "big talk" with similarly "big action"—in other words, an inability to make voice represent more than merely unauthenticated
noise.

The text of the novel's protagonist, the delineation of Janie's life
story, has presented problems for critics who view her sometimes
painful experience as concluding ultimately in a self-possessed liberation symbolized by and, indeed, accomplished by means of her
achievement of a powerful cultural voice. Such a reading is problematic, as my subsequent discussion will show, primarily because Janie
does not (after insisting in her conversation with Pheoby that she will)
narrate her own story in the novel.

In the novel's narration, Janie's voice is virtually silent. In my examination of the texts of those who shape and control her life, I suggested that each text's ultimate effectiveness is contingent upon the
degree to which it perverts the primary relation between voice and
action. Janie's failure to narrate her own story might appear, at first
glance, to be another in a series of examples in the novel of unauthenticated voice. Is it possible, then, to argue that Janie has truly
achieved a self-determined identity when the narration of the novel

evidences her failure to coordinate voice (her insistence that she will tell the story) with action (her narration thereof)?

Perhaps the most effective means of discussing Janie's text is to employ, as Barbara Johnson does, a deconstructive critical approach. Instead of suggesting that Janie's voice and identity are functions of her self-division, however, I want to show that her achievement of identity is signaled by her narrative *silence*. By the time she returns to Eatonville, she has learned that *individual* voice is either tyrannical or ineffectual. As a result, her own text—the narration of her life story in the novel—is situated in a self-determined space between precultural and Afro-American cultural expressive practices. This situation has led the narrative strategies of *Their Eyes Were Watching God* to exhibit not an independent voice such as Janie's individual (first-person) narration, but, rather, a discourse derived from a commingling of the principles of two distinct forms of communication: Afro-American call and response which demands a unity of voices, and "natural" communication in which action begets voice. This union allows Janie's voice to be expressed not through her individual narration, but through the meshing of her (largely unheard) voice with the cultural voices of others. Hence, rather than exhibiting an independent voice, the novel's narration evidences the protagonist's voice as (apparent) absence and silence.

Janie's narrative voice (or, more to the point, her unconventional "voice") has led critics who view voice as the signal of self-actualized power either to insist that the narration of Hurston's novel is flawed or to offer sometimes clearly forced and ultimately unconvincing interpretations that attempt to explain her failure to act narratively as a speaking subject in a conventional sense. Darwin Turner's deservedly infamous discussion of Hurston's life and career in *In a Minor Chord* presents the first contemporary example of the former critical tendency. He insists that the effectiveness of the novel is "weakened [by a] careless shift of point of view."[23] Turner is referring specifically to the novel's rendering of Nanny's personal history in the first person. (Apparently, Turner is unaware of other such shifts in narrative perspective in the novel—for example, Janie's own brief narration of the beginning of her tale.)

Several critics writing after Turner, despite their disagreement with his negative presentation of Hurston as a human being and an artist, nevertheless share his views of the narration of *Their Eyes Were Watching God*. Hurston's biographer, Robert Hemenway, for example, says of the novel: "the narration shifts awkwardly from first to third person."[24] In a parenthetical aside, Lillie Howard argues that the third person narration of the novel is "awkwardly done . . . since, ostensibly, Janie is telling her own story" (410). And in what is to date the most extensively articulated criticism of the narration of Hurston's text, Robert Stepto indicates that the tale's framing is the "one great flaw" of *Their Eyes Were Watching God:*

> . . . Hurston created the essential illusion that Janie has achieved her voice. . . . But the tale undercuts much of this, not because of its content . . . but because of its narration. Hurston's curious insistence on having Janie's tale—her personal history in and as a literary form—told by an omnisc[i]ent third person, rather than a first-person narrator, implies that Janie has not really won her voice and self after all—that her author . . . cannot see her way clear to giving Janie her voice outright. . . . [W]hen told in this fashion control of the tale remains, no matter how unintended, with the author alone. (166)

Stepto's is a serious and widely shared criticism that has not been sufficiently addressed. In her essay "New Directions for Black Feminist Criticism," Deborah McDowell decries Stepto's virtual exclusion of black women writers from his study *From Behind the Veil* which purports to be "a history . . . of the historical consciousness of an Afro-American art form—namely, the Afro-American written narrative" (x). McDowell refers to Stepto's analysis of *Their Eyes Were Watching God* as "a token two-paged discussion," and insists that sexism caused him not to "feel that the novel merited its own chapter or the thorough analysis accorded the other [male authored] works he discusses."[25]

However, McDowell fails to mention Stepto's remarks about Hurston's novel which state his explicit justification for the brevity of his discussion:

> . . . one might say that the example of *Their Eyes* calls for a narrative in which the primary figure (like Janie) achieves a space beyond those defined by the tropes of ascent and immersion, but (unlike Janie) also achieved authorial control over both the frame and tale of his or her personal history. In short, *Their Eyes*, as a narrative strategy in a continuum of narrative strategies, directs us most immediately to Ralph Ellison's *Invisible Man*. Janie is quite possibly more of a blood relative to Ellison's narrator than either the "male chauvinist" or "feminist" readers of the tradition would care to contemplate. (166-67)

According to Stepto, his failure to discuss Hurston's novel at length results from his view that *Their Eyes Were Watching God* is strategically close to *Invisible Man*, and because Ellison's is the more accomplished work, it is, hence, more worthy of discussion. For Stepto, Hurston's is a courageous, but, ultimately failed, attempt to combine what he feels are the major tropes of the Afro-American narrative—ascent and immersion. McDowell's critique unfortunately fails to address the former's sharp criticism of Hurston's novel.

Her failure undermines the effectiveness of her response to Stepto's seemingly sexist exclusion of women from his study. For it prevents her from addressing the actual sexist biases of the tropes that Stepto employs as major rhetorical figures in Afro-American narrative. Constructions such as immersion and ascent—given women's traditionally bound and domestic space in American culture—almost necessarily eliminate the possibility of Stepto's including narratives by Afro-American women written before the 1980s in his study.

In Toni Morrison's corpus, for example, the inherent difficulties of measuring the success or failure of works in terms of ascent and/or immersion of female characters is immediately apparent. *The Bluest Eye* informs us that while Pecola's brother Sammy can escape the horrors of his family by running away from home, Pecola is forced by her sex to remain in her storefront house.[26] In *Sula*, though the women (particularly Sula and her grandmother Eva) possess a greater freedom of movement than Pecola, the text shrouds their journeys in mystery as though such female freedom does not make for a "proper" novel about women.[27] It is only when Morrison portrays a male protagonist in *Song of Solomon* that the tropes of ascent and immersion are applicable to her corpus. Because Stepto chooses to represent Afro-American narrative in terms of these gender-specific tropes, he has virtually no alternative other than to exclude women.

Several commentators on *Their Eyes Were Watching God* have attempted to address criticisms such as Stepto's by offering fully detailed discussions of the potency of Janie's voice. Such attempts have, for the most part, proven far from satisfying. Wendy McCredie's article, "Authority and Authorization in *Their Eyes Were Watching God*," offers a case in point. As her reading reaches its conclusion, McCredie encounters an inconsistency between her claim that the novel delineates the growth of Janie's control of her own voice and self and the fact that the protagonist fails to narrate her own tale. She writes:

[Janie] no longer needs authorization to speak effectively.
Nevertheless, Zora Neale Hurston *does authorize* both Janie and

her voice. By Hurston's writing down, author(iz)ing, Janie's life, Janie's entire past becomes present—not just her past at a specific point in her narration. Time no longer limits Janie. She will live forever in the continual self-authorizing present of *Their Eyes Were Watching God*. (28)

For pages McCredie attempts to substantiate her thesis that Hurston's novel presents "the story of Janie's struggle to articulate, to appropriate her own voice, and through her voice, herself" (25). Her brief concluding remarks attempt, however, virtually to dismiss a necessity that Janie *exhibit* the power of her voice by controlling the narration of *Their Eyes Were Watching God*. According to the parameters by which McCredie measures Janie's power of voice—that is, its ability to authorize Janie—the protagonist's failure to exhibit her oratorical skills must, if McCredie is correct about the potential of her voice, be seen as problematic. Certainly, McCredie's essay suggests that Hurston is infinitely more concerned with delineating her heroine's struggle to articulate than with presenting such struggles as "timeless." As Hurston's text actually presents itself, then, its narrative strategies undercut what McCredie views as the theme of the novel: its protagonist's achieved self-authorization through voice. Her reading, thus, does little to counteract the long-standing view that Hurston's execution of her novel is flawed.

At this point, it is essential that critics of *Their Eyes Were Watching God* formulate readings of the novel that explain Janie's silence, her failure to assume the role of narrator. Deborah McDowell's essay, while it does not itself explain Hurston's strategies, suggests a method that is helpful in the formation of an explanation. She advocates a contextual approach to Afro-American women's literature grounded in Afro-American history and culture.[28] I, too, feel that the narration of the novel, its expression of itself, must be viewed in relation to other systems of Black expressivity. Like other commentators—such as McCredie, Stepto, and Wolff—I believe Hurston's novel is very much concerned with discussing the possible potency of voice and the consequences of its absence. Measuring the troublesome narration of Hurston's novel against tropes of Black expression can lead one to realize that its narrative strategies—long held to be faulty—are, rather, a stunningly successful act in the *denigration* of the novel as an expressive form.

VI

ONE OF the best-known aspects of Black expression is the importance of the call-and-response interaction between speaker and audience, or, soloist and chorus. In *Talkin and Testifyin*, the Afro-American linguist Geneva Smitherman defines call and response as "spontaneous verbal and nonverbal interaction between speaker and listener in which all the speaker's statements ('calls') are punctuated by expressions ('responses') from the listener."[29] Smitherman describes such interaction as "a basic organizing principle in Black American culture generally, for it enables traditional black folk to achieve the unified state of balance or harmony which is fundamental in the traditional African world view" (104). This traditional world view, which I discussed extensively in the Introduction, emphasizes a fundamental interdependence of all entities: spirit and matter, the spiritual and physical worlds, leader and tribe, etc. In Afro-American expressivity, such interdependence takes form in an audience verbally and nonverbally inspiring a speaker to achieve oratorical heights. As Smitherman suggests, "call-and-response seeks to synthesize speaker and listeners in a unified movement" (108). The pattern "permeates" Afro-American vernacular communication and reaffirms Black culture's insistence on interactive unity.

The audience not only aids a speaker's performance, but also *performs* in its own right. Every member of the black audience is required to participate actively in communication. The audience, in fact, is a speaker, and the speaker, thriving on the response of the audience, is herself a listener. Smitherman describes this antiphony as follows: "there is no sharp line between performers or communications and the audience, for virtually everyone is performing and everyone is listening" (108).

In Western culture, a favored model of communication is linear. That is to say, the speaker is held to deliver information to a quiet, courteous audience which applauds occasionally at emphatically made points and at the conclusion of the communication. For the most part, any failure on the part of the audience to exhibit polite, mannered (*silent*) behavior is viewed as an interruption of communication. On the other hand, communication in Black culture is best symbolized by the geometric figure of the circle. The barriers between speaker and audience erected in Western culture do not exist in Afro-American communication. Not only does the black audience listen to the text—it helps to *create* it.

Zora Neale Hurston infuses *Their Eyes Were Watching God* with antiphonal verbal exchanges that correspond to the call-and-response pattern prevalent in all forms of Afro-American expressivity.[30] Such elements, while more obvious in the narrative events, also contribute significantly to the rendering of Janie's tale. In this tale's frame, the narrator indicates that the protagonist's oratorical ability is related unquestionably to the response of her audience, Pheoby. After the pages of Janie's first-person narration, the reader is told: "Pheoby's hungry listening helped Janie to tell her story" (23). As Janie's audience, Pheoby—according to the rules of Afro-American communication— must actively encourage Janie's performance. Such encouragement can be verbal or, as in the case of "Pheoby's hungry listening," non-verbal. While the text does not indicate Pheoby's specific form of response, it does insist that she *is responding*, and, moreover, that her response enhances Janie's performance.

In direct contrast to Janie's antiphonal interaction are the violence-bolstered impositions of prepared texts on Janie by Nanny and Joe Starks. Both Nanny and Starks demand from Janie a silent obedience as opposed to active participation in the communication, or the development, of texts that they present. For example, Nanny, in response to what she views as Janie's ingratitude and lack of attentiveness to her insistence that she marry Killicks, strikes her granddaughter: "She slapped the girl's face violently, and forced her head back so that their eyes met in struggle" (28-29). It is at this point, when her audience has been forcibly silenced and physically subdued, that Nanny imposes on Janie her text: her life story and her resultant "great sermon about colored women sittin' on high."

While Black culture insists that the relation of a message should be a shared experience between speaker and audience, Nanny's slap has forced her granddaughter into the role of passive, silent audience: "Old Nanny sat there [while telling her story] rocking Janie like an infant" (32). Not only, then, is the subject of Nanny's text—that is, of Afro-American women "classing" themselves off from the less affluent masses—contrary to the unifying impulses of black culture, but so, too, is her method of communication.

Even more extreme in his failure to adhere to Black expressive cultural norms is Joe Starks who, like Nanny, operates in accord with irrefutably Western values. As I suggested earlier, he is like Nanny in positing for Janie a place on high, above and beyond the black masses. He employs physical and psychological violence to deny her access to typically Afro-American cultural means of instruction and self-expression. In an oral culture, knowledge is, of course, transmitted verbally. The Afro-American historian John Blassingame asserts that folktales "represented the distillation of folk wisdom and were used as an instructive device."[31] By preventing Janie's hearing and involvement in such Afro-American expressivity, Starks strives to cut her off from her culture's wisdom. The narrative tells us: "Janie loved the conversation and sometimes thought up good stories . . . , but Joe had forbidden her to indulge" (85). Attempting to confine her to the exclusive role that he has assigned, Starks forbids Janie to participate either in the communality or the orality of her culture. Educated not in black culture but, rather, in the ways of white folks, he cannot comprehend his wife's failure to appreciate the gifts he provides:

> She wasn't even appreciative of his efforts and she had plenty cause to be. Here he was just pouring honor all over her; building a high chair for her to sit in and overlook the world and she here pouting over it! (98)

At this point in her life, Janie desires not a "high chair" overlooking her people, but an intimate involvement *with* them. She craves interaction, both with the thought picture creators of her community and with her husband. She dislikes the fact that her marriage is dominated by Starks, and tells him: "You sho loves to tell me whut to do, but Ah can't tell you nothin' Ah see" (110). No more willing than Nanny to acknowledge in Janie an autonomous voice, Starks refuses to grant her any personal freedom whatsoever. Rather than seeing her as an equal, Starks "wanted her submission [to his authority] and he'd keep on fighting until he felt he had it" (111). Nanny's refusal to allow Janie control over her own life forces her granddaughter's infant-like silence. Starks' refusal leads to Janie's double consciousness.

After Starks' death, Janie meets and very cautiously falls in love with Vergible "Tea Cake" Woods. Instead of forcing a text upon Janie, he insists that she learn to appreciate herself, a self-regarding posture that will allow her to "partake wid everything." He appears to be the personification of her earlier garden dream, the man "She was saving up feelings for." In other words, Tea Cake seems the idea bee-man:

> She couldn't make him look just like any other man to her. He looked like the love thoughts of women. He could be a bee to a blossom—a pear tree blossom in the spring. He seemed to be crushing scent out of the world with his footsteps. Crushing aromatic herbs with every step he took. Spices hung about him. He was a glance from God. (161)

It is with this bee-man that Janie attempts to establish a type of interactive relationship she has long craved. She describes to Pheoby the contrast between Tea Cake and Starks in a way that I have discussed above: "Dis ain't no business proposition, and no race after property and titles. Dis is uh love game" (171). Unlike her arranged marriage to Killicks and her status as attractive possession of Mayor Starks, Janie is with Tea Cake solely for love. Hence, she approaches the type of "pollination" that she observed as a youth in her backyard.

The fact that Tea Cake ultimately fails to achieve the status of ideal male as delineated by late-twentieth century literary critics does not detract from the effectiveness of his gifts. He offers Janie an active participation in the traditions and rituals of her culture. He also provides the means for Janie to create a sincere appreciation of her own physical and spiritual beauty. This knowledge allows her to experience, through the customs and lore of her people, her culture's power and beauty. Rather than viewing the third-person narration to the tale of a culturally achieved, oratorically skilled Janie as evidence of a flaw in Hurston's execution of her narrative, one might suggest that the narration of *Their Eyes Were Watching God* confirms Janie's status as a communally oriented, culturally informed Afro-American woman.

What is, perhaps, most essential to such a reading of the complex narration of Hurston's novel is contained in the first chapter. Pheoby tells her recently arrived friend that the "zigaboos" who oversee her return are "so het up over ho' business till they liable to hurry theyself to Judgement to find out about you if they don't soon know" (17). Pheoby then advises Janie to "make haste and tell 'em 'bout you and Tea Cake"; in other words, she suggests that Janie assume the role of porch storyteller that Starks had denied to her on several occasions. Janie, thus, has urging and opportunity to flaunt her profound verbal ability, to exhibit, as she had while living on the muck, her mastery of the conventions and tropes of black expressivity. Instead, she says to Pheoby:

> Ah don't mean to bother wid tellin' 'em nothin', Pheoby. 'Tain't worth de trouble. You can tell 'em what Ah say if you wants to. Dat's just de same as me 'cause mah tongue is in mah friend's mouf. (17)

The "mass cruelty" (10) of the Eatonville porch sitters marks the second occasion following Tea Cake's death on which Janie is "up in the mouth" of an Afro-American community. Before her return to Eatonville, Janie is verbally attacked at her trial by a group of Tea Cake's friends who believe that her murder of her husband was malicious: "She felt them pelting her with dirty thoughts. They were there with their tongues cocked and loaded" (275).

Having already been exposed in her dealings with Nanny and Starks to the injurious potential of voice, Janie apparently has learned to protect herself from its damaging effects. Janie is uninjured psychologically by this attack of venomous tongues; their combined voice is exposed as impotent, incapable either of obtaining for itself an audience in the courtroom or of intimidating Janie. The exhibition of malicious voice, however, does place the culturally versed protagonist in a frustrating position. Instead of telling (porch) "lies," she is fighting them. These lies, referred to by the narrative as "a tongue storm" (276), represent this group's attempt to demonstrate its power. But, armed herself with a knowledge of the ineffectualness of malicious voice, Janie realizes that these "cocked and loaded" tongues were powerless, that, like Starks' continued references to her age, they were "the only real weapon left to weak folks" (275).

Despite a hasty reconciliation with Sop-de-Bottom and others of her attackers, Janie recognizes that she does not belong among these people for whom voice, in addition to serving as a conveyor of cultural wisdom, is also employed as a self-defensive, malicious shield. Just as she does when she is the victim of Starks' and Tea Cake's weakness-inspired malice, Janie resolves not to play the martyr. Rather, after burying Tea Cake, she quickly leaves the muck, abandoning, at the same time, the search for people that had characterized her life after Starks' death.

When she returns to Eatonville, then, Janie's posture with respect to involvement with the masses has been significantly altered. She distances herself emotionally from the folk, the source of whose malice is transparent: jealousy and weakness. Armed with her knowledge of such negative motives, a self-confident Janie feels no compulsion to defend or justify her actions to Eatonville's cynical nay-sayers who have "got me up in they mouth now" (16). She is aware of her own voice's authenticating power and is, thus, uninterested in justifying her action on the porch where the creators of exaggerated thought pictures have drawn their fabricated, hyperbolic self-images.

Her statement to Pheoby also exhibits the fact that though she has distanced herself from the group, she nevertheless clings to her culture's insistence on communality. While she is unable to unite with the porch critics, her words suggest her unquestionable connectedness with her "kissin'-friend." This connection is made apparent by Janie's willingness to allow Pheoby to tell her story to the porch sit-

ters. She insists that her individual narration of her own text is not
essential to its accurate depiction. When she has completed her story,
she tells Pheoby: "Ah know all dem sitters-and-talkers gointuh worry
they guts into fiddle strings till dey find out whut we been talkin'
'bout. Dat's all right, Pheoby, tell 'em" (284). In effect, Janie's narration of her story in the novel's frame represents an extended, di-
dactic "call" whose message she herself summarizes in the following
way:

> . . . you must tell 'em dat love ain't somethin' lak uh grindstone
> dat's de same thing everywhere and do de same thing tuh every-
> thing it touch. Love is lak de sea. It's uh movin' thing, but still
> and all, it takes its shape from de shore it meets, and it's different
> with every shore.
>   . . . It's uh known fact, Pheoby, you got tuh go there to know
> there. Yo' papa and yo' mama and nobody else can't tell yuh and
> show yuh. Two things everybody's got tuh do fuh themselves.
> They got tuh go tuh God, and they got tuh find out about livin'
> fuh theyselves. (284-85)

Here, Janie seems to assume the role of prophet. In this role, she wishes
to share with her people her hard-won knowledge of the world. Hers
is a text vastly different from either Nanny's or Starks' in that it insists upon the necessity of acquiring a personal knowledge of the world
to complement—and make intelligible—cultural wisdom. But because of her own experiences with the masses, Janie is forced to position herself outside of the community that her knowledge would
benefit. She cannot, therefore, relate her text personally. Consequently, she enlists the assistance of Pheoby, a gesture which helps
to make comprehensible the complex narrative strategies of *Their Eyes
Were Watching God.*

These narrative strategies represent Hurston's application of the
Afro-American verbal behavior call-and-response—in a modified
form—to the genre of the novel. They suggest a manner in which two
voices can be combined successfully into a *single voice* to communi-
cate a *single text.* Janie's figurative discussion of the means by which
her story will be narrated by Pheoby suggests that her text can indeed
be related by such a unified voice. She says to Pheoby: "Ah don't
mean to bother wid tellin' 'em nothin', Pheoby. . . . You can tell 'em
what Ah say if you wants to. *Dat's just de same as me 'cause mah
tongue is in mah friend's mouf*" (17, my emphasis). Her text will not
be related to the porch critics by Janie personally, but by a "kissin'-
friend" Pheoby with whose voice her own will be unified by virtue

of a common perspective. Her voice will speak *with* Pheoby's, *through* Pheoby's. This strategy allows Janie the sanctity of a necessary distance from the group, while exhibiting (to the informed reader) her adherence to the principles of shared textual communication of her culture.

The narrative strategies of Hurston's novel are motivated, I think, by Hurston's desire to represent shared voice as a narrative possibility for the genre of the novel. Janie has learned that human voice is not in and of itself empowering, that quite often it signifies powerlessness, a response to threatening circumstances or an evasion of actual realities. Hurston's refusal to allow Janie to serve as exclusive, first-person narrator does not, as Stepto argues, "impl[y] . . . that Janie has not really won her voice and self after all," but, rather, demonstrates the protagonist's profound self-control and her knowledge of the impotence of the solitary voice. What Hurston does on the level of narration is to offer an example of an Afro-American pattern of verbal communication that represents *collective interaction* rather than *individual dictation*. The narrative strategies of her novel serve as a manifestation of Janie's insistence that distinct voices can be conjoined by means of emotional and psychological affinity, that, indeed, "mah tongue is in mah friend's mouf." It is a narration informed by the protagonist's knowledge and spirit, but not controlled by her voice.

In "The Blackness of Blackness" Henry Louis Gates argues that Hurston employs free indirect discourse in *Their Eyes Were Watching God* in order to "signify upon the tension between the two voices of Jean Toomer's *Cane* . . . by adding to direct or indirect speech a strategy through which she can privilege the black oral tradition, which Toomer has found to be problematic, and dying" (290). A most appropriate figure for such discourse is the image of unified tongues which suggests a potential blending of direct (first-person) and indirect (third-person) narration. Hurston's *denigration* of the genre of the novel by means of her imaginative employment of the principles of shared voice symbolized in the call-and-response verbal behavior argues forcefully that the black oral tradition is not dying at all but, rather, remarkably vibrant and powerful. Her narrative strategies suggest further that the black oral tradition is so powerful that it can be employed to adapt successfully the Western genre of novel in order to reflect Afro-American cultural impulses rather than mainstream Western ones. The narration of *Their Eyes Were Watching God* has been so long misunderstood because critics—even those knowledgeable about Afro-American culture and Hurston's commitment to demonstrating its beauty—have measured Janie's oratorical abilities by Western, as opposed to Afro-American, expressive criteria.

Janie does act in the role of prophet predicted for her at the scene of her natural education. Her life story—and its complex narration— suggest the manner in which the problematic state of Afro-American double consciousness (and its discursive corollary, double voicedness) can be resolved: by adherence to the communal principles of black culture. In a white-dominated America where principles antithetical to those of Black culture are often imposed upon Afro-Americans, the type of resolution suggested by Hurston's novel can be accomplished only by a re-connection of opposites that Western culture has conceptualized as irrevocably dissociated. Janie's achievement of an integrated self is made possible by her knowledge of the natural relationship between voice and action, by her unwillingness to privilege one and dismiss the other. Her final act as described in the novel, in fact, is an act of consolidation:

> . . . Tea Cake came prancing around her where she was and the song of the sigh flew out of the window and lit in the top of the pine trees. Tea Cake, with the sun for a shawl. Of course he wasn't dead. He could never be dead until she herself had finished feeling and thinking. The kiss of his memory made pictures of love and light against the wall. Here was peace. She pulled in her horizon like a great fish-net. Pulled it from around the waist of the world and draped it over her shoulder. So much of life in its meshes! She called in her soul to come and see. (286)

Janie's pulling into herself of the horizon suggests her achievement of indivisibility, the reconciliation of formerly disparate dimensions. She no longer will be forced into the posture of self-division, nor will she view the universe as divided. Inside and outside coalesce. Thus, aspects of human existence and of the universe which transportation to America has led Afro-Americans to view as distinct and other (Nature, the spiritual world, action) are understood by Janie to complement their antipodes (cultural, the physical world, voice). She realizes, for example, that Tea Cake's physical death has not ended his existence, that her own soul keeps him alive. She is able to conflate physical and spiritual into one, interactive, interdependent system and, thus, to resolve a double consciousness into a unified, black sensibility.

2

"The Evil of Fulfillment": Scapegoating And Narration in *The Bluest Eye*

I had found my tongue.

Toni Morrison
The Bluest Eye

. . . all the voice in answer he could wake
Was but the mocking echo of his own.

    *   *   *   *

He would cry out on life, that what it wants
Is not its own love back in copy speech,
But counter-love, original response.
And nothing ever came of what he cried . . .

Robert Frost
"The Most Of It"

. . . just as the male artist's struggle against his precursor
takes the form of what [Harold] Bloom calls revisionary
swerves, flights, misreadings, so the female writer's battle
for self-creation involves her in a revisionary process. Her
battle, however, is not against her (male) precursor's read-
ing of the world but against the reading of her.

Sandra Gilbert and Susan Gubar
The Madwoman in the Attic

IN THE previous chapter I attempted to chart Zora Neale Hurston's successful *denigration* of the novel. *Their Eyes Were Watching God* provides particularly compelling evidence in support of Hurston's claim that "everything that [the Afro-American] touches is re-interpreted for his own use." Such reinterpretation of expressive forms requires, as I have argued, not only a sensitive exploration of the lives of black characters, but also an energetic revision of the Western forms themselves. Hurston's placement of her novel in the Afro-American expressive cultural tradition in general, and in the Afro-American literary tradition in particular, is signalled by that novel's employment (and successful resolution) of the Du Boisian concept of double consciousness in both its content and its narrative strategies.

In the present chapter, I shall focus on Toni Morrison's *The Bluest Eye*. Morrison's narrative stands as her initial attempt at generic *denigration*, as her first effort to create what she has elsewhere called "A genuine Black . . . Book."[1] But while, as in the case of Hurston's text, it is possible to read in Morrison's novel clear signs of a merging of narrative voices, the narrative events of *The Bluest Eye*—and particularly Pecola's schizophrenic double voicedness exhibited when she believes she has been granted the "bluest eyes in the whole world"[2]— portray double consciousness as a constant and, for Pecola at least, a permanently debilitating state.

The following discussion will attempt to account for the reasons *The Bluest Eye* can present merged Afro-American consciousness only in its strategies of narration. Before such accounting is possible, however, it is necessary first to discuss the specifics of Morrison's placement of herself within the Afro-American literary tradition. This placement, I will argue, evidences a self-conscious rejection of the models of such preeminent figures as James Baldwin and Ralph Ellison, and a clear exploration of the types of thematic and formal concerns found in Hurston.

I

IN "ROOTEDNESS : The Ancestor as Foundation" Morrison insists that ancestors play an essential role in individual works in the Afro-American canon. She states:

> it seems to me interesting to evaluate Black literature on what the writer does with the presence of the ancestor. Which is to say a grandfather as in Ralph Ellison, or a grandmother as in Toni Cade Bambara, or a healer as in Bambara or Henry Dumas. There is always an elder there. And these ancestors are not just parents, they are sort of timeless people whose relationships to the characters are benevolent, instructive and protective, and they provide a certain kind of wisdom.[3]

Despite the apparent optimistic assurance of this statement, Morrison is well aware that "the presence of the ancestor" is not always viewed by the Afro-American writer as "benevolent, instructive and protective." Indeed, she argues—just a few sentences following the above declaration—that the works of Richard Wright and James Baldwin exhibit particularly identifiable problems with the ancestor. For Morrison, Wright's corpus suggests that he "had great difficulty with that ancestor," and Baldwin's that he was "confounded and disturbed by the presence or absence of an ancestor" (343). (Although Morrison does not specify which texts she has in mind, one assumes that she is referring to Wright's *Native Son* and *Black Boy*, and to Baldwin's *Go Tell It On The Mountain* and "Notes of a Native Son.")[4]

Morrison's singling out of Wright and Baldwin as figures in whose work ancestors represent troubling presences (or absences) is not, it seems to me, a random act. For in addition to both writers' *intra*textual struggles with ancestors, the Wright-Baldwin personal and literary relationship represents the most fabled *inter*textual association in Afro-American letters. Baldwin's attacks on his acknowledged precursor Wright offer intriguing Afro-American examples of what Harold Bloom has termed "the anxiety of influence."[5] In "Alas, Poor Richard," for example—an unconscionably vicious final assault on the recently deceased precursor—Baldwin asserts that the harsh criticism of *Native Son* that occupies the final pages of his essay "Everybody's Protest Novel" represented his attempt to create canonical space for his own perceptions of Afro-American life. He states: "I had used [Wright's] work as a kind of spring-board into my own. His work was a roadblock in my road, the sphinx, really, whose riddles I had to answer before I could become myself."[6]

Though it is certainly far from a sympathetic postmortem, "Alas, Poor Richard" does exhibit a great deal of sensitivity to the complex system of violent verbal revision that characterizes the Western (male) literary tradition. For Baldwin discusses not only his own problematic relationship to his precursor Wright, but also his view that he will himself inevitably represent for a younger writer an ancestral roadblock which that younger writer will need to clear away in order to create canonical space for himself or herself. He admits to not looking forward to being himself thrust into the role of villainous ancestor that he fashioned so successfully for Wright: "I do not know how I will take it when my time [to be attacked as ancestral roadblock] comes" (197).

With the publication in 1970 of *The Bluest Eye*, it becomes evident that Baldwin's "time" had indeed come, perhaps much more quickly than he had imagined. Morrison, of course, makes no overt attack on ancestral figures of the sort that occurs in Baldwin's "Many Thousands Gone" or, for that matter, Ralph Ellison's "The World and the Jug." But her first novel does contain clear evidence of her (sometimes subtle) refigurations of key elements of Baldwin's and Ellison's corpuses. Specifically, Morrison refigures Baldwin's discussion of Wright in "Many Thousands Gone" and the Trueblood episode in Ellison's *Invisible Man*. Only by understanding the nature of Morrison's disagreements with and formal revisions of Ellison and Baldwin can we fully comprehend her rejection of these "strong"[7] male figures as literary ancestors.

II

THE THRICE-REPEATED primer that serves, in its varying degrees of decipherability, as part of *The Bluest Eye*'s prefatory material assumes a central position in the critical discourse surrounding Morrison's novel. In "Dick-and-Jane and the Shirley Temple Sensibility in *The Bluest Eye*," for example, Phyllis Klotman argues that the various versions of the primer "are symbolic of the lifestyles that the author explores in the novel either directly or by implication."[8] Klotman goes on to suggest her view of the specific referents of each version of the primer:

> The first [version] is clearly that of the alien white world. . . . The second is the lifestyle of the two black MacTeer children, Claudia and Frieda, shaped by poor but loving parents trying desperately to survive. . . . The Breedlove's lives . . . are like the third— the distorted run-on—version of "Dick and Jane." (123)

Another reading that suggests that the primer offers an interpretive key to Morrison's text, Raymond Hedin's "The Structuring of Emotion in Black American Fiction," astutely discusses Morrison's manipulation of the contents of the primer. Hedin says:

> Morrison arranges the novel so that each of its sections provides a bitter gloss on key phrases from the novel's preface, a condensed version of the Dick and Jane reader. These phrases . . . describe the [American] cultural ideal of the healthy, supportive, well-to-do family. The seven central elements of Jane's world—house, family, cat, Mother, father, dog, and friend—become, in turn, plot elements, but only after they are inverted to fit the realities of Pecola's world.[9]

Hedin is correct in his suggestion that the body of *The Bluest Eye* represents an intentional inversion of the primer. Morrison's further manipulations of the primer are, indeed, even more striking. She employs the primer not only as prefatory material to the text proper, but also to introduce the chapters of *The Bluest Eye* that are recounted by the novel's omniscient narrative voice. The seven epigraphic sections are, as Hedin implies, thematically tied to the chapters which they directly precede. For example, the chapter which introduces the Breedlove family to the reader is prefaced by the primer's reference to Jane's "very happy" family:

HEREISTHEFAMILYMOTHERFATHER
DICKANDJANETHEYLIVEINTHEGREE
NANDWHITEHOUSETHEYAREVERYH (34)

But the family presented in the subsequent pages of the novel is the very antithesis of the standardized, ideal (white) American family of the primer. The reader is informed, in fact, of the Breedlove's overwhelming unhappiness and self-hatred. The chapter discusses, among other things: the "calculated, uninspired, and deadly" (35) fights of the Breedlove parents; the father Cholly's alcoholism and the mother Polly's perversely self-serving Christianity; the son Sammy's intense hatred of his father and the fact that he frequently runs away from home; and the daughter Pecola's tragic desire for blue eyes. The reader learns, in short, of the Breedlove's psychological and physical "unattractiveness," of the family's utter failure to conform to the standards by which the beauty and happiness of the primer family (and, by extension, American families in general) are measured.

But it is possible to make further claims for Morrison's employment of the primer as epigraph. In her systematic analysis of an inversive relationship between pretext (the primer) and text (her delineation of Afro-American life), the author dissects, *deconstructs*, if you will, the bourgeois myths of ideal family life. Through her deconstruction, she exposes each individual element of the myth as not only deceptively inaccurate in general, but also wholly inapplicable to Afro-American life. The emotional estrangement of the primer family members (an estrangement suggested by that family's inability to respond to the daughter Jane's desire for play) implies that theirs is solely a surface contentment. For despite Hedin's suggestion that this family is represented as "healthy" and "supportive," it appears to be made up of rigid, emotionless figures incapable of deep feeling.

Afro-American attempts to live in accord with these ultimately unhealthy standards occasion, as my subsequent discussion will demonstrate, not only an emotional barrenness similar to that of the primer family, but also intense feelings of failure and worthlessness such as those experienced by the Breedloves. By exhibiting that such negative feelings are direct functions of Afro-American adoptions of these myths, Morrison attempts to break the spell of the hypnotic propaganda of an overly materialistic America. She seeks, by means of her deconstruction, to mitigate the power of (American propagandistic) words and to make possible an emotion-privileging Afro-American environment. In her attempt to alter the reader's perception of what should be viewed as normative and healthy, Morrison's perspective is similar to that of her character Claudia when she discusses what would be for her an ideal Christmas. Claudia states:

> nobody ever asked me what I wanted for Christmas. . . . *I did not want to have anything to own, or to possess any object.* I wanted rather to *feel* something on Christmas day. The real question would have been, "Dear Claudia, *what experience would you like* on Christmas?" I could have spoken up, "I want to sit on the low stool in Big Mama's kitchen with my lap full of lilacs and listen to Big Papa play his violin for me alone." The lowness of the stool made for my body, the security and warmth of Big Mama's kitchen, the smell of the lilacs, the sound of the music, and, since it would be good to have all of my senses engaged, the taste of a peach, perhaps, afterwards. (21, my emphasis)

In privileging feelings and experience over ownership of objects, Claudia—and Morrison—rejects bourgeois standards of happiness. The false security of the "pretty," "green and white house" of the primer and its materialism are repudiated in favor of "experience"— the smell of lilacs, Big Papa's music, the genuine emotional security of Big Mama's kitchen.

Morrison's deconstruction of the primer and her exposure of an inversive relationship between pretext and text suggest that the author uses the primer consciously to trope certain conventions prominently found in eighteenth-, nineteenth-, and early-twentieth-century Afro-American texts. The convention that Morrison revises here is that of the authenticating document, usually written by whites to confirm a genuine Black authorship of the subsequent text. The white voice of authority—a William Lloyd Garrison in the case of Frederick Douglass' *Narrative*, a William Dean Howells in the case of Paul Laurence Dunbar's *Lyrics of Lowly Life*—has traditionally authenticated the black voice in Afro-American literature.

Robert Stepto has suggested that such white pretextual authorization of the black voice has had a significant influence in shaping the Afro-American literary enterprise. Indeed, his study *From Behind the Veil*[10] examines the various functions of strategies of authentication in selected (male-authored) Afro-American texts predicated on conscious revisions and refigurations of precursor texts. The increasing level of artistic sophistication Stepto observes in these narratives are, for him, a function of the Afro-American writers' increasing ability to manipulate strategies and documents of authentication.

The Afro-American narrative moves, according to Stepto, from white authentication of blackness to, with the examples of Ralph Ellison and Richard Wright, black self-authentication. Morrison's manipulation of the pretextual material in *The Bluest Eye*'s prefatory primer signals, it seems to me, another step in the development of the Afro-American narrative as conceived by Stepto. Morrison returns to an earlier practice—of the white voice introducing the black text—to demonstrate, as I have suggested, her refusal to allow white standards to arbitrate the success or failure of the Afro-American experience. Her manipulation of the primer is meant to suggest, finally, the inappropriateness of the white voice's attempt to authorize or authenticate the Afro-American text or to dictate the contours of Afro-American art.

Morrison's attitudes about Afro-American expressive art differ significantly from those of Ralph Ellison. For unlike Ellison, Morrison appears to have little interest in comparisons of her work to that of white authors, and views such comparisons as "offensive" and "irrelevant." In Claudia Tate's *Black Women Writers at Work*, Morrison says: "I find such criticism dishonest because it never goes into the work on its own terms. . . . [Such criticism] is merely trying to place the [Afro-American] book into an already established [read: white] literary tradition."[11] In "Rootedness" Morrison offers, in direct contrast to Ellison (and Baldwin), what are the terms by which she believes her work should be judged:

> I don't like to find my books condemned as bad or praised as good, when that condemnation or that praise is based on criteria from other paradigms. I would much prefer that they were dismissed or embraced based on the success of their accomplishment within the culture out of which I write. (342)

Morrison demands that her work be judged according to Afro-American expressive criteria.

Such comments from Morrison stand in direct contrast to statements by Ellison. In "The World and the Jug"—an essay whose expressed goal is a delineation of the fundamental difference of his fiction from that of Wright—Ellison refutes Irving Howe's claim that Wright is his literary ancestor. He states:

> . . . perhaps you will understand when I say he did not influence me if I point out that while one can do nothing about choos-

ing one's "relatives," one can, as artist, choose one's "ancestors."
Wright was, in this sense, a "relative"; Hemingway an "ancestor." Langston Hughes, whose work I knew in grade school and
whom I knew before I knew Wright, was a "relative"; Eliot, whom
I was to meet only many years later, and Malraux and Dostoiev-
sky and Faulkner, were "ancestors" . . . [12]

Ellison denies an Afro-American literary family represented by Wright
and Hughes in favor of a (white) Western ancestry characterized by
Hemingway and Faulkner and predicated on what he considers to be
the greater quality of their achievements as artists. He insists, then,
that a common (Afro-American) culture background is not determinative of literary lineage.

Unlike Ellison, Morrison rejects a (white) Western ancestry in favor
of an (exclusively) Afro-American one. She strives to create not American or Western, but an identifiably Afro-American (or Black) Art, works
which are identifiable as such because she "incorporate[s] into my
fiction [elements] that are directly and deliberately related to what
I regard as the major characteristics of Black art" (341). Just as she
refuses to voice assent to critical assessments of her work that judge
it by (white) Western standards or compare it to that of white authors, so, too, does Morrison refuse to allow the white voice and perception of the primer to authorize or authenticate the supremely self-
conscious example of Black Art that is *The Bluest Eye.*

Such a rejection of white criteria of judgment of Afro-American art
and life is, unfortunately, not possible for the blacks who populate
the pages of Morrison's first novel. The differences between her views
of Afro-American art and those of Ellison (and Baldwin) are evident
not only in statements such as those cited above, but also in her depiction in *The Bluest Eye* of the dangers inherent in Afro-American
acceptance of white standards.

III

THE BLACK characters of *The Bluest Eye* appear to accept Western
standards of beauty, morality, and success despite (for the most part)
being unable themselves to achieve these standards. The first such
apparent failure chronicled in the text involves the MacTeer home's
state of physical and seeming emotional disrepair. In direct contrast
to the primer house which is "green and white," "has a red door" and
is "very pretty" (7) is the "old, cold, and green" MacTeer house (12).

The structure's physical disrepair is symbolized in its inability to protect its inhabitants from cold (and cold germ-bearing) winds. Its apparent emotional impoverishment is exemplified for the novel's first-person narrator by her mother's apparently insensitive reaction to her daughter's contraction of a cold and her resultant vomiting. Claudia says:

> My mother's voice drones on. She is not talking to me. She is talking to the puke, but she is calling it my name: Claudia. She wipes it up as best she can and puts a scratchy towel over the large wet place. I lie down again. The rags have fallen from the window crack, and the air is cold. I dare not call her back and am reluctant to leave my warmth. My mother's anger humiliates me; her words chafe my cheeks, and I am crying. . . . By and by I will not get sick; I will refuse to. But for now I am crying. I know I am making more snot, but I can't stop. (13-14)

With a sufficient distance from this painful childhood experience, Claudia is able to see the inappropriateness of the images of cold and misery by which she characterizes her youth. As an adult she is able to see that her mother "is not angry at me, but at my sickness" (14). Further, she is able to observe that in the anguish of her former pain was:

> a productive and fructifying pain. Love, thick and dark as Alaga syrup, eased up into that cracked window. I could smell it—taste it—sweet, musty, with an edge of wintergreen in its base—everywhere in that house. It stuck, along with my tongue, to the frosted windowpanes. It coated my chest, along with the salve, and when the flannel came undone in my sleep, the clear, sharp curves of air outlined its presence on my mouth. And in the night, when my coughing was dry and tough, feet padded into the room, hands repinned the flannel, readjusted the quilt, and rested a moment on my forehead. So when I think of autumn, I think of somebody with hands who does not want me to die. (14)

This passage suggests Claudia's rejection of white evaluative standards vis-à-vis Afro-American life. Thus, her childhood, formerly conceived in a vocabulary of pain—her mother's droning voice, the scratchy wet towel, the coldness of the air—has been reconceptualized as filled with protective, "sweet," "thick and dark" love of a mother "who does not want me to die." The passage recalls Nikki Giovanni's discussion in the poem "Nikki-Rosa" of "Black love" and the inability of white criteria to sense its contours:

childhood experiences are always a drag
if you're Black
you always remember things like living in Woodlawn
with no inside toilet
and if you become famous or something
they never talk about how happy you were to have
your mother
all to yourself and
how good the water felt when you got your bath
from one of those
big tubs that folk in chicago barbecue in . . .

         *   *   *   *

And though you're poor it isn't poverty that concerns you
and though they fought a lot
it isn't your father's drinking that makes any difference
but only that everybody is together and you
and your sister have happy birthdays and very good
Christmases
and I really hope no white person ever has cause
to write about me
because they never understand
Black love is Black wealth and they'll
probably talk about my hard childhood
and never understand that
all the while I was quite happy.[13]

Like Giovanni's persona, Claudia discovers that despite the difficulties of poverty in an opulent America, "all the while I was quite happy."

Such a rereading of her life evidences Claudia's ultimate achievement of an informed black perspective. But her achievement is not unproblematic, to be sure. Perhaps the most poignant (and certainly most "charged" in an intertextual sense) of the incidents that result in Claudia's ability to reread her own life is her attempt to understand the rationale for standards that insist on white physical superiority.

Claudia's efforts can profitably be viewed as tentative first steps toward initiation into the larger American society. Her search to comprehend the myth of white physical superiority while attempting, at the same time, to hold onto her views of her own people's beauty and cultural worth, exposes hers as a situation "betwixt and between" that the anthropologist Victor Turner has labeled liminality or marginality. In *Dramas, Fields, and Metaphors*, Turner discusses marginality in ways that help explain Afro-American double consciousness. Marginals, according to Turner:

> are simultaneous members (by ascription, optation, self-definition, or achievement) of two or more groups whose social definitions and cultural norms are distinct from, and often even opposed to, one another. . . . What is interesting about such marginals is that they often look to their group of origin, the so-called inferior group, for communitas, and to the more prestigious group in which they mainly live and in which they aspire to higher status as their structural reference group.[14]

Certainly one way to conceive of the Afro-American's attempt to resolve double consciousness is as a struggle to be initiated into the larger American society. Such a struggle does not necessarily conclude in acceptance by that society (what Turner terms "aggregation"), to be sure. In other words, Afro-American double consciousness is not always resolved. As Turner insists, marginals—people situated betwixt and between antithetical, often antagonistic cultures—"have no cultural assurance of a final resolution of their ambiguity" (233).

Social marginality (or double consciousness) can, then, be a permanent condition. To begin to resolve such ambiguity, Turner argues, it is necessary to seek both the origin and an understanding of the often self-aggrandizing myths of the "more prestigious group." The questing marginal must seek to understand the origins of myths, "how things came to be what they are" (233). Consequently, adults' gifts of white dolls to Claudia are not, for the young girl and future narrator, pleasure-inducing toys but, rather, signs (in a semiotic sense) that she must learn to interpret correctly. Such interpretation requires mining the dolls' surfaces (pink skins, blue eyes, blond hair)—a literal search for source(s):

> I had only one desire: to dismember [the doll]. To see of what it was made, to discover the dearness, to find the beauty, the desirability that had escaped me, but apparently only me. Adults, older girls, shops, magazines, newspapers, window signs—all the world had agreed that a blue-eyed, yellow-haired, pink-skinned doll was what every girl child treasured. "Here," they said, "this is beautiful, and if you are on this day 'worthy' you may have it". . . . I could not love it. But I could examine it to see what it was that all the world said was lovable. Break off the tiny fingers, bend the flat feet, loosen the hair, twist the head around,

and the thing made one sound—a sound they said was the sweet
and plaintive cry "Mama," but which sounded to me like the bleat
of a dying lamb, or, more precisely, our icebox door opening on
rusty hinges in July. (20-21)

One of this passage's dominant images—that of ritualistic sacrifice—foreshadows Pecola's employment as scapegoat by *The Bluest
Eye*'s black community. This passage also offers material which enables us to contrast Claudia's and Pecola's encounters with the myth
of white superiority. Gifts of white dolls arouse in Claudia not affection—which would suggest acceptance of the myth—but, rather, a
sadistic curiosity: she dissects white dolls and, later, transfers this
urge to little white girls, in confrontation with images of beauty that
imply that her own almost antithetical appearance is exceedingly unattractive.

Pecola, on the other hand, also faced with the pervasiveness of
Western culture standards of beauty, accepts unquestioningly the
myth's validity. Her family's perception of its physical appearance is
represented by the omniscient narrator as significantly different than
that of other blacks who appear to accept Caucasian features as the
norm:

No one could have convinced them [the Breedloves] that they
were not relentlessly and aggressively ugly. . . . You looked at
them and wondered why they were so ugly; you looked closely
and could not find the source. Then you realized that it was from
conviction, their conviction. It was as though some mysterious
all-knowing master had given each one a cloak of ugliness to wear,
and they each accepted it without question. The master had said,
"You are ugly people." They had looked about themselves and
saw nothing to contradict the statement; saw, in fact, support
for it leaning at them from every billboard, every movie, every
glance. "Yes," they had said. "You are right." And they took their
ugliness in their hands, threw it as a mantle over them, and went
about the world with it. (34)

Jacqueline DeWeever has argued that *The Bluest Eye*'s obvious
preoccupation with the often devastating effects of the pervasive
Western standards of beauty on black Americans represents a foregrounding of a relatively minor scene in Ellison's *Invisible Man*.[15] In
the scene in question, Ellison's protagonist encounters a sign in a
Harlem store window with the following inscription: "You too can
be truly beautiful. Win greater happiness with whiter complexion. Be

outstanding in your social set."[16] It is certainly the case that *The Bluest Eye* manifests Morrison's revision of several aspects of Ellison's text—in particular, as I will later discuss in detail, the Trueblood episode in which the effects of incest are explored. But it seems to me most fruitful to observe this thematic concern with comparisons of black and white physical appearance in terms of the novel's female precursorial text, *Their Eyes Were Watching God.*

Morrison's discussion of an all-knowing master's decree that the Breedlove clan is ugly recalls most specifically not the invisible man's Harlem window shopping, but the infatuation of Hurston's Mrs. Turner with Caucasian features. Hurston says of the muck storekeeper:

> Mrs. Turner, like all other believers had built an altar to the unattainable—Caucasian characteristics for all. Her god would smite her, would hurl her from pinnacles and lose her in deserts. But she would not forsake his altars. . . . [She held] a belief that somehow she and others through worship could attain her paradise—a heaven of straight-haired, thin-lipped, high-nose boned white seraphs. The physical impossibilities in no way injured faith. That was the mystery and mysteries are the chores of gods.[17]

Certainly Pecola's and Mrs. Turner's wishes are not exactly parallel, but they are unquestionably similar. Both believe that through energetic prayer their desires for the obliteration of the Negroid—in Pecola's case, her black eyes, in Mrs. Turner's, the Afro-American race altogether—can be achieved. Mrs. Turner, already possessing (she believes) the beauty that accompanies Caucasian features, prays that the rest of the blacks—whose pigmentation, immorality and lack of civility offend her—be whitened in a miraculous act of God. But Pecola, whose features—her "high cheek bones," "shapely lips," "insolent nostrils," and dark complexion—are undeniably black, desires from her god a seemingly much smaller miracle: to be given the bluest eyes in the world.

Just as fervently as Mrs. Turner prays for a wholesale black metamorphosis, so, too, does Pecola ask to be blessed with a symbol of beauty. Having been taught by school primers and Madison Avenue advertisers that beauty and happiness are possible only for whites, Pecola believes that the possession of the blue eyes of a white girl would significantly alter her desperately painful familial situation:

> It had occurred to Pecola some time ago that if her eyes, those eyes that held the pictures, and knew the sights—if those eyes of hers were different, that is to say, beautiful, she would be dif-

ferent. . . . If she looked different, beautiful, maybe Cholly would be different, and Mrs. Breedlove too. Maybe they'd say, "Why, look at pretty-eyed Pecola. We mustn't do bad things in front of those pretty eyes" . . .

Each night, without fail, she prayed for blue eyes. Fervently, for a year she had prayed. Although somewhat discouraged, she was not without hope. To have something as wonderful as that happen would take a long, long time. (40)

Like Mrs. Turner, Pecola realizes that patience is required if her dreams are to be realized.

In "Eruptions of Funk: Historicizing Toni Morrison," Susan Willis suggests that "[t]he problem at the center of Morrison's writing is how to maintain an Afro-American cultural heritage once the relationship to the black rural south has been stretched thin over distance and generations."[18] If Willis is correct about the primary focus of Morrison's work, then surely Pecola's reaction seems to be the result of her spatial and psychological distance from Black cultural survival mechanisms that have served to preserve Afro-American racial pride. But Pecola's difficulties notwithstanding, *The Bluest Eye* does suggest that this legacy—however perverse its manifestations—is alive in other members of Pecola's community. For despite the apparent compliance signalled by its reaction to white standards, this community's reactions do evidence a (silent) rejection of white myths.

The survival of Afro-American mechanisms of self-preservation can be noted, for example, in Claudia's description of the outcome of her search for the source of white beauty. She says that the impulse to dismember white dolls gives way to "The truly horrifying thing":

. . . the transference of the same impulses to little white girls. The indifference with which I could have axed them was shaken only by my desire to do so. To discover what eluded me: the secret of the magic they weaved on others. What made people look at them and say, "Awwww," but not for me? . . .

If I pinched them [little white girls], their eyes—unlike the crazed glint of the baby doll's eyes—would fold in pain, and their cry would not be the sound of an icebox door, but a fascinating cry of pain. (22)

Claudia's somewhat sadistic dismemberment of white dolls and her subsequent torture of white girls are meant to recall, it seems to me, Bigger Thomas' axed mutilation of the dead body of Mary Dalton (presented by Richard Wright as a symbol of young white female beauty) in *Native Son.*[19] Morrison's refiguration of Wright's scene, as we shall see, is her means of adding her voice to the discourse surrounding Bigger's murder, the most renowned of which belongs to James Baldwin.

Claudia's impulses lend nominal weight to Baldwin's claim in "Many Thousands Gone" that "no Negro living in America . . . has not . . . wanted . . . to break the bodies of all white people and bring them low."[20] But while Baldwin suggests that such violent impulses are "urges of the cruelest vengeance" and motivated by "unanswerable hatred" (30), Claudia's acts, while they are, in part, sadistic in nature (she apparently enjoys "the fascinating cry of pain" of her victims), are motivated in the main by a need to locate the source of a white physical superiority that is not immediately apparent to her. Baldwin believes that, in general, the Afro-American refusal to give in to such urges and "smash any white face he may encounter in a day" results from a noble embrace of humanity. He states:

> the adjustment [from desiring to attack whites physically to attempting peaceful coexistence with them] must be made—rather, it must be attempted, the tension perpetually suspended—for without this he [the Afro-American] has surrendered his birthright as a man no less than his birthright as a black man. The entire universe is then peopled only with his enemies, who are not only white men armed with rope and rifle, but his own far-flung and contemptible kinsmen. Their blackness is his degradation and it is their stupid and passive endurance which makes his end inevitable. (30)

For Baldwin, such "adjustment" allows the Afro-American to claim (or reclaim) his humanity, a humanity which is, in Baldwin's words, "his birthright." This adjustment not only permits the Afro-American to demystify and de-villainize whites, but also to love his or her own people (a love of which, according to Baldwin, Bigger Thomas is incapable).

Claudia's "adjustment," however, has significantly different causes and consequences:

> When I learned how repulsive this disinterested violence [directed toward white girls] was, that it was repulsive because it was disinterested, my shame floundered about for refuge. The best hiding place was love. Thus the conversion from pristine sadism, to fabricated hatred, to fraudulent love. It was a small step to Shirley Temple. I learned much later to worship her . . . ,

knowing, even as I learned, that the change was *adjustment with-out improvement.* (22, my emphasis)

Claudia's "conversion" is motivated not by an embrace of humanity but, rather, by "shame." Apparently, the white-controlled societal forces that promote a single standard of beauty for which Claudia is attempting to find a rationale provide no sufficient answers to the questing marginal's quandaries about the origins of this standard. She learns only to feel ashamed of the curiosity that led to her "dis-interested violence," and that her failure to accept without question the standards of white America is considered "repulsive."

Claudia terminates her search for the source of white myths and replaces the violent urges she had previously directed at whites with "fraudulent love." But the suppression of violent urges by Afro-Amer-icans has significantly different implications for Morrison than for Baldwin. For Morrison, the Afro-American's humanity is not what is at stake, and "fraudulent love" of whites, the ultimate result of this rejection of violence, is not better or more authentically human. It is only different, only "adjustment" (an intentional repetition of Bald-win's terminology, it would appear) "without improvement."

The one feature that distinguishes Pecola (and her family) from the other Afro-Americans in the novel is the authenticity of her adoption of Western standards. The deeds of other characters—the adults' gifts of white dolls to black girls, "The eye slide of black women as [white girls] approached them on the street and the possessive gentleness of their touch as they handled them" (22)—would appear to suggest an authentic love of whites and acceptance of white standards. But like Claudia's "fraudulent love," this apparent love is not real; rather, it is simply the response to "The Thing" (62) that makes blacks feel guilt and shame about overt expression of Afro-American pride. In her provocative refiguration of Baldwin, Morrison implies that there is a wholescale Afro-American adoption of a self-protective mask. She suggests this further in her description of a group of boys who en-circle Pecola and shout at her, "Black e mo. Black e mo. Yadad-dsleepsnekked":

They had extemporized a verse made up of two insults about matters over which the victim had no control: the color of her skin and speculations on the sleeping habits of an adult, wildly fitting in its incoherence. That they themselves were black, or that their own fathers had similarly relaxed habits was irrele-vant. It was their contempt for their own blackness that gave the first insult its teeth. They seemed to have taken all of their *smoothly*

cultivated ignorance, their *exquisitely learned self-hatred*, their
elaborately designed hopelessness and sucked it all up into a fiery
cone of scorn that had burned for ages in the hollows of their
minds—cooled—and spilled over lips of outrage, consuming
whatever was in its path. They danced a macabre ballet around
the victim, whom, for their own sake, they were prepared to sacrifice to the flaming pit. (55, my emphasis)

This passage vividly suggests the pattern of mask wearing that permeates the Afro-American community depicted in *The Bluest Eye*. The
existence of such masking helps the reader to comprehend the devastating effects on Pecola of the community's employment of her as
scapegoat.

In her own view, as well as in that of the omniscient narrator, Pecola's appearance is not what distinguishes her from her black peers.
Rather, she is held up as a figure of supreme ridicule strictly because,
in her detachment from her cultural heritage, she exists unprotected
from the disastrous effects of standards that she cannot achieve. She
has not properly learned the rules of black (urban) life, or, rather, she
has learned them too well. While other blacks pay *nominal* homage
to the gods who created the standards by which America measures
beauty and worth, and appear, as a consequence, to have "collected
self-hatred by the heap," they actually maintain strong feelings of
self-worth. They hide these feelings from gods who are interested only
in surface—and not spiritual—devotion.

These people, in other words, represent a community that maintains, as does Janie in the face of Joe Starks' very similar tyranny in
Their Eyes Were Watching God, the Afro-American survival technique
of self-division. The community's worship at the altar of white beauty
is only gesture, only acts "smoothly cultivated" to fool the master,
to appease the gods. Because Pecola never learns of the potential benefits of masking and self-division in a white-dominated America, she
represents a perfect target of scorn for the blacks who are armed with
this knowledge. These Afro-Americans, in fact, use Pecola as ritual
object in their ceremonies designed to exhibit to the master their "rejection" of blackness.

The Bluest Eye, then, can be said to concentrate on the factors which
provoke Pecola's victimization in her own community. As we move
through the seasonally cyclical, inverted world that is represented in
Morrison's text, we see Pecola travel through various socioeconomic
sectors of the community and be abused by each in turn. Only by
understanding the specific provocations for the sacrifice of Pecola

Breedlove can we comprehend the role of masking and double consciousness in the tragedy of the novel. Such an understanding will enable us to grasp the reasons that Morrison presents the (divided) Afro-American psyche as unhealed in the text's narrative events.

IV

THE PASSAGE that depicts the apparent self-hatred of the boys who surround and taunt Pecola precisely suggests her role as scapegoat, a role that several critics have discussed in explications of *The Bluest Eye*. The study most devoted to such a reading of Morrison's text is Chikwenye Ogunyemi's "Order and Disorder in Toni Morrison's *The Bluest Eye*." While it is laced with inanities and facile misreadings of the text,[21] Ogunyemi's essay offers a sound analysis of the system of scapegoating operative in the novel. He states: "Running through the novel is the theme of the scapegoat: Geraldine's cat, Bob the dog, and Pecola are the scapegoats supposed to cleanse American society through their involvement in some violent rituals."[22] He goes on to insist that the abuse heaped upon Pecola—from the circle of taunting boys to her father's molestation of her—can be characterized, in each instance, as a ritual of purgation. Such purgation, or cleansing of the spiritual self, is evident in Claudia's eloquent conclusion of the text:

> All of our waste . . . we dumped on her and . . . she absorbed. And all of our beauty, which was hers first and which she gave to us. All of us—all who knew her—felt so wholesome after we cleaned ourselves on her. We were so beautiful when we stood astride her ugliness. Her simplicity decorated us, her guilt sanctified us, her pain made us glow with health, her awkwardness made us think we had a sense of humor. . . . We honed our egos on her, padded our characters with her frailty, and yawned in the fantasy of our strength. (159)

For my purposes here, a most helpful general discussion of the phenomenon of scapegoating which aids in the illumination of the motivations for such purgative abuse of Pecola is offered by Erich Neumann in *Depth Psychology and a New Ethic*. According to Neumann, scapegoating results from the necessity for the self and/or the community to rid itself of the "guilt-feeling" inherent in any individual or group failure to attain the "acknowledged values" of that group. This guilt feeling, or "shadow" as Neumann terms it, is discharged from the individual or communal self by means of:

the phenomenon of the projection of the shadow which cannot be accepted as a negative part of one's own psyche and is therefore . . . transferred to the outside world and is experienced as an outside object. It is combated, punished, and exterminated as "the alien out there" instead of being dealt with as "one's own inner problem."[23]

In combating the shadow that has been externalized and can, thus, be perceived as Other, the group is able to rid itself ceremonially of the evil that exists within both the individual member and the community at large. To be fully successful, such exorcism requires a visibly imperfect, shadow-consumed scapegoat:

> evil can only be made conscious by being solemnly paraded before the eyes of the populace and then ceremoniously destroyed. The effect of purification is achieved by the process of making evil conscious through making it visible and by liberating the unconscious from this content through projection. On this level, therefore, evil, though not recognised by the individual as his own, is nevertheless recognised as evil. To put it more accurately, evil is recognised as belonging to the collective structure of one's own tribe and is eliminated in a collective manner . . . (51)

Neumann's observations apply to "mass" or general man who, in his estimation, "cannot . . . acknowledge . . . 'his own evil' at all, since consciousness is still too weakly developed to be able to deal with the resulting conflict. It is for this reason," according to Neumann, "that evil is invariably experienced by mass man as something alien, and the victims of shadow projection are therefore, always and everywhere, the aliens" (52).

Neumann goes on to suggest that minorities and aliens typically provide the objects for "the projection of the shadow." This projection is, for Neumann, "symptomatic of a split in the structure of the collective psyche" (52). The self is split, in other words, into the good, desirable, unshadowed ideal self and the evil, undesirable, shadowed black self. Neumann argues that this division is motivated by:

> unconscious feelings of guilt which arise, as a splitting phenomenon, from the formation of the shadow. It is our subliminal awareness that we are actually not good enough for the ideal values which have been set before us that results in the formation of the shadow; at the same time, however, it also leads to an unconscious feeling of guilt and to inner insecurity, since the shadow confutes the ego's pipedream that is identical with the ideal values. (53)

Neumann's formulations of the scapegoat are richly suggestive in an analysis of both black-white relations and the difficulties inherent in an Afro-American sensibility that Du Bois characterizes as divided. For the Afro-American to split herself into shadow (evil, "black") and unshadowed (ideal, "American") selves, in a country which has traditionally viewed her as the (shadowed) personification of evil, is to invite such Afro-American self-contempt as is evident in *The Bluest Eye*. In circumstances where evil—which, for our purposes here, can be defined as a pronounced failure to achieve the ideal values and standards that have been set up by the tribe as exclusively desirable—must be eradicated from the community, that evil is often conceptualized both in the Euro-American psyche and in the divided Afro-American sensibility as the specifically and culturally black.

This eradication of black evil by whites is observable in such extreme instances as the lynching and mutilation of the genitals of black men under the guise of protecting white Southern womanhood. A milder (or, at least, less physically violent) intraracial form reveals itself in the passing for white of light-skinned blacks as depicted, for example, in James Weldon Johnson's *The Autobiography of an Ex-Coloured Man* and in Nella Larsen's *Passing*.[24] In both cases blackness, as a valuable human condition, is denied and destroyed. *The Bluest Eye* offers less extreme (perhaps), but nonetheless cogent examples of this hopelessly futile effort on the part of Afro-Americans to exorcize what the divided psyche often holds as the evil of blackness. Morrison's novel also vividly suggests the resultant scapegoating that occurs as a function of what Neumann terms "the projection of the shadow."

In Pecola's victimization at the hands of a circle of young black males, we see clear evidence of a projection of the shadow of evil upon her. These boys' insults are described as a function of their ability to disregard their similarity to their victim; the verse they compose to belittle her ("Black e mo. . . . Yadaddsleepsnekked") reflects their own skin color and, quite possibly, familial situations. Claudia tells the reader of the boys' "smoothly cultivated ignorance": "That they themselves were black, or that their own father had similarly relaxed habits was irrelevant" (55). This ignorance renders them incapable of recognizing the irony implicit in their castigation of Pecola by means of a verse that, because it chronicles the allegedly depraved conditions of their own lives, is also self-discrediting. This irony is lost to the boys because of the success of their projection of the shadow of blackness onto Pecola.

This manner of projection is also observable in Pecola's encounter with Geraldine and her son Junior. Morrison tells the reader that the most treasured bit of education that Geraldine has received has been:

> how to behave. The careful development of thrift, patience, high morals, and good manners. In short, *how to get rid of the funkiness.* The dreaded funkiness of passion, the funkiness of the wide range of human emotions.
>
> Whenever it erupts, this Funk, they [black women like Geraldine] wipe it away; where it crusts, they dissolve it; wherever it drips, flowers, or clings, they find it and fight it until it dies. They fight this battle all the way to the grave. The laugh that is a little bit too loud; the enunciation a little too round; the gesture a little too generous. They hold their behind in for fear of a sway too free; when they wear lipstick, they never cover the entire mouth for fear of lips too thick, and they worry, worry, worry about the edges of their hair. (68, my emphasis)

As I have mentioned earlier, Susan Willis argues that alienation—both in terms of "an individual's separation from his or her cultural center" as well as in the form of a frowning upon the natural Afro-American characteristics of kinky hair and thick lips—typifies the lives of Morrison's characters. For example, Willis says of Pecola's mother, Polly Breedlove:

> As a housemaid in a prosperous lakeshore home, Polly Breedlove lives a form of schizophrenia, where her marginality is constantly confronted with a world of Hollywood movies, white sheets and tender blond children. When at work or at the movies, she separates herself from her own kinky hair and decayed tooth. The tragedy of a woman's alienation is its effect on her role as mother. Her emotions split, she showers tenderness and love on her employer's child, and rains violence and disdain on her own. (265)

Polly's self-division—characterized by Willis as "a form of schizophrenia" and as a "separat[ion from] herself" —is nowhere more poignantly exhibited than in the scene to which the critic alludes in which Pecola accidently spills a blueberry pie that her mother had made onto the newly cleaned floor of Polly's employer's kitchen. In the process, she frightens the young daughter of Polly's employer. Her mother's reaction indicates some of the consequences of her schizophrenia:

> Most of the [pie] juice splashed on Pecola's legs, and the burn must have been painful, for she cried out and began hopping about

just as Mrs. Breedlove entered with a tightly packed laundry bag.
In one gallop she was on Pecola, and with the back of her hand
knocked her to the floor. Pecola slid in the pie juice, one leg folded
under her. Mrs. Breedlove yanked her up by the arm, slapped her
again, and in a voice thin with anger, abused Pecola. . . .

"Crazy fool . . . my floor, mess . . . look what you . . .
work . . . get on out . . . now that . . . crazy . . . my floor,
my floor." Her words were hotter and darker than the smoking
berries. (86-87)

Polly's reactions evidence no interest whatsoever in her own child's
welfare, not a bit of concern about the berry burns that caused her
to cry out in pain. Instead, she strikes Pecola, and displays infinitely
more anxiety about the condition of "my floor" than about her
daughter.

Further, her subsequent gentle soothing of her employer's crying
child and attention to her soiled dress contrast—painfully—to her
further besoiling of Pecola's dress and refusal to offer her daughter
any parental—or even human—compassion. Most telling of all the
occurrences in this scene is the interchange between Mrs. Breedlove
and the white girl after Pecola (and the MacTeer sisters) depart:

"Who were they, Polly?"
"Don't worry none, baby."
"You gonna make another pie?"
" 'Course, I will."
"Who were they, Polly?"
"Hush. Don't worry none," she whispered, and the honey in her
words complemented the sundown spilling on the lake. (87)

In addition to the clear contrast between Polly's reaction to the white
girl and her daughter—"the honey in her words" to the employer's
daughter as opposed to the smoking berry heat of her abuse of Pecola—this scene presents the maid's refusal to share with the white
girl Pecola's identity because of her shame at being identified with
the clumsy, pathetic girl who knocks the blueberry pie onto the floor.

The projection of the shadow, and its resultant scapegoating, then,
can lead to the sacrifice of the black offspring, to parental detachment from the child, and to complete adoption of white standards as
suggested by the "whispered . . . honey in [the] words" of Polly to
the Fisher girl. Such projection can also inspire, as in the example of
Geraldine, a futile effort to erase the black self entirely.

Geraldine desires to repress and deny "the funk," to exhibit no characteristically or stereotypically Afro-American qualities such as thick lips, nappy edges, and "rounded enunciation." To get rid of funkiness is, for Geraldine, to get rid of blackness and, in an America where blackness is equated with evil, to embrace the ideal national virtues of "thrift, patience, high morals, and good manners." To turn again to Neumann's discussion of scapegoating, we can conceptualize Geraldine's efforts as an attempt to exorcise the shadow of her own blackness. This energetic attempt to eliminate the funk does not allow her the pleasure of loving either her husband, whose sexual advances are unsatisfying inconveniences, or her son, whose emotional needs she meets with an affectionless efficiency.

So when she encounters Pecola in her house—this girl who represents for the entire community the literal embodiment of the shadow of blackness—and sees that the object of all her affection—her cat—is dead, Geraldine's reaction is one of a self-protective anger and horror. The text tells us:

> She looked at Pecola. Saw the dirty torn dress, the plaits sticking out on her head, hair matted where the plaits had come undone, the muddy shoes with the wad of gum peeping out from between the cheap soles, the soiled socks, one of which had been walked down into the heel of the shoe. . . . She had seen this little girl all of her life. . . . They [girls like Pecola] had stared at her with great uncomprehending eyes. Eyes that questioned nothing and asked everything. Unblinking and unabashed, they stared at her. The end of the world lay in their eyes, and the beginning, and all the waste in between.
> . . . Grass wouldn't grow where they lived. Flowers died. Shades fell down. . . . Like flies they hovered; like flies they settled. And this one had settled in her house. (75)

For Geraldine Pecola represents the repulsiveness of poverty, the vileness of blackness, the veritable eruption of funk. She equates Pecola with germ-infested pests, with flies that invade and soil carefully disinfected houses and elaborately prepared picnics. Pecola is everything that Geraldine is fighting to suppress. She is, for Geraldine, "funk," shadow, the blackness of blackness. When Geraldine tells Pecola to leave her house—" 'Get out,' she said, her voice quiet. 'You nasty little black bitch. Get out of my house.' " (75)—she is also, in effect, attempting to rid herself of her fears of her own evil, of her own unworthiness, of her own shadow of blackness.

Geraldine's efforts constitute, it seems to me, a splitting of herself into a good, moral, funkless self which she works diligently to maintain, and an evil, immoral, nappy-edged black self that she suppresses and attempts to expel. That this suppression and attempted exorcism of blackness render her incapable of enjoying life or of loving her family—or herself—seems to her a small price to pay for the warding off of the ignominy of an association with evil. Thus we see in Geraldine's characterization an example of defensive self-division similar to Janie's during her marriage to Joe Starks in *Their Eyes Were Watching God.* But while Janie, as I argued in the previous chapter, divided herself into inside and outside in order to hold on to the natural and to the culturally black, Geraldine's self-division is caused by her attempt to expel her natural "funkiness" or blackness.

With the examples of Geraldine and Polly, it becomes clear that, as is the case with Hurston's novel, an exploration of Du Boisian double consciousness is at the center of the narrative events depicted in *The Bluest Eye.* But, as in Hurston's text, Morrison's exploration of the Du Boisian formulation does not reflect an uncategorical acceptance of the older writer's views of the Afro-American psyche. According to Du Bois, the Afro-American seeks to ease the pain of participation in antithetical cultures by means of conflation of blackness and Americanness. He speaks, as I have noted, of an Afro-American

> longing . . . to merge his double self into a better and truer self. In this merging he wishes neither of the older selves to be lost. He would not Africanize America. . . . He would not bleach his Negro soul in a flood of white Americanism.[25]

Morrison presents evidence which disputes Du Bois' claims. Her characters' projections of the shadow of blackness, their unquestioning acceptance of American standards of beauty and morality, suggest that they have, indeed, bleached their black souls "in a flood of white Americanism." Theirs are not merged, but hopelessly divided selves, selves which attempt an erasure of blackness. In her exploration of divided and funk-rejected characters, Morrison both revises Du Bois and seems to refigure instances from Hurston's *Their Eyes Were Watching God.*

But while Geraldine's and Polly's shadow projections reflect suggestively the pattern of scapegoating in *The Bluest Eye,* they fail to attain the myriad symbolic implications of what must be considered the most deplorable and permanently damaging instance of scapegoating in the novel: Cholly's rape of his daughter Pecola. It is certainly possible to analyze Cholly Breedlove's incestuous act in ways that are similar to the above discussion of Geraldine and Polly: namely, as his attempt to relieve the persistent pain of the ignominy of his own sexual initiation by involving his daughter in an even more ig-nominious sexual act.[26] But such an analysis, while it might prove useful to a further elaboration of scapegoating in *The Bluest Eye*, would fail to address what seems to me to be the intertextually charged na-ture of Morrison's depiction of incest. In particular, I believe that Morrison is consciously (and *critically*) revising the Ellisonian depic-tion of incest in the Trueblood episode of *Invisible Man*. Her revision of Ellison, as the following discussion will attempt to demonstrate, provides particularly compelling evidence to support feminist claims about the power of feminist literary and critical texts to alter sub-stantatively our readings of male canonical works.

V

THE BREEDLOVE family in Morrison's text possesses a parodic rela-tion to Ellison's incestuous clan. The relation is initially suggested in the names of the respective families. Ellison's designation suggests that the sharecropper and his family are the true (genuine) "bloods" (an Afro-American vernacular term for culturally immersed blacks). The Breedloves' name, however, is bestowed with bitter irony; theirs is a self-hating family in which no love is bred. In both texts, the economically destitute families are forced to sleep in dangerously close(d) quarters. In *Invisible Man* cold winters—and a lack of money with which to buy fuel—force the nubile Matty Lou into bed between her still-procreative parents. In the case of *The Bluest Eye*, Pecola sleeps in the same room as her parents, a proximity which necessitates her hearing the "Choking sounds and silence" of their lovemaking (49).

Further, there are stark similarities between mother and daughter in both texts which contribute to the incestuous act. In Ellison's novel, as Houston Baker argues in "To Move Without Moving: Creativity and Commerce in Ralph Ellison's Trueblood Episode" (about which I will have more to say below), the daughter Matty Lou is her mother "Kate's double—a woman who looks just like her mother and who is fully grown and sexually mature."[27] (On a night which Trueblood describes as "dark, plum black" (53) such similarities would seem to have been a principle factor in the sharecropper's incestuous act.) And Cholly Breedlove's lust is awakened by Pecola's scratching of her leg in a manner that mirrored "what Pauline was doing the first time he saw her in Kentucky" (128).

It is possible, with the above evidence in place, to begin to suggest the specifics of what seems to me to be Morrison's purposefully feminist revision. Read intertextually, *The Bluest Eye* provides—as I shall demonstrate below—an example par excellence of what the feminist critic Annette Kolodny has called "revisionary reading [that] open[s] new avenues for comprehending male texts."[28] The Ellisonian conceptualization of incest differs markedly from what, through the example of Morrison's text, it seems to represent for the female imagination. The gender-determined differences between the presentations of incest can, I believe, be successfully accounted for if we turn briefly at this point to contemporary feminist discussions of female reading of male canonical works.

One of the contemporary feminist criticism's initial goals was the analysis of the implications for women readers of the overwhelmingly male authored and oriented Western literary and critical canons. Among the best early examples of feminist readings of male literary works is Judith Fetterley's landmark study, *The Resisting Reader*. In her in roduction to this study, Fetterley asserts her belief that women have historically been taught to read like men. Prior to the recent burgeoning of feminist criticism, the reading of the canon's decidedly phallocentric works such as (to cite examples which Fetterley uses) Ernest Hemingway's *A Farewell to Arms* and F. Scott Fitzgerald's *The Great Gatsby* encourages women's agreement with the inscribed anti-female slant of the works. Having been taught to accept the phallocentric as indisputably universal, the woman reader unconsciously internalizes the often-misogynistic messages of male texts. She loses, as a result, any faith in the validity of her own perceptions of life and, according to Fetterley, accepts male (mis)representation of women without protest. In short, she learns to read like a man: "In such [male] fictions the female reader is co-opted into participation in an experience from which she is explicitly excluded; she is asked to identify with a selfhood that defines itself in opposition to her; she is required to identify against herself."[29]

In the face of such derogative and self-negating instruction, a female must, in order to successfully participate as a woman in the reading experience, "become a resisting rather than an assenting reader and, by this refusal to assent, . . . begin the process of exorcizing the male mind that has been implanted" in women (xxii). The removal of the male implant results, for Fetterley, in "the capacity for what Adrienne Rich describes as re-vision—'the act of looking back, of seeing with fresh eyes, of entering an old text from a new critical direction'" (xxii). Feminist re-vision, according to Fetterley, offers the terms of a radically altered critical enterprise and the liberation of the critic: "books will . . . lose their power to bind us unknowingly to their designs" (xxii-iii).

Houston Baker's "To Move Without Moving" represents an excellent example in support of Fetterley's view of the (sometimes dangerously) persuasive powers of texts. For in this essay, the critical canon's most elaborate explication of the Trueblood episode of *Invisible Man*, we can observe the power of texts quite literally to bind even the most intellectually nimble readers/critics to their designs. Baker's unquestionably provocative recent study *Blues, Ideology, and Afro-American Literature* (in which the analysis of the Trueblood section appears) exhibits, particularly in a stunning reading of the economics of female slavery and the figuration of a community of female slaves in Linda Brent's *Incidents in the Life of a Slave Girl*,[30] his awareness of the ways in which feminist theory can help illuminate literary texts. This sensitivity to feminist concerns is, unfortunately, missing from his readings of Ellison. Instead, Baker's essay mirrors the strategies by which Trueblood (and Trueblood's creator) validates male perceptions of incest while, at the same time, silencing the female voice or relegating it to the evaluative periphery.

Baker's begins his reading by citing Ellison's discussion in the essay "Richard Wright's Blues" of "The function, the psychology, of artistic selection."[31] This function, according to the novelist, "is to eliminate from art form all those elements of experience which contain *no compelling significance.*"[32] While Baker cites this statement by Ellison for undoubtedly significant reasons—to suggest, ultimately, an essential parallel between Ellison and his folk artist creation Trueblood—his choice provides a means to discuss the shortcomings of his own and Ellison's treatments of the subject of incest.

If it is accurate to perceive of the artistic process as an act of omission of insignificant life experiences, then it is equally true that the critical process consists, in part, of eliminating from consideration those elements of the literary text that are without significant ideological or symbolic import. While I wish to avoid straying too far into issues of relativism that have been masterfully debated by others, Ellison's statements, situated as they are in Baker's essay, lead (I think necessarily) to an inquiry as to why neither Ellison's text nor Baker's critique of it treat the female perspective on and reaction to incest as containing any "compelling significance."

In the case of the novel, Trueblood's incestuous act is judged almost exclusively by men. This male judgment is offered by a cast which includes the black school administrators who wish to remove the sharecropper from the community and Trueblood's white protectors who pressure the administrators to allow the sharecropper to remain in his home and who "wanted to hear about the gal [Matty Lou] lots of times" (52). They form, as it were, an exclusively male evaluative circle which views Trueblood's act as either shamefully repugnant (as in the case of the black college administrators and the black preacher) or meritoriously salacious (as in the case of the white protectors who provide Trueblood and his family with material goods).

Except for the mother Kate's memorably violent reaction to seeing her husband atop their daughter, the female perspective on True-blood's act is effectively silenced and relegated to the periphery in the sharecropper's recounting of the story. Just as the Trueblood women run to the back of the cabin upon the approach of the car bearing Mr. Norton and the unnamed protagonist of *Invisible Man*, so, too, do Matty Lou's and the town's doubtlessly unified female community's emotional responses to the incestuous act remain (conveniently, it would seem) out of the reader's sight. Never in Trueblood's rendering of the story are Matty Lou's feelings foregrounded or even actually shared with the reader. Further, Trueblood is well aware of the silent scorn that the women who help Kate attend to the unconscious Matty Lou bear for him. When he returns home after an exile precipitated, in his view, by the inability of others to distinguish between "blood-sin" and "dream-sin," he orders the scornful community of women that has formed in response to his "dirty lowdown wicked dog" act off of his property: "There's a heap of women here with Kate and I runs 'em out" (66). Having effectively run out the openly critical female community and silenced, by means of his abominable act, his wife and daughter, Trueblood is able to interpret his act in an extremely self-serving way, untroubled by the radically incompatible perspectives of women. He can assert, for example, that the reason "Matty Lou won't look at me and won't speak a word to nobody" (66) is that she is ashamed to be pregnant. And he can, despite his belief that he is a good family man, fail to see the bitter irony in his assessment of his family situation: "Except that my wife an' daughter won't speak to me, I'm better off than I ever been before" (67).

From a feminist perspective, Baker's reading of the Trueblood episode proves as problematic as the sharecropper's because he, too, relegates the woman's voice to the evaluative periphery and sketches his own circle of males to justify and validate the sharecropper's act. Through an imaginative employment of male voices of authority from Freud to Victor Turner and Clifford Geertz, Baker asserts that one of the dominant themes of *Invisible Man* is "black male sexuality" (180). He speaks salutarily of the (re)productive energy of the black male phallus in Trueblood's tale: "The black phallus—in its creative, ambulant, generative power, even under conditions of castration—is like the cosmos itself, a self-sustaining and self-renewing source of life" (183). It is in terms of Trueblood's phallic "generative power" that Baker discusses the symbolic import of the sharecropper's incestuous act:

> The cosmic force of the phallus thus becomes, in the ritual action of the Trueblood episode, symbolic of a type of royal paternity, an aristocratic procreativity turned inward to ensure the royalty (the "truth," "legitimacy" or "authenticity") of an enduring black line of descent. In his outgoing phallic energy, therefore, the sharecropper is . . . indeed, a "hard worker" who takes care of "his family needs." . . . His family may, in a very real sense, be construed as the entire clan or "tribe" that comprises Afro-America. (183)

Baker invokes an almost exclusively male chorus to support his reading of the Trueblood episode. He cites, for example, Geertz's discussion of the Balinese conception of "self-operating penises, ambulant genitals with a life of their own"[33] in order to corroborate the sharecropper's statements which indicate the "natural unpredictability" of male arousal. He also cites Freud's speculations about incest which argue that prehistorical man "established a taboo on sexual intercourse with the women of their own clan" in order to "prevent discord among themselves and to ensure their newly achieved form of social organization" (179). While statements from Geertz and Freud help Baker to substantiate points about the uncontrollability of phallic energy and about Trueblood's dream signalling a historical regression (points which support the sharecropper's claim that he cannot be blamed for his "dream-sin"), they fail, because they invoke worlds in which women are indisputably at the mercy of the phallic and legislative powers of men, to allow the critic to consider the response of the victim to her father's act.

And though Baker makes a valiant effort to endow the hastily considered Matty Lou with positive qualities, viewing her—along with her mother—as one of the "bearers of new black life" (185), she remains in the critic's interpretation of the episode—as she does in the sharecropper's narrative—simply an absence. While Baker's essay adds immeasurably to our understanding of Ellison's art and of the sharecropper as vernacular artist, it fails, unfortunately, to consider the subsequently silenced victim of Trueblood's unrestrained phallus. Only by failing to grapple seriously with the implications of Trueblood's representation of Matty Lou's state following the incestuous act— "Matty Lou won't look at me and won't speak a word to nobody"—

can Baker conceive at the consequences of the taboo-breaking act as generally beneficial.

Unlike Baker's reading of the Trueblood episode of *Invisible Man* in which incest is conceptualized as material and tribal gain, Morrison's revision depicts it as painfully devastating loss. Actually, her reading of Ellison's text must be remarkably similar to Baker's, for in refiguring Trueblood in the character of Cholly Breedlove, she surrounds her creation with images consistent with the critic's conception of the Ellisonian character as majestic Afro-American vernacular artist free from social restraints. Morrison says of her character:

> Only a musician would sense, know, without even knowing that he knew, that Cholly was free. Dangerously free. Free to feel whatever he felt—fear, guilt, shame, love, grief, pity. Free to be tender or violent, to whistle or weep. . . . He was free to live his fantasies, and free even to die, the how and the when of which held no interest for him . . .
>
> It was in this godlike state that he met Pauline Williams. (125-26)

Only an Afro-American artist with the blues sensibility that Baker argues for Trueblood can organize and transform into meaningfully unified expression the utter chaos of Cholly's life. But Morrison—the remarkably skilled novelist who does transform Cholly's life into art—provides the blues song that is *The Bluest Eye* with a decidedly feminist slant. For while Ellison furnished his depiction of incest with a vocabulary of naturalism and historical regression that permit it to be read in relation to undeniably phallocentric sociocultural interpretations of human history, Morrison's representation is rendered in what are, for a writer with Morrison's lyrical gift, startlingly blunt terms.

Trueblood's presence inside his sexually inexperienced daughter's vagina is described in ways that suggest a significant symbolic import. The sharecropper's dream of sexual contact with a white woman while in the home of an affluent white man necessarily brings to mind images of lynching and castration of Afro-American males by white men because of the threat of black male sexuality. Consequently, Trueblood's actual presence inside his daughter assumes less importance in the text than his dream encounter with an unnamed white woman. Morrison, however, provides her depiction of incest with no such historically symbolic significance:

> [Cholly's] mouth trembled at the firm sweetness of the flesh. He closed his eyes, letting his fingers dig into her waist. The rigid-

ness of her shocked body, the silence of her stunned throat, was better than Pauline's easy laughter had been. The confused mixture of his memories of Pauline and the doing of a wild and forbidden thing excited him, and a bolt of desire ran down his genitals, giving it length, and softening the lips of his anus. Surrounding all of this lust was a border of politeness. He wanted to fuck her—tenderly. But the tenderness would not hold. The tightness of her vagina was more than he could bear. His soul seemed to slip down to his guts and fly out into her, and the gigantic thrust he made into her then provoked the only sound she made—a hollow suck of air in the back of her throat. (128)

Cholly is far from the majestic figure that Baker argues for Trueblood during his efforts to "move without movin' " in his daughter's vagina. And though Morrison does endow the incestuous male figure with the capacity for sympathy—citing, for example, the "border of politeness" that accompanies his lust—Cholly's "wild," "confused" act lacks the inscribed symbolic weight of Trueblood's transgression. While the sharecropper's inability to withdraw from his daughter's vagina represents, according to Baker, Trueblood's "say[ing] a resounding 'no' to castratingly tight spots of his existence as a poor farmer in the undemocratic south" (187), the tight sexual space represents for Cholly the forbidden area that must be forcibly entered and exited. The text of *The Bluest Eye* informs us: "Removing himself from her was so painful to him he cut it short and snatched his genitals out of the dry harbor of her vagina" (128).

Morrison, finally, seems to be taking Ellison to task for the phallocentric nature of his representation of incest which marginalizes and renders as irrelevant the consequences of the act for the female victim. *The Bluest Eye* serves as a revisionary reading of the Trueblood episode of *Invisible Man*. Morrison writes her way into the Afro-American literary tradition by foregrounding the effects of incest for female victims in direct response to Ellison's refusal to consider them seriously. And so while the victims of incest in both novels ultimately occupy similarly silent, asocial positions in their respective communities, Morrison explicitly details Pecola's tragic and painful journey, while Ellison, in confining Matty Lou to the periphery, suggests that her perspective contains for him "no compelling significance."

Unlike Ellison, Zora Neale Hurston is immensely interested in exposing patriarchy's inherent oppressiveness. In the following discussion, I will offer an intertextual reading of *The Bluest Eye* and *Their Eyes Were Watching God* in order to suggest the ways in which Hurston's text can be seen as a direct, "benevolent" precursor to Morrison's first novel. Material for such a claim can be most clearly observed in a further analysis of Pecola and of the text's narrative strategies.

VI

ONE WAY to begin to analyze the intertextual relationship between Hurston's and Morrison's texts is to compare the titles of the novels. Henry Louis Gates has suggested in "The Blackness of Blackness" that such an interpretive strategy leads to a full understanding of Ellison's signifying, in *Invisible Man*, on his precursor Wright. He asserts:

> [Ellison's] signifying . . . starts with the titles: Wright's *Native Son* and *Black Boy*, titles connoting race, self and presence, Ellison tropes with *Invisible Man*, invisibility an ironic response, of absence, to the would-be presence of "blacks" and "natives," while "man" suggests a more mature and stronger status than either "son" or "boy."[34]

It is similarly possible to chart a relationship between *The Bluest Eye* and *Their Eyes Were Watching God* by analyzing their respective titles. "Their eyes were watching God" connotes a communal observation of the wondrously curious acts of a god who is undeniably present in the world; "the bluest eye" implies loneliness (the single "eye"/I), blueness in the Afro-American vernacular sense, and implicitly suggests that solitude—distance from the tribe—is a function of aspirations for the non-black, for blue eyes. In other words, Pecola's (and, I would argue, Geraldine's and Polly's) status as "The bluest I" results from her adoption of white standards of perception. Hurston's title and text, then, suggest a common, culturally based method of (non-Western) perception of the world. Morrison's, on the other hand, imply solitude, distance from the group and, consequently, a means of viewing the world that is at odds with the Afro-American cultural heritage.

Morrison's apparent refigurations of Hurston's text are further observable in her various uses of nature in *The Bluest Eye*. Janie's fate is intricately bound to nature: the pear tree image dominates Hurston's novel. What is arguably the most important scene in the first half of the novel is Janie's education under the tutelage of a voice-capable nature which teaches her about natural marriage. Her improving self-image and defensive self-division are possible only when she rediscovers nature. Janie's remarkable harmony with nature stands

in direct contrast to Pecola's natural discord. While the sexual awakening of Hurston's heroine occurs in the spring and corresponds with
natural reproductive cycles, Pecola's sexual maturation, signaled by
the commencement of her menstruation, occurs in the fall during a
brief stay in the MacTeer household. The beginnings of both protagonist's physical maturity occasion inquiries about love and marriage.
Janie's questions are answered by an instructive nature:

> She saw a dust-bearing bee sink into the sanctum of a bloom;
> the thousand sister-calyxes arch to meet the love embrace and
> the ecstatic shiver of the tree from root to tiniest branch cream-
> ing in every blossom and frothing with delight. So this was a
> marriage! She had been summoned to behold a revelation. (24)

Pecola, on the other hand, finds no answers in a family where love
is not bred or in a northern city where she has little or no access to
nature or to the wisdom of her culture. Just as Nanny reads signs of
Janie's maturation into her kiss by Johnny Taylor, so, too, do Frieda
and Claudia view the menstruating Pecola as "grown-up-like" (28).
But this physical maturity is not accompanied by a fuller knowledge
of the workings of her own body or of love and marriage, as Pecola's
questions to her temporary bedmates suggest:

> After a long while [Pecola] spoke very softly. "Is it true that I can
> have a baby now?"
>   "Sure," said Frieda drowsily. "Sure you can."
>   "But . . . how?" Her voice was hollow with wonder.
>   "Oh," said Frieda, "somebody has to love you."
>   "Oh."
> There was a long pause in which Pecola and I thought this over.
> It would involve, I supposed, "my man," who, before leaving me,
> would love me. But there weren't any babies in the songs my
> mother sang. Maybe that's why the women were sad: the men
> left before they could make a baby.
>   Then Pecola asked a question that had never entered my mind.
> "How do you do that? I mean, how do you get somebody to love
> you?" But Frieda was asleep. And I didn't know. (29)

Answers to Pecola's quandries are unavailable. Having never felt
the love of anyone, she has no idea how to "get somebody to love"
her. When she ponders how romantic adult love might be manifested,
the only example available is that of her bickering parents. She wonders if their relationship represents the norm:

What did love feel like? she wondered. How do grown-ups act
when they love each other? . . . Into her eyes came the picture
of Cholly and Mrs. Breedlove in bed. He making sounds as though
he were in pain, as though something had him by the throat and
wouldn't let go. Terrible as his noises were, they were not nearly
as bad as the no noise at all from her mother. It was as though
she was not even there. Maybe that was love. Choking sounds
and silence. (49)

In contrast to Janie's instruction where she is able to observe the "love
embrace" of elements of nature, Pecola has as her only example the
"Choking sounds and silence" of her parents' sexual intercourse. Thus,
while Janie gains valuable information about marriage during the
period of sexual awakening, Pecola acquires only misinformation: that
love must necessarily be characterized solely by pain and absence. It
is possible, then, to perceive of Pecola's fate—at least with respect to
her sexual awakening—as directly contrasting that of Janie. Such
contrast is further observable in a more elaborate discussion of the
authors' presentation of nature in their respective texts.

Phyllis Klotman argues that "nature serves as the unifying element
in the novel."[35] It is true that, in terms of its strategies of narration,
Morrison's text employs nature's seasons to provide *The Bluest Eye*
with a sense of unity and wholeness. But nature here is represented
as being at best indifferent to man. Claudia's first words in the novel
suggest nature's apathy where humanity is concerned:

Quiet as it's kept, there were no marigolds in the fall of 1941.
We thought, at the time, that it was because Pecola was having
her father's baby that the marigolds did not grow. A little examination and much less melancholy would have proved to us
that our seeds were not the only ones that did not sprout; nobody's did. Not even the gardens fronting the lake showed marigolds that year. But so deeply concerned were we with the health
and safe delivery of Pecola's baby we could think of nothing but
our own magic: if we planted the seeds, and said the right words
over them, they would blossom, and everything would be all right.
. . . For years I thought my sister was right: it was my fault. I
had planted them too far down in the earth. It never occurred to
either of us that the earth itself might have been unyielding. . . . What is clear now is that of all of that hope, fear, lust,
love, and grief, nothing remains but Pecola and the unyielding
earth. (9)

Claudia's prefatory remarks imply an affinity between Pecola and the "unyielding earth," but it is one based on their common unpreparedness for reproduction. Nothing, not even the MacTeer girls' amateurish acts of conjuring, can encourage the barren earth to stimulate the growth of marigold seeds. The barren earth of Lorain, Ohio, directly contrasts with the actively reproductive nature of the young Janie's backyard in which the protagonist of *Their Eyes Were Watching God* observes the potential of "ecstatic shiver[s]" in natural marriage.

Another contrast between the two novels is observable in Morrison's apparent revision of the optimism inherent in Tea Cake's final gift to Janie. After she kills him in self-defense, Janie finds among her third husband's belongings a package of seeds. She plans to plant these seeds outside her Eatonville home:

> The seeds reminded Janie of Tea Cake more than anything else because he was always planting things. She had noticed them on the kitchen shelf when she came home from the funeral and had put them in her breast pocket. Now that she was home, she meant to plant them for remembrance. (283)

By planting the seeds, Janie will ensure that her memory of Tea Cake—whose given name, Verigible Woods, indicates his intense affinity with nature—will never die. In *Their Eyes Were Watching God*, the planting of seeds serves as a means of preserving life. Hurston's text ends with the suggestion that such preservation is indeed possible: "Tea Cake came prancing around her where she was and the song of the sigh flew out of the window and lit on the top of the pine trees. . . . Of course he wasn't dead. He could never be dead until she herself had finished feeling and thinking" (286).

Morrison's text appears to revise Hurston's use of seeds, insisting that the natural world of the North has no ability (or desire) to save or preserve human life. The planting of seeds in *The Bluest Eye* serves to demonstrate not nature's harmony with humanity and the possibility of preserving (at least the memory of) life, but, rather, a barren earth's indifference to humanity's needs.

Nevertheless, as I have shown, Pecola is continually associated with domesticated animals who are themselves employed by members of *The Bluest Eye*'s black community as scapegoats. But, just as she is associated with nonhuman entities such as dogs, cats, and "the unyielding earth," she is also connected metaphorically to birds. For example, after her encirclement by the boys and Maureen Peal's unexpected attack, Claudia says of Pecola: "She seemed to fold into herself, like a pleated wing" (38). This bird-like response to abuse recalls Nanny's explanation to Janie of the diligence of her efforts to move from the white Washburn family's property and purchase her own home:

> Ah raked and scraped and bought dis lil piece uh land so you wouldn't have to stay in de white folks' yard and *tuck yo' head befo' other chillun at school.* . . . *Ah don't want yo' feathers always crumpled by folks throwin' up things in yo' face.* (37, my emphasis)

Nanny's loving sacrifice is an effort to keep her granddaughter from suffering the ignominy of being perceived by the black community as a white folks' nigger, as an Afro-American who is influenced and controlled by a white perception of reality.

Pecola's tragic plight, on the other hand, stems primarily from her inability to achieve a positive reading of blackness in an urban setting dominated by pervasive white standards. Stuck in "de white folks' yard" of self-promotional propaganda, and unable to liberate herself from the oppressive influence of white American standards, Pecola cannot, unlike Milkman Dead in Morrison's *Song of Solomon,* "give up the shit that weighs [her] down" and "surrender . . . to the air."[36] This pervasive whiteness, coupled with her victimization at the hands of self-protective Afro-Americans who view her as the shadow of blackness, causes her almost literal transformation into the type of victimized bird that Nanny's efforts save her granddaughter from becoming. As the narrative continues, Pecola is represented as a grotesque, flightless bird:

> The damage done [by the community's abuse] was total. She spent her days, her tendril, sap-green days, walking up and down, up and down, her head jerking to the beat of a drummer so distant only she could hear. Elbows bent, hands on shoulders, she flailed her arms like a bird in an eternal, grotesquely futile effort to fly. Beating the air, a winged but grounded bird, intent on the blue void it could not reach—could not even see—but which filled the valleys of the mind. (158)

She remains tragically tied to white standards of beauty and is, even in her insanity, striving for "the blue void . . . [she] could not reach."

VII

THE RESULT of Pecola's victimization by her own community is a tragic schizophrenia, a psychotic double voicedness. This double voicedness results from her belief that she has been granted the beauty that she believes accompanies blue eyes. After her rape by her father and her encounter with the misanthropic Soaphead Church (which she believes concludes with her achievement of blue eyes), Pecola manufactures a friend in order to validate her newfound beauty.

Perhaps the greatest significance of Pecola's self-division to a discussion of the relation of Morrison's text to the Afro-American literary tradition is as a revision of Du Bois' conceptualization of the Afro-American psyche. For Pecola clearly loses the battle—as Du Bois conceives of it —to conflate in her person blackness and Americanness. Her loss is reflected in her schizophrenic confirmation of the beauty of (unachieved) blue eyes and in her total rejection of blackness. And so while Janie's divided consciousness is healed at the conclusion of *Their Eyes Were Watching God* to the point that she is able to "pull . . . in her horizon . . . from around the waist of the world and drape . . . it over her shoulder" (286) as a symbol of her self-unity and unity with the natural world, Pecola, burdened as she is with a permanently and debilitatingly dissociated sensibility, is depicted as involved in a futile effort to achieve the unreachable, imperceptible "blue void."

Pecola's splitting into two voices corresponds directly to the two-voiced narration of *The Bluest Eye.* The text of Morrison's novel has been narrated by two distinct voices: by Claudia and by an omniscient presence. For the greater part of the novel, these voices are in their focus and levels of emotional involvement in the matters they relate unquestionably distinct from one another. Claudia, who narrates the first chapter in each section of the novel, relates matters about her own life and that of her family, as well as information concerning Pecola about which she knows firsthand: her own dismemberment of white dolls; Mr. Henry's fondling of her sister; Mrs. Breedlove's abuse of her daughter in the Fischer home; and her sister's and her own attempts to save Pecola's baby. On the other hand, the omniscient narrator, whose voice controls the chapters that Claudia does not narrate, conveys pertinent information about the histories of characters much older than Claudia, as well as information about Pecola of which Claudia could not possibly be aware: Cholly's reaction to the white hunters who discover him and Darlene in the woods;

Polly's fascination with movies; Geraldine's attempts to suppress the funkiness of passion; Cholly's motivation for raping his daughter; and Pecola's schizophrenic discussion with herself.

But after the onset of Pecola's schizophrenic double-voicedness, the distinctive narrative voices of *The Bluest Eye* apparently merge into a single voice. Suddenly Claudia is privy to information which she clearly could have learned only from the omniscient narrator. She plainly comprehends, for example, the complex ritual of scapegoating in which the entire community has involved Pecola:

> All of us . . . felt so wholesome after we cleaned ourselves on her. . . . Her inarticulateness made us believe we were eloquent. Her poverty kept us generous. Even her waking dreams we used—to silence our own nightmares. And she let us, and thereby deserved our contempt. We honed our eyes on her, padded our characters with her frailty, and yawned in the fantasy of our strength. (159)

She is informed, further, of Pecola's desire for blue eyes—information that Pecola has shared only with God and with her imaginary friend—and of the Maginot Line's love for the abused protagonist. Claudia also knows the specifics of Cholly's incestuous act, and speaks of its motivation in the same terms as the omniscient narrator: as a function of his freedom.

> Cholly loved her [Pecola]. I'm sure he did. He, at any rate, was the only one who loved her enough to touch her, envelop her, give something of himself to her. But his touch was fatal, and the something he gave her filled the matrix of her agony with death. Love is never any better than the lover. Wicked people love wickedly, violent people love violently, weak people love weakly, stupid people love stupidly, but the love of a free man is never safe. There is no gift for the beloved. The lover alone possesses his gift of love. (159-60)

Not only, then, does Claudia's voice occupy the position previously reserved for the omniscient narrator, it also evidences a scope and breadth of knowledge that had heretofore belonged only to that omniscient voice.

This merging of narrative voices recalls Janie's memorable phrase when she assigns to Pheoby the role of narrator of her story to the Eatonville community: "mah tongue is in mah friend's mouf." It does indeed appear that the scope of the omniscient narrator's knowledge has, in the concluding pages of *The Bluest Eye*, been imparted to Claudia, that the last paragraphs of the novel evidence the conflation of their voices, of their "tongues." But the situation of such a conflation of narrative voices suggests that this healing of double voicedness occurs as a direct function of Pecola's own schizophrenia. Just as the improved self-image of the community depicted in Morrison's text results from its sacrifice and projection of the shadow of blackness onto Pecola, so, too, it seems, can a healed narrative double voicedness be achieved only through the sacrifice of the female protagonist in the novel's narrative events. The sacrifice of Pecola—a young girl who measures her own worth in terms of idealized white standards of beauty and morality, and goes mad as a result—is, it would appear, necessary for the achievement of the Afro-American expressive ideal of merged consciousness, of unified voice.

Despite its undoubtedly tragic conclusion, *The Bluest Eye* can be said to serve as another illustration of the Afro-American enterprise devoted to the *denigration* of the genre of the novel. Morrison's successful *denigration* of the form is accomplished not simply in her employment of dual narrative voices, but, especially, in the ultimate merging of these voices in the conclusion of her text. And so while she can depict healed consciousness as a possibility for any of the characters of *The Bluest Eye* only through the example of Claudia (whose subsequent achieved black consciousness enables her to serve as a narrator of the novel), Morrison has, through her manipulation of the white voice of the primer, through her apparent revisions of precursor texts, and through her depiction of narrative voices as ultimately conjoined, added to the Afro-American literary canon another supreme example of a Genuine Black Book.

3

Authorial Dreams of Wholeness: (Dis)Unity, (Literary) Parentage, and *The Women of Brewster Place*

*I wrote because I had no choice, but that was a long road
from gathering the authority within myself to believe that I
could actually be a writer. The writers I had been taught to
love were either male or white. And who was I to argue that
Ellison, Austen, Dickens, the Brontës, Baldwin and Faulkner weren t masters? They were and are. But inside there
was still the faintest whisper: Was there no one telling my
story? And since it appeared there was not, how could I
presume to? . . . [Reading]* **The Bluest Eye** *[was] the
beginning [of my ability to conceive of myself as a
writer]. . . . The presence of the work . . . said to a young
black woman, struggling to find a mirror of her worth in
this society, not only is your story worth telling but it can
be told in words so painfully eloquent that it becomes a song.*

Gloria Naylor
"A Conversation" (with Toni Morrison)

IN HIS essay "Art as a Cultural System," Clifford Geertz says of the
coalescence of form and content in art:

> The unity of form and content is, where it occurs and to the de-
> gree it occurs, a cultural achievement, not a philosophical tau-
> tology. If there is to be a semiotic science of art it is that achieve-
> ment it will have to explain.[1]

While my discussion of form-content coalescence (and concurrent explorations of double consciousness) is certainly not offered as a "sci-
ence" of Afro-American textual reading, it does, I hope, serve to ex-
emplify the semiotic notion that art forms, as Geertz puts it,
"materialize a way of experiencing, bring a particular cast of mind
out into the world of objects, where men can look at it" (99). What
my readings in this study allow men and women to look at, if these
readings are successfully lucid, is Black culture's insistence on unity,
even in the face of powerfully divisive opposition.

The unity of form and content in Gloria Naylor's *The Women of Brewster Place* is, like that of its female-authored precursors, essentially related to its exploration of the redemptive possibilities of female coalescence. But because it is a work that consists of the narratively *disconnected* stories of individual women, such coalescence does not involve simply an individual protagonist's inside and outside as it does in *Their Eyes Were Watching God* and *The Bluest Eye.* Rather, it involves demonstrating—both by exhibiting essential psychological and circumstantial affinities between the women and by offering significant evidence of these women's recognition of such affinities—that the protagonists of the individual texts actually form, at the novel's conclusion, a community of women. As is the case in both of the texts on which this study has concentrated to this point, textual explorations of female unity in Naylor's novel are unmistakably related to the work's narrative strategies, strategies whose ends are underscored by the novel's subtitle, "A Novel in Seven Stories": to demonstrate that the narratively disconnected texts of individual protagonists can be forged into a unified whole.

Naylor's narrative tasks are seemingly complicated by the means she chooses to demonstrate an achieved Afro-American woman's community. In a novel in which unrealistic dreams are the source of much of the female characters' pain, the author's depiction of the scene of female coalescence—the women's unified efforts to tear down the wall that separates Brewster Place from the rest of the city—as the grief-inspired dream of one of these characters prevents a reading of Naylor's portrait of female nexus as either an actual narrative event or a realistic possibility. *The Women of Brewster Place*'s totalizing gesture, then, evidences the work's textual disjunctions. If Naylor's novel displays a unity of form and content, it is a unity based on a common *disunity,* on a shared failure to achieve wholeness.

My subsequent discussion will demonstrate that despite its various disjunctive elements, *The Women of Brewster Place*'s relation to the novels previously discussed in this study is not essentially a parodic one. In other words, Naylor's novel does not employ *Their Eyes Were Watching God* or *The Bluest Eye* as misinformed works whose correction offers—as is the case with Baldwin's "corrections" of Wright and Morrison's revisions of both the primer and Ellison's Trueblood episode—dramatic entry into the Afro-American literary tradition. Rather, these texts, along with other key Afro-American works which provocatively explore women's lives and the impediments to the development of cooperative Afro-American communities (namely, Ntozake Shange's *for colored girls*[2] and Jean Toomer's *Cane*), provide the textual foundation and material for the author's provocative explorations of the potential richness of narrative disunity.

II

ELAINE SHOWALTER'S essay "Feminist Criticism in the Wilderness" argues that one means of advancing the study of women's literature is to describe and systematically account for the presence of both female and male precursorial influence in women's texts. She says:

> Our current theories of literary influence . . . need to be tested in terms of women's writings. If a man's text, as Bloom and Edward Said have maintained, is fathered, then a woman's text is not only mothered but parented; it confronts both paternal and maternal precursors and must deal with the problems and advantages of both lines of inheritance. . . . [A] woman writing unavoidably thinks back through her fathers as well [as her mothers].[3]

The notion of a female author's confrontation with a dual ancestry, of her text's "parented" status, is certainly applicable to the Afro-American woman's literary tradition which has—as much as its white woman's counterpart—been forced to develop (until very recently) in the shadows of an overwhelmingly male canon. My preceding chapter offers a detailed account of Toni Morrison's confrontations with such a dual parentage.

Morrison's refiguration of Ellison provides a suggestive literary example of the feminist revisionary impulse whose radically subversive goals the critic Sandra Gilbert characterizes in the following way: "We [feminists] must redo our [Western] history . . . , we must review, reimagine, rethink, rewrite, revise, and reinterpret the events and documents that constitute [a thousand years of Western culture]."[4] Showalter, however, appears to condemn feminist criticism's revisionary emphasis, arguing that it "retards our progress in solving our own theoretical problems" and speaking approvingly of the fact that feminist criticism has "gradually shifted its center from revisionary readings to sustained investigation of literature by women" (247). Showalter's views to the contrary notwithstanding, it seems to me that such a revisionary emphasis was a necessary moment in the history of contemporary feminist criticism. It allowed feminist critics and writers to expose the phallocentric myths that have long contaminated Western culture and literary history, clearing space for the types of sustained investigations Showalter desires.

Taken together, Gilbert's and Showalter's comments suggest a profitable way to conceptualize the primary differences between Morrison's and Naylor's first novels. *The Bluest Eye* stands as a revisionary reading whose textual struggles with white and Afro-American male-authored texts clear imaginative space for Naylor's sustained investigation of Afro-American women's life in *The Women of Brewster Place*. Morrison's stunning critical revision of Ellison's phallocentric *Invisible Man*, the Afro-American literary canon's most highly esteemed text, offers subsequent writers like Naylor a freedom from such corrective revisionary chores and an opportunity to establish less adversarial relationships with male writers whose work seriously and conscientiously considers Afro-American women.

Showalter argues that a parented woman's text "must deal with the problems and advantages of both lines of inheritance." It is difficult to discern in Morrison's revisionary ratios anything but the "problems" offered by *The Bluest Eye*'s paternal precursor. With Naylor's text, however, one can observe both the provocative "advantages" and perplexing "problems" represented by *Cane*. (Interestingly, as we shall see, what is for Naylor perhaps the most significant advantage of *Cane* also serves as its most perplexing problem.) Toomer's influence is felt first in *The Women of Brewster Place*'s opening sentence: "Brewster Place was the bastard child of several clandestine meetings between the alderman of the sixth district and the managing director of Unico Realty Company."[5] The sentence is a direct echo of the first sentence of *Cane*'s "Seventh Street"—the text that introduces the movement northward of the narrative's focus: "Seventh Street is a bastard of Prohibition and War."[6]

The narrative structure of *The Women of Brewster Place* is, in fact, akin to *Cane*'s first section. For the novel presents, like the first section of Toomer's text, the self-titled stories of female protagonists followed by a concluding story that explores a female community's reaction to an ominous natural event. There is, thus, evidence of Naylor's refiguration of *Cane*'s content. But any literary descendant of Toomer more interested in the *form* of his presentation of women than in the *content* of such presentations—as I believe Naylor is—must confront the perplexing problem of *Cane*'s form: that is, its apparent disjunctiveness and refusal to fit comfortably into any Western generic category. Clearly, no current generic designation is appropriate to describe the curious admixture of vernacular songs, imagistic verse, experimental fiction and drama that make up *Cane*. An artist attempting to use Toomer's text as a model must come to terms, I believe, with how it achieves its "chaotic" unity.

Naylor's technical refigurations of Toomer, which I shall discuss more fully toward the close of this chapter, manifest her creative responses to the problem of *Cane*'s form. Before such responses can be demonstrated, however, it is necessary to chart her more content-oriented refigurations of *The Women of Brewster Place*'s maternal precursorial text, *The Bluest Eye*. Only when one comprehends the later work's revisionary gestures with respect to elements of Morrison's novel can one successfully describe Naylor's recapitulation of a Toomerian effect to compose a specifically Afro-American text.

III

PERHAPS THE most fruitful starting point in an exploration of Naylor's relationship to Morrison is the author's own comments about *The Bluest Eye* and its potential assistance to a beginning writer. In a *New York Times Book Review* article entitled "Famous First Words" in which various authors answer the question "What is your favorite opening passage in a work of literature, and why?", Naylor cites Claudia's preface to *The Bluest Eye*.

> Each writing seminar I teach begins with having my students read Toni Morrison's *Bluest Eye*. I believe that by taking apart the first novel of any great writer, we can see plainly what strategies failed since it is a first work and where the germ of artistic brilliance lies since it is that particular author. With this passage [Claudia's preface], one of the novel's opening sections, I can demonstrate all the major elements of a writer's art simply through an exegesis of three short paragraphs. While the novel handles a weighty subject—the demoralization of black female beauty in a racist society—it *whispers* in the mode of minimalist poetry, thus resulting in the least common denominator for all classics: the ability to haunt. It alerts my students to the fact that fiction should be about storytelling, the "why" of things is best left to sociologists, the "how" is more than enough for writers to tackle, especially beginning writers.[7]

Naylor's statement is significant for my present discussion for two reasons: (1) it discloses its author's view of how one begins the struggle to become a successful writer, and (2) it justifies in a quite curious way its own insistence that Claudia's preface constitutes the most analytically provocative "first words" of Morrison's novel. In the first instance, Naylor suggests that becoming a writer requires development of a very specific *interpretive* skill. According to Naylor, the beginning writer must become analytically sophisticated enough to expose the artistic "flaws" in the "weak" first products of great writers. While Baldwin's discussions of his problematic relation to Wright are perhaps best understood in terms of Freudian theories of Oedipal struggles between fathers and usurping sons, Naylor's comments are more fully elucidated when they are viewed as calls for deconstructive exegesis.[8]

Although she disagrees with deconstructionist theories about the perfectibility of expressive forms (her statement suggests a view that great writers *are* great by virtue of their ability to conceive and execute successfully inde(con)structible narratives), Naylor seems nevertheless to feel that the apparent unity of a lesser work of even the greatest writers falls apart under the weight of an exegesis that concentrates on exposing textual disjunctions. Her view, for example, that "by taking apart the first novel of any great writer, we can see plainly what strategies failed" compares analytically with Jonathan Culler's suggestion that "[d]econstructive readings characteristically undo narrative schemes by focusing instead on internal difference."[9] Such readings, in other words, expose the disunity of apparently unified narrative structures. By taking apart the precursor text in order to reveal its failed strategies of narration in the manner Naylor suggests, the aspiring author operates much like the deconstructive critic who, according to Culler, "attends to structures that resist a text's unifying narrative schemes" (251).

Apparently, however, such self-oriented utilizations of texts as Naylor and Culler suggest also occasion what Harold Bloom characterizes as creative misreadings. For Bloom, the novice writer attempts to appropriate and then correct a precursor's meaning, an act which, because there is no such thing as "interpretations but only misinterpretations,"[10] leads necessarily to misreadings that serve to advance the novice writer's perspectives at the expense of those of the precursor. While Naylor makes no mention of what she feels are the specific flaws in *The Bluest Eye*'s narrative strategies, her strategic misreadings of Morrison's text, and their self-interested purpose, are, I believe, plainly evident in her discussion of Claudia's preface.

In asserting her view that Claudia's preface is of greater importance than the primer to Morrison's subsequent text, Naylor even goes so far as to argue that Claudia's preface contains qualities that clearly belong to the primer. She says that the first sentence of Claudia's preface, "Quiet as it's kept, there were no marigolds in the fall of 1941,"[11] "is the DNA [of the novel], spawning the second sentence, the second the third,"[12] though Morrison herself, in her employment of the primer's sentences as epigraphs to sections of the text, plainly implies a more essential generative relationship (albeit an inversive one) between primer and text.

The motivation for Naylor's misreading is not far to seek, for it lies in the most pronounced differences between *The Bluest Eye* and *The Women of Brewster Place*. White presence and influence are represented in Morrison's novel as powerful institutional forces that render blacks unable to assert any positive sense of self. Morrison's imaginative employment of the primer convincingly suggests the debilitating effects of such white influence on black Americans. But because Naylor's text depicts an Afro-American community virtually free from the presence and direct influence of whites, it fails to recognize the *denigrative* impulses that fuel Morrison's art. In short, while Naylor can correctly interpret Morrison's text as a sustained investigation of the lives of black women (as a novel, in other words, whose theme is demoralized black female beauty), she apparently cannot see, and therefore misreads, its revisionary impulses vis-à-vis the primer.

Thus, despite its obvious indebtedness to *The Bluest Eye*—an indebtedness whose most suggestive manifestations I will further discuss below—*The Women of Brewster Place* is clearly not interested in tackling what Naylor herself believes is the major theme of her precursor's novel: racism's effects on Afro-American women. In fact, Naylor clearly and purposefully avoids the subject, not in an unconscious act of defensive self-promotion or Bloomian misprision, but, I think, in order to examine (or, perhaps more accurately, to posit) *in*tracial origins of Afro-American women's pain as a corollary to Morrison's more deeply investigated depiction of its *inter*racial sources. Reading Naylor's novel as an ancillary text to *The Bluest Eye* might successfully explain its otherwise troubling silence where white culpability is concerned and its equally troubling extirpation of the racially energized tropes that it borrows from Morrison. I am suggesting, then, that *The Women of Brewster Place* is fully comprehensible only when it is read *intertextually*, with Morrison's text assuming a precursorial or pretextual relationship to the subsequent novel. For in fascinating, but distinct, ways, Naylor's art as represented in her first novel is as fueled by her deconstruction ("taking apart") and refiguration of *The Bluest Eye* as that novel is itself propelled by its dissection of its own prefatory primer.

First, however, it is perhaps necessary to distinguish fully between Bloom's views of misreading and my own as they pertain to a cooperative, noncompetitive textual system of black women's creativity. For Bloom, tropological refiguration and textual misreading of precursor texts by subsequent writers represent defensive, heroic attempts to establish priority over canonized writers. There are, however, other possible explanations for tropological refiguration. It is certainly difficult to imagine that Naylor's revisions are intended as heroic corrections of Morrison when the weight of historical evidence emphatically insists upon the accuracy of the older writer's assessment of white culpability in the continuing tragedies of Afro-Americans. Her refigurative gestures might best be explained, I think, as investigations of intraracial sources of Afro-American women's pain in the context of what Donald Gibson calls the "pressures" of a particular historical moment.

Gibson's discussion in *The Politics of Literary Expression* of the mimetic impulses of Afro-American writers offers a provocative juxtaposition to Bloom's theories. For Gibson argues that "black writers have produced literature that reflects their situations as social beings existing within a particular historical framework and subject to the pressures of a special nature resulting therefrom."[13] Instead of an anxiety of self-promotion, Gibson speaks of the pressures on Afro-American writers to depict (one would assume *accurately*) the social realities of their people "within a particular historical framework." Social conditions, according to Gibson, are the primary determinants of the scope and focus of individual Afro-American texts. While I do not agree uncategorically with Gibson's assessments,[14] I do believe that the most fruitful means of comprehending noncompetitive revision in Afro-American expressive systems in general, and in the texts I am examining in particular, is by examining the social and historical differences between the contexts in which the various figures are being used. When I refer to Naylor's novel as an ancillary text to *The Bluest Eye*, I mean not only that much of its content is derived from Morrison's novel, but, more importantly, that a full understanding of *The Women of Brewster Place*'s refigurative gestures is possible only when the reader is cognizant of the differences between the social conditions in which the texts were composed.

It is evident just from the writers' presentations of white presence in the respective communities depicted in the novels that they are discussing decidedly different times. Despite these differences, however, Naylor chooses to repeat several of Morrison's figures. For example, her discussion of the history of Brewster Place in the prefatory section entitled "Dawn" clearly is a revision of Morrison's description of the Breedlove family and household. Both texts explicitly contrast the socioeconomic mobility of white former inhabitants with the state of virtual imprisonment of the current black residents. Morrison accounts for the Breedlove's inhabitance of a dilapidated storefront in the following way:

> The Breedloves did not live in a storefront because they were having temporary difficulty adjusting to the cutbacks at the plant. They lived there because they were poor and black, and they stayed there because they believed they were ugly. (34)

In *The Women of Brewster Place*, blacks are also, in effect, confined to urban ghetto space:

> They [black Brewster dwellers] clung to the street with a desperate acceptance that whatever was here was better than the starving southern climates they had fled from. Brewster Place knew that unlike its other [white] children, the few who would leave forever were the exception rather than the rule, since they came because they had no choice and would remain for the same reason. (4)

Unlike the non-black immigrants in both texts—unlike the Hungarian baker in *The Bluest Eye* who was "modestly famous for his brioche and poppy-seed rolls" and the "gypsies [who] used it [the Breedlove home] as a base of operations" (30), and, in Naylor's text, the similarly "dark haired and mellow-skinned" people who had brought to Brewster Place "the pungent smells of strong cheeses and smoked meats" (2)—the blacks who populate the subsequently abandoned space of the American ghetto are permanently bound there. In both texts, then, Afro-Americans are, despite their journeys north from what Naylor calls "starving southern climates" (4), unable to partake of putatively superior opportunities for economic advancement.

The Women of Brewster Place presents the confinement to ghetto space of the Breedlove family as a reality for an entire Afro-American community. However, Naylor's refigurations are, to be sure, repetition with a difference. Unlike the black community in *The Bluest Eye*, all of whose residents suffer because of pressures to live in accord with white standards, Brewster Place is a physically and legislatively isolated urban island which is, for the most part, untouched by a direct white influence. Consequently, while Morrison's novel criticizes white-controlled institutional forces for their roles in causing the development of negative Afro-American self-images, Naylor's work looks

elsewhere for the sources of black women's pain. An examination of
the section of *The Women of Brewster Place* entitled "Cora Lee" offers
evidence not only about where Naylor locates that source, but also
about the nature of historically determined tropological refiguration.

IV

"CORA LEE" represents the clearest example of Naylor's reuse and refiguration of the deconstructed parts of *The Bluest Eye*. In this story,
Naylor's eradication of the interracial import of figures which she
borrows from Morrison is fully evident, and offers perhaps the best
means of conceptualizing the nature and precise motivation of such
acts. The story's initial paragraphs which discuss a young girl's over-
abundant love of dolls appear, when considered in relation to Morrison's depiction of Claudia's negative reaction to dolls, to represent
perhaps the signal moment of critical revision in the Afro-American
woman's narrative tradition. The text tells us of Cora Lee:

> Her new baby doll. They [her parents] placed the soft plastic and
> pink flannel in the little girl's lap, and she turned her moon-shaped
> eyes toward them in awed gratitude. It was so perfect and so
> small. She trailed her fingertips along the smooth brown fore-
> head and down into the bottom curve of the upturned nose. She
> gently lifted the dimpled arms and legs and then reverently placed
> them back. Slowly kissing the set painted mouth, she inhaled its
> new aroma while stroking the silken curled head and full cheeks.
> She circled her arms around the motionless body and squeezed,
> while with tightly closed eyes she waited breathlessly for the first
> trembling vibrations of its low, gravelly "Mama" to radiate
> through her breast. (107)

This reaction to Christmas gifts of dolls is directly and intentionally
antithetical to Claudia's response to white dolls:

> The . . . dolls, which were supposed to bring me great pleasure,
> succeeded in doing quite the opposite. When I took it to bed, its
> hard, unyielding limbs resisted my flesh—the tapered fingertips
> on those dimpled hands scratched. If, in sleep, I turned, the bone-
> cold head collided with my own. It was a most uncomfortable,
> patently aggressive sleeping companion. To hold it was no more
> rewarding. The starched gauze or lace on the cotton dress irri-
> tated any embrace. (20)

The (white) doll is, for Claudia, nothing short of a formidable foe—unyielding, uncomfortable, unrewarding—to which she is clearly unable to respond positively. Her inability to regard the doll positively demonstrates, it seems to me, Claudia's general rejection of sex-role stereotyping—she apparently has no natural attraction to sugar, spice, or everything typically thought of as nice for young girls—just as her subsequent dissection of these dolls suggests her conscious repudiation of white myths of superiority. The (brown) doll in "Cora Lee," however, is a dimpled figure to which Cora attends with a near-religious devotion and reverence; its plastic form yields not only pleasant, plastic aromas, but also gratifyingly responsive voice—"the first trembling vibrations of its low, gravelly 'Mama.' "

Cora's exuberant reaction to the doll's voice contrasts dramatically with Claudia's almost scientific investigation of the source of her doll's voice:

> the thing made one sound—a sound they [the adults] said was the sweet and plaintive cry "Mama," but which sounded to me like the bleat of a dying lamb, or, more precisely, our ice-box door opening on rusty hinges in July. Remove the cold and stupid eyeball, it would bleat still, "Ahhhhh," take off the head, shake out the sawdust, crack the back against the brass bed rail, it would bleat still. The gauze back would split, and *I could see the disk with six holes, the secret of the sound. A mere metal roundness.* (20–21, my emphasis)

Unlike Cora Lee, who believes that the doll's voice is unquestionably a response to the affectionate and reverent nature of her embrace, Claudia—for whom the plastic figure's voice signifies death (the bleatings of dying lambs) and dilapidation (her refrigerator's door opening on rusty hinges)—learns that her doll's voice is a mechanical response to pressure. Claudia discovers upon further investigation "the secret of the sound," the source, if you will, of plastic voice: "A mere, metal roundness."

Naylor's revisionary gestures are further observable in her refiguration of Claudia's destruction of dolls. Because Claudia's de-(con)struction yields sufficient information about the source of her doll's voice, she believes that further dissection may offer answers as to the source of the myth of white superiority. Like Claudia, Cora destroys dolls that are to her undesirable. But while Claudia's de(con)struction results directly from feelings of racial pride and from a desire or need for knowledge, Cora's destruction of dolls is a function of her inability or unwillingness to mature—of her determined avoidance of knowledge. The text informs us:

she spent all of her time with her dolls—and they had to be baby dolls. She told [her parents] this with a silent rebellion the year they had decided she was now old enough for a teenaged Barbie doll; they had even sacrificed for an expensive set of foreign figurines with porcelain faces and real silk and lace mantillas, saris, and kimonos. The following week they found the dolls under her bed with the heads smashed in and the arms twisted out of the sockets. (107-8)

Cora Lee destroys the dolls intended for an increasingly mature child in an effort to maintain a willful ignorance of the world and of herself. She has no interest in dolls against which she can measure signs of her own increasing physical maturity, or even in gaining raimentary knowledge of foreign cultures. Rather, quite unlike Claudia, Cora is interested in baby dolls as cuddly, helpless figures which she can think of as possessing an unvarying need for her attention, and whose static natures are a perfect complement to her own inability to mature.

While their presentations of young girls' responses to dolls are, at the very least, antithetical, I would argue that Naylor is not seeking to call into question the accuracy of Morrison's depiction of the destructive efforts of white standards. Rather, Naylor's refigurations represent her submitting of her precursor's figure to the pressures of a different historical moment. Morrison's discussions of her motivations for writing *The Bluest Eye* not only serve to substantiate Gibson's claim that black writers "have produced literature that reflects their situations as social beings," but also offer information which aids our understanding of her specific figuration of the doll trope. In a cover story of *Newsweek* devoted to her, Morrison says of *The Bluest Eye*'s genesis: "It was 1967 and the slogan 'Black is beautiful' was in the air. I loved it, but something was missing."[15] Her essay "The Making of *The Black Book*" offers a clear elaboration of what she felt was "missing" in the slogan:

the phrase evaded the issue and our plight by being a reaction to a white idea, which means it was a white idea turned inside out, and a white idea turned inside out is still a white idea. The concept of physical beauty as a virtue is one of the dumbest, most pernicious and destructive ideas of the Western world, and we should have nothing to do with it. Physical beauty has nothing to do with our past, present or future.[16]

The phrase "Black is beautiful" clearly is not, in several respects, black enough for Morrison. That is, it accepts white evaluative notions of worth—not the superiority of Caucasian beauty, but the "Western" belief that physical beauty, as determined by whatever subjective standards, connotes human worth—and, for Morrison, exposes its advocates' continued submission to white authority. What is missing in the slogan for Morrison, then, is a *denigrative* component that would allow Afro-Americans to promote black pride in accord with Black cultural truths, with something that "has . . . to do with our past, present or future." The doll trope in *The Bluest Eye*, then, serves as Morrison's means to criticize the white institutional tendency to promote a single standard of beauty, and to invalidate the idea that physical beauty connotes intrinsic human value.

When Naylor employs the doll trope in *The Women of Brewster Place*, the greatest problems in the Afro-American community are of a different nature. These problems concern not the beauty of blackness, but, some have argued, the self-destruction of the black underclass. Michele Wallace succinctly characterizes the "profound crisis" in the Afro-American community as its "accelerating rates of high school dropouts, imprisonment, teenage births, unemployment, [and] impoverished female-headed families."[17] Naylor's manipulation of the doll trope reflects her testing of the figure under the historical conditions Wallace describes in an overtly revisionary gesture. This revisionary gesture stands not as a competitive correction of the precursor's meaning, but as an erudite acknowledgment of the fact that few tropological configurations are indisputably "true" or "correct" in perpetuity.

Naylor's interest in exploring what Wallace calls the Afro-American community's "profound crisis" is observable in the subsequent pages of the story "Cora Lee." The title character, who is unable to appreciate her parents' gifts of dolls that befit her movement toward physical maturity, is also incapable later in her life of caring responsibly for her own growing children. Her immaturity occasions her childish conceptualization of the male phallus as—in her mother's euphemistic phrase—"the thing that felt good in the dark" (109). She takes little thought of the economic and psychological consequences for her children of her perpetually bringing infants into the world. Cora Lee remains, despite the undeniably horrendous family life she has created for her children, magically attracted to infants who, like her dolls, depend solely upon her for sustenance. While she attends "religiously" (112) to her infant children, because of her own emotional stagnation she has not the slightest notion of how to care for or nurture children when they are no longer babies. Her older children are for her simply incomprehensible nuisances who interrupt her soap opera viewing and destroy furniture and clothes. They are, in her candid (and much-expressed) view, "little dumb asses" (118).

Cora apparently has no idea of her own culpability in her children's repugnant behavior—truancy, destruction of property, digging in garbage for sweets. Her ignorance of the fact that their scholastic weaknesses result largely from her failure to provide adequate inspiration or discipline is observable in her response to their insistence that they have no homework and, consequently, should be permitted to play outdoors: " 'Awful strange,' she muttered darkly. 'No one ever has any homework. When I was in school, we always got homework.' " (111)

Despite such unsettling beginnings, "Cora Lee" traces its protagonist's ultimate movement toward what Naylor calls "hopeful echoes of order and peace" (127). Such a transformation is encouraged, somewhat ironically, by Kiswana Browne, the novel's resident dreamer, and by a black production of *A Midsummer Night's Dream*, Shakespeare's masterful exploration of the ambiguities of the space between reality and dream. Cora Lee ultimately moves from an almost total incomprehension of her non-infant children and of her role as mother to what is, for her, a rather profound knowledge of maternal responsibilities. On what the text refers to as "a night of wonders" (127), Cora resolves to create a supportive academic environment for her children:

> School would be over in a few weeks, but all this truant nonsense had to stop. She would get up and walk them there personally if she had to—and summer school. How long had the teachers been saying that they needed summer school? And she would check homework—every night. And P.T.A. Sonya wouldn't be little forever—she'd have no more excuses for missing those meetings in the evening. Junior high; high school; college—none of them stayed little forever. And then on to good jobs in insurance companies and the post office, even doctors and lawyers. Yes, that's what would happen to her babies. (126)

But, unlike the heavily textured Shakespeare comedy that Cora Lee and her family attend in which, in the words of the critic Anne Barton, a "new social order . . . has emerged from the ordeal of the wood,"[18] the protagonist's patterns of parenthood will not change appreciably. Despite the "hopeful echoes" resonating through her apartment, Cora nevertheless sleeps with the anonymous "shadow" lover "who had let himself in with his key" (127) and, apparently—if we can trust Mattie's dream as accounted in the section "The Block Party"

in which Cora Lee appears pregnant—begins again the cycle of pregnancy, infant adoration, and post-infant neglect which has characterized her adult life.

Such a reading of "Cora Lee" is made possible not only by the el-
evated, totally unrealistic (considering the narrator's comments about
a severely limited black social mobility) nature of the mother's plans
for her children—"even doctors or lawyers"—but also by her reaction to the presence of the shadow. Because of the physical and psychological abuse she suffers at the hands of her older children's fathers, Cora has learned to view her subsequent sexual partners as
shadows, men "who came in the dark and showed her the thing that
felt good in the dark, and often left before the children awakened"
(113). Upon seeing her latest sexual partner in bed at the close of a
day of self-discovery, she "turned and firmly folded her evening like
gold and lavender gauze deep within the creases of her dreams, and
let her clothes drop to the floor" (127). The title character's slovenly
disrobing contrasts directly with her neat folding of her children's
ragged clothing (and her figurative folding of her evening) and suggests, it would appear, her own return to a neglectful mode of
parenthood.

"Cora Lee" not only contains within its pages evidence of reuse of
Morrison's text which aids our comprehension of the nature of
Naylor's "taking apart" of *The Bluest Eye*, but also offers the means
of locating what appears to me to be the dominant theme of *The Women
of Brewster Place*. "Cora Lee" is, like most of the other narrative sections, an exploration of unfulfilled and (within the context of the world
its author creates) unachievable dreams of Afro-American women.
Naylor's novel does not examine the societal forces which are responsible for the unfulfilling nature of many black women's lives in
as systematic and illuminating a fashion as Morrison's novel. What
it does offer, however, is the author's explorations of her characters'
own culpability in the tragedies of their lives. The primary thematic
differences between Naylor's and Morrison's novels can perhaps be
briefly summarized in the following way: *The Bluest Eye* portrays the
ramifications of the imposition of myth upon a people; *The Women
of Brewster Place*, by contrast, describes the myriad problems for Afro-
Americans (particularly women) who refuse to abandon unachievable
dreams.

In a review of *The Women of Brewster Place*, Judith Brazburg argues
that "The Two" and "The Block Party," the concluding sections of
the novel, "address the question from Langston Hughes' poem, 'What
happened to a dream deferred?' which is posed on the prefatory pages

of the novel."[19] In fact, however, each of the novel's sections details the deferred dreams of Afro-American women. These dreams are evident in textual information from Etta Mae Johnson's desperate need for social respectability that "stuff[ed] up her senses" to the point that she totally misreads the intentions of a visiting minister (70) and Kiswana Browne's mother's characterization of her daughter as one who "constantly live[s] in a fantasy world—always going to extremes—turning butterflies into eagles" (85), to Mattie Michael's dream of female community that concludes the novel. Naylor's most successfully rendered depictions of the consequences of disappointed dreams occur in "Lucielia Louise Turner." This section offers not only profound insight into Naylor's precise intentions where the novel's major theme is concerned, but also the author's subtle refigurations of both Morrison and Zora Neale Hurston.

V

NAYLOR'S EXPLORATIONS of the consequences of deferred Afro-American women's dreams direct us intertextually not only to Hughes' poem, but also to Hurston's assertions with respect to women and dreams in the opening pages of *Their Eyes Were Watching God.* In contrast to men who, according to Hurston, wait passively for—and only occasionally achieve—their desires:

> women forget all those things they don't want to remember, and remember everything they don't want to forget. The dream is the truth. Then they act and do things accordingly.[20]

According to Hurston, women possess a greater capacity than men to actively pursue their desires. This greater capacity results from an ability to filter from consciousness an awareness of any matters that would hamper the dream's pursuit. It is this ability that allows Janie to ignore her initial misgivings about Joe Starks, for example, and to endure decades of mistreatment at his hands, hoping all the while either that he would be metamorphosed into her dream of an ideal man, or, when the evidence of this dream's unattainability becomes so overwhelming that it cannot be conveniently forgotten, that some other man can successfully fulfill this role.

In his essay "Zora Neale Hurston and the Nature of Female Perception," Lloyd Brown employs Simone de Beauvoir's discussions in *The Second Sex* of the female "realm of imagination" to analyze the consequences of female dreams, and self-deception in *Their Eyes Were Watching God*. He says:

> de Beauvoir argues . . . [that] dreams are the women's means of compensating for a sense of subordination (immanence) through the "realm of imagination," and as such they are a form of transcendence, the "ultimate effort—sometimes ridiculous, often pathetic—of imprisoned women to transform her prison into a heaven of glory, her servitude into sovereign liberty." Hurston's own narrative actually centers on the essential ambiguities which de Beauvoir attributes here to the woman as dreamer, with dreams as both triumphant transcendence and pathetic flight into imagination.[21]

In my chapter on *Their Eyes Were Watching God*, I stated my objections to Brown's reading of Tea Cake's and Janie's relationship. But Brown's discussion of the essential ambiguities involved in the transcendent female dream is remarkably astute. I would, however, take his assertion a step further. With respect to its negative consequences, not only does the female flight into imagination represent at times a "pathetic" attempt to transform a painful experience, but it also serves to compel women to commit plainly injurious acts of self-deception. Even after her recognition of her prodigious shortcomings, Janie still refuses to be governed by what she learns is the truth:

> "Maybe he ain't nothin'," she cautioned herself, "but he is something in my mouth. He's got tuh be else Ah ain't got nothin' tuh live for. Ah'll lie and say he is. If Ah don't, life won't be nothin' but uh store and uh house." (118-19)

Her instinctive removal to the realm of imagination permits her transformation of the dream—Starks as bee man—to a lie about actuality—the insistence, despite a wealth of empirical evidence to the contrary, that she maintain her former image of her husband as a means of preserving any semblance of self-worth.

The text of *Their Eyes Were Watching God* makes it abundantly clear that sincere feelings of self-worth are impossible under such conditions of self-deception, and that only actual transcendence permits the subordinated female to discern her own human virtues. Janie's transcendence begins when she finds Tea Cake, the man who most closely resembles her dream of an ideal mate. In "Lucielia Louise Turner," the section of *The Women of Brewster Place* in which Naylor most expertly depicts the Afro-American woman dreamer's tragedy and subsequent self-affirmation, the beleaguered female's transcendence is made possible by the efforts of a female "kissin'-friend," Mattie Michael.

"Lucielia Louise Turner" traces, among other things, its title character's efforts to maintain her dream-draped image of her lover whose "deep musky scent . . . brought back the ghosts of the Tennessee soil of her childhood" (92). Eugene is like Joe Starks in that he coerces his lover's submission to his authority, a submission which results directly in her abortion of the fetus of a baby she desperately wants, and indirectly in the death of their two-year-old daughter.

The utter failure of Ciel's actions to produce their desired ends— Eugene's willingness to remain in the relationship—becomes obvious when he announces that he is leaving her and their daughter Serena for putative employment on the docks of Maine. This announcement, coupled with his refusal to allow mother and daughter to accompany him and his confusion about the location of Newport, shatters the image that Ciel has held of her mate as effectively as Starks' slap destroys Janie's illusions about her second husband:

> She looked at Eugene, and the poison of reality began to spread through her body like gangrene. It drew his scent out of her nostrils and scraped the veil from her eyes, and he stood before her just as he really was—a tall, skinny black man with arrogance and selfishness twisting his mouth into a strange shape. (100)

As in *Their Eyes Were Watching God*, the pollinated female perception gives way to what Naylor terms "the poison of reality"—the recognition of the male's self-interested, manipulative control that results in a woman's fruitless endurance of pain. Ciel's recognition of Eugene's inadequacies is followed by a period of "brief mourning for the loss of something denied to her" and an "overpowering need to be near someone who loved her" (100). But her awakening is accompanied by an even more painful reality—the screams and subsequent death of her electrocuted daughter Serena.

"Lucielia Louise Turner" offers a provocative juxtaposition of two vastly different scenes of ritualistic cleansing: Ciel's failed attempts to completely clean a pot of cooked rice, and Mattie Michael's successful exorcism of pain from the grieving body of a woman she had helped to raise. The first such instance is occasioned by Eugene's statement, "I lost my job today," which signals, in Ciel's mind, the end of the tenuous peace that had existed in her apartment since his return. Upon hearing the announcement, Ciel, standing at the sink cleaning rice, transforms her culinary efforts into a (somewhat sadistic) rite of purification:

> The water was turning cloudy in the rice pot, and the force of
> the stream from the faucet caused scummy bubbles to rise to the
> surface. These broke and sprayed tiny starchy particles onto the
> dirty surface. Each bubble that broke seemed to increase the vol-
> ume of the dogged whispers she had been ignoring for the last
> few months. She poured the dirty water off the rice to destroy
> and silence them, then watched with a malicious joy as they dis-
> appeared down the drain. (94)

In this doubly symbolic rite, Ciel equates "scummy bubbles" with the
repressed and "dogged whispers" of discord that were again entering
the relationship. By sadistically drowning the whisper-containing
bubbles, by silencing, in other words, the voice of reality, she displays
a preference for illusion, silence, and dream and an unwillingness to
confront directly the implications of the voice's message. Like Janie,
Ciel fights stubbornly to maintain her image of her mate. Confronted
by the ultimate failure of her purification rite, Ciel realizes that some
sacrifice on her part is required in order to satiate Eugene, to whom
she turns in "silent acquiesc[ence]" and asks, "All right, Eugene, what
do you want me to do?" (94) In an effort to maintain her relationship
with this undependable, egregiously self-centered man, Ciel resolves
to be governed by his will, even though such a resolve will result in
her abortion of the fetus that grows inside her.

Ciel's refusal or inability to rid herself of her dream vision of
Eugene leads to her particularly profound sense of self-division both
during and after the abortion. Naylor tells us that during the abortion, for example:

> Ciel was not listening [to the droning voice of the abortionist].
> It was important that she keep herself completely isolated from
> these surroundings. All the activities of the past week of her life
> were balled up and jammed on the right side of her brain, as if
> belonging to some other woman. And when she had endured this
> one last thing for her, she would push it up there, too, and then
> one day give it all to her— Ciel wanted no part of it.
>   The next few days, Ciel found it difficult to connect herself up
> again with her own world. Everything seemed to have taken on
> new textures and colors. . . . There was a disturbing split sec-
> ond between someone talking to her and the words penetrating
> sufficiently to elicit a response. (95-96)

Ciel's affective split or double consciousness is motivated, as were her
efforts to silence the whispers of the scummy bubbles, by her desire

to prevent reality from impinging upon her desperately held dreams about Eugene and, ultimately, herself. Such dreams concern, then, not only her lover's character, but also self-protective illusions about herself necessitated by her submission to the control of this shallow man. In effect, Ciel piles lie upon lie in an effort to forestall her own recognition of the fact that her life with Eugene, in Janie's apt phrase, "ain't nothin'." As a result of her refusal to confront the stark reality of her life, Ciel splits into two selves. One self plans and endures the physical and emotional pain of abortion "as if [the activities] be-long[ed] to some other woman." This other woman, Ciel's other self, will eventually have to come to terms with these acts.

When Serena dies, Ciel is forced to confront not only the pain of her loss of a child, but also her own self-destructive acts—her inability to perceive Eugene correctly and thereby prevent the abortion of a fetus. No longer able to assign the blame for her undesirable actions to her other, future self, she is overwhelmed by an intense grief whose pain she had long deferred. The intensity of her grief propels her past pain and to the nadir of emotional insensibility. The text tells us of Ciel's failure to cry when Serena dies that others believed was a sign of "some special sort of grief": "Ciel was not grieving for Serena. She was simply tired of hurting. And she was forced to slowly give up the life that God had refused to take from her" (101).

Mattie Michael, the title character of the novel's first section—whose maternal instincts where Ciel is concerned result from pre-Brewster days—recognizes intuitively her surrogate daughter's condition. In a heroic display of personal fortitude, Mattie forcefully intervenes:

> "Merciful Father, no!" she bellowed. There was no prayer, no bended knee or sackcloth supplication in those words, but a blasphemous fireball that shot forth and went smashing against the gates of heaven, raging and kicking, demanding to be heard. "No! No! No!" (102-3)

The deeply religious Mattie voices a resounding "no" to Ciel's impending death, a cry with heaven-shaking reverberations. It is not her words or voice that save Ciel from a premature, grief-stricken demise, however, but, rather, her actions—her painful but somehow soothing rocking and embrace. "Propelled," as Naylor says, by Ciel's almost inaudible moans, Mattie's resuscitating motion transports her younger friend through history so that she is able to observe the timelessness of her loss:

> Mattie rocked her out of that bed, out of that room, into a blue vastness just underneath the sun and above time. She rocked her

over Aegean seas so clean they shone like crystal, so clear the
fresh blood of sacrificed babies torn from their mother's arms
and given to Neptune could be seen like pink froth on the water.
She rocked her on and on, past Dachau, where soul-gutted Jew-
ish mothers swept their children's entrails off laboratory floors.
They flew past the spilled brains of Senegalese infants whose
mothers had dashed them on the wooden sides of slave ships.
And she rocked on. (103)

Mattie's rocking allows Ciel to connect the pain of her own maternal
losses with an apparently timeless—and, in a sense, equally gainless
—history of maternal pain. Mattie's rocking "above time" offers Ciel—
dying because of an emptiness caused by the loss of children and
illusions—a recognition of her connection with women throughout
history, a sense, in other words, of membership in a timeless community of women united by common suffering

Ciel's imaginative flight does not end, however, with such insights.
Mattie rocks Ciel from visions of the general—perceptions of the
timelessness of her pain—to the specific—a direct confrontation with
her illusions about life and about herself which rendered her incapable of preventing her personal tragedies. These illusions, in fact,
had made her a hesitant participant in her tragedies' unfolding:

[Mattie] rocked her into her childhood and let her see her murdered dreams. And she rocked her back, back into the womb, to
the nadir of her hurt, and they found it—a slight silver splinter,
embedded just below the surface of the skin. And Mattie rocked
and pulled—and the splinter gave way, but its roots were deep,
gigantic, ragged, and they tore up flesh with bits of fat and mus-
cle tissue clinging to them. They left a hole, which was already
starting to pus over, but Mattie was satisfied. It would heal.
(103-4)

The removal of the symbolic splinter leads to Ciel's ability to observe
clearly the terrible consequences of this splinter's lengthy presence.
These consequences include her inability to confront the origins of
her repressed anguish—her unnamed "murdered dreams"—and her
creation of self-protective illusions which encourage her continual
victimization.

The salvation of Ciel is not accomplished solely by means of
Mattie's allowing her to perceive timeless maternal pain and destructive personal illusions. Its ultimate achievement requires a communal act that is the section's second rite of purification. Ciel's vom-

iting after the splinter is uprooted is described as possessing spiritually purgative qualities: "The bile that had formed a tight knot in
Ciel's stomach began to rise and gagged her as it passed her
throat. . . . After a while she heaved only air, but the body did not
seem to want to stop. It was exorcising the evilness of pain." (104)
This exorcism of the evilness of pain represents one aspect of a rite
of purification; its completion involves Mattie's bathing of the young
woman who has regressed to a state of physical helplessness akin to
that of an infant:

> And slowly she bathed her. She took the soap, and, using only
> her hands, she washed Ciel's hair and the back of her neck. She
> raised her arms and cleaned the armpits, soaping well the downy
> brown hair there. She let the soap slip between the girl's breasts,
> and she washed each one separately, cupping it in her hands. She
> took each leg and even cleaned under the toenails. Making Ciel
> rise and kneel in the tub, she cleaned the crack of her behind,
> soaped her pubic hair, and gently washed the crease in her va-
> gina—slowly, reverently, as if handling a newborn. (104)

Mattie's and Ciel's are complementary acts of purification—the
cleansing of the outside and the inside of the female respectively. Theirs
is a wordless antiphonal rite in which Ciel's moans inspire Mattie's
life-sustaining rocking, a rite which concludes with Ciel's crying "cold
and good" tears. These tears provide the final stage of purification
for Ciel's heretofore dying self which the text now describes as her
"freshly wet, glistening body, baptized now" (105). Inside and outside, previously disjoined because Ciel's maintenance of a willing ignorance about the reality of her life, perform as an interactive, complementary system set in motion by the affectionate rocking and
bathing of Mattie, and supported by Ciel's cleansing of her spiritual
self and her will to live.

   This scene provides, it seems to me, an explanation of the failures
of similarly salvific gestures in *The Bluest Eye*. More precisely, it helps
us to comprehend the failure of Claudia's and Frieda's efforts to save
Pecola's incestuous seed. The MacTeer girls attempt, through an amateurish bit of conjure (the burial of money and garden seeds, and
the incantation of "magic words") to save Pecola's baby which the
rest of the community wants dead. The adult narrator Claudia attri-
butes their effort's failure to nature's general unresponsiveness to humanity, and not to any incantatory shortcomings on their part. However, if read in terms of Naylor's scene, Claudia's and Frieda's efforts
seem, despite the girls' obvious sincerity, hopelessly inadequate. For

in the face of Pecola's intense self-hatred and the disdain of an entire community where Pecola and her pregnancy are concerned, discursive acts such as the MacTeer girls' incantations of putative (but, curiously, unspoken in the novel) "right words" cannot avoid being anything but insufficient. What is required, as Naylor's text suggests, is the bonding of women, or what Ntozake Shange calls in *for colored girls'* final scene of an achieved female community—which, not coincidentally, is directly preceded by a male's murder of children—"a layin on of [female] hands."[22] This communal laying on of hands results in the liberation of the female self and "the holiness of myself released" (62). Ciel's baptized and reborn self, like the holy and released female community in Shange's choreopoem, can courageously confront the problems inherent in being a black woman in America.[23]

VI

HOWEVER PROFITABLE individual acts of sisterly love such as those described in the final pages of "Lucielia Louise Turner" prove, they do not have the power to alter significantly the deleterious conditions for Brewster Place's female as a group. *The Women of Brewster Place's* penultimate story, "The Two," makes this point abundantly clear. In this story, Naylor's revision of Morrison achieves its most profound and unsettling configurations. Such repetition takes form, for example, in aspects of characterization such as Ben's daughter's physical deformity and his surrogate daughter Lorraine's physical carriage which refigure, from *The Bluest Eye*, Polly Breedlove's rusty nail-inspired limp and her offspring Pecola's carriage which, according to Claudia, resembled a "pleated wing" (61). In fact, it appears that Naylor conflates in the figure of Lorraine many of the manifest weaknesses of the characters of Morrison's novel. If, as I have argued, Pecola serves as scapegoat in a community's rites of purgation, then Lorraine's ultimate status in *The Women of Brewster Place* includes, in different instances, both purgative scapegoat and brutalized martyr whose demise apparently serves to unify a (female) community.

But while the sacrifice of Pecola—despite its obviously reprehensible motivation and outcome—does unite, in a sense, Lorain's black citizens, the decidedly feminist Afro-American women's community that forms in the final story of Naylor's novel, "The Block Party," is not represented as an actual narrative event at all but, rather, as merely the dream of Mattie Michael. In a novel where the products of the female "realm of imagination" have proven disastrous, the author's

representation of what feminist texts such as Shange's choreopoem
suggest are the most nurturing environment for women as a female
character's dream calls into question Naylor's views of the possibilities—or perhaps even the uncategorical desirability—of such exclusively women's communities.

The major incidents from *The Bluest Eye* that Naylor refigures
in "The Two" are Pecola's schoolyard encounter with a gang of boys
and her rape by her father. As I have argued, Morrison's description of Pecola's taunters who, "like a necklace of semiprecious
stones . . . surrounded her" (55), is inextricably related to their employment of Pecola as scapegoat upon whom they project the evilness
of the shadow of blackness. But in Naylor's refiguration, the group
of male tauntors that confronts Lorraine is threatened not by her undeniable blackness as in Pecola's case, but, rather, by her homosexual
orientation which places her, C. C. Baker's gang fears, "beyond the
length of [phallic] power" (162).

Though many of her uses of Morrison's figures effectively bracket
race, Naylor's description of Lorraine's expedition into black male
gang territory is charged with an acute understanding of white racism's culpability in the creation of C. C. Baker and his gang of urban
thugs. She says of Lorraine:

> She had stepped into the thin strip of earth [the alley near the
> wall] that they had claimed as their own. Bound by the last
> building on Brewster and a brick wall, they reigned in that unlit
> alley like dwarfed warrior-kings. Born with the appendages of
> power, circumcised by the guillotine, and baptised with the steam
> from a million nonreflective mirrors, these young men wouldn't
> be called upon to . . . scatter their iron seed from a B-52 into
> the wound of the earth, point a finger to move a nation, or stick
> a pole into the moon—and they knew it. They only had that three-
> hundred-foot alley to serve them as stateroom, armored tank, and
> executioner's chamber. So Lorraine found herself, on her knees,
> surrounded by the most dangerous species in existence—human
> males with an erection to validate in a world that was only six
> feet wide. (169-70)

In a country which has, throughout its history, consistently rewarded
"manly" displays of courage and machismo, the attitudes of C. C.
Baker's gang seem, no matter how repugnant, almost relentlessly logical. Indeed, male psychological abusiveness and murderous potentials that are suggested in the other texts of Naylor's novel—Sam
Michael's vicious beating of his daughter Mattie; Eugene's psycho-

logical abuse of Ciel; the fractured jaws, loosened teeth and permanent scars suffered by Cora Lee at the hands of men frustrated by the
natural time demands of children—effectively prefigure the abhor-
rent display of misogyny and homophobia involved in the gang's bru-
talization of Lorraine. While the Afro-American literary tradition is
replete with delineations of sexual violence directed at women,
Naylor's description of the brutal gang rape of Lorraine is without
question one of the most unsettling. As an intertext of *The Bluest Eye*,
the scene combines, as I have stated, Cholly's rape of Pecola with Bay
Boy and friends' verbal abuse and encircling of the young protagonist. Both Pecola's verbal victimization by the young boys and, later,
her rape, are accompanied by her silence—her wordless "cover[ing]
her eyes with her hands" (56) in the circle of male scorn and her
voiceless response to Cholly's sexual abuse. The text informs the reader
about her wordless response to her father's sexual abuse: "the only
sound she made [was] a hollow suck of air in the back of her throat"
(128).

Naylor's depiction of Lorraine's victimization also focuses on her
silence. But unlike Pecola, who appears not to possess the proper vocabulary to respond to such abuse, Lorraine does attempt to verbalize
a response—a plea to the boys' humanity. Throughout the rape, she
was:

> trying to form the one word that had been clawing inside of her—
> "Please." It squeezed through her paralyzed vocal cords and fell
> lifelessly at their feet. Lorraine clamped her eyes shut and, using
> all of her strength within her, willed it to rise again.
> "Please."
> The sixth boy took a dirty paper bag lying on the ground and
> stuffed it into her mouth. She felt a weight drop on her spread
> body. Then she opened her eyes and they screamed and screamed
> into the face above hers—the face that was pushing this terrible
> pain inside of her body. The screams tried to break through her
> corneas out into the air, but the tough rubbery flesh sent them
> vibrating back into her brain, first shaking lifeless the cells that
> nurtured her memory. (170-71)

Her appeal to her attackers' humanity proved fruitless. Lorraine's voice
has no life, no effect in the barbarous male circle formed to exhibit
phallic power.

As a consequence of the profound mental chaos that follows her
rape, she attacks the male figure who moved "in perfect unison with
the sawing pain that kept moving inside of her" (172). In an attempt

to stop the pain, Lorraine kills Ben, Brewster Place's janitor who had
served as a father figure for the otherwise painfully isolated woman.
During an argument with her lover Theresa, Lorraine, who believes
that her homosexuality does not represent a sense of difference significant enough to permanently isolate her from the larger Afro-
American community, speaks of herself as someone "who just wants
to be a human being—a lousy human being, who's somebody's
daughter or somebody's friend or even somebody's enemy" (165). She
tells Theresa that she is able to achieve such feelings only in Ben's
basement apartment:

> they [the world at large, Brewster residents in particular] make
> me feel like a freak out there, and you try to make me feel like
> one in here. That [sic] only place I've found some peace, Tee, is
> in that damp old basement, where I'm not different. (165)

The alliance between Lorraine and Ben is based primarily on their
feelings of difference, absence, and loss. Ben's northern journey to
Brewster is motivated, at least in part, by his inability to protect his
infirm daughter from sexual exploitation at the hands of her white
employer. Lorraine travels to Brewster largely because of her fear of
difference and because of the pain of her father's violent reaction to
her homosexuality. Each character fulfills for the other the role of
absent family so they no longer feel they are "livin' in a world with
no address" (149).

Lorraine achieves a positive sense of self with the assistance of Ben,
which leads to what Theresa views as "a firmness in her spirit that
hadn't been there before" (155). Her insane lashing out at Ben, then,
appears to reflect simply the chaotic and deeply disturbed nature of
Lorraine's psyche. But if it is correct to view Lorraine's victimization
as exemplary of the Afro-American woman's plight in a male-domi-
nated world (as textual evidence I will cite below seems to indicate),
then it seems also possible to regard Ben, the novel's only fully sketched
male character, as in some respects representative of the Afro-American male. For though Ben's sensitivity where Lorraine is concerned
is genuine and commendable, he is no more able in a northern urban
environment to protect his surrogate daughter from sexual abuse than
he was to defend his own offspring from the deep South's landowner's
sexual exploitation. In fact, his wife frames her view of Ben's inadequacies in terms remarkably similar to the narrator's discussion of
C. C. Baker and his gang's impressions of manhood. When Ben la-
ments being rendered unable by the power dynamics of his relationship to Mr. Clyde either to avenge his daughter's suffering or to force

it to cease—frustratedly saying, "If I was half a man I woulda—"
(153), his wife:

> came across the porch and sneered into his face. "If you was half
> a man, you coulda given me more babies and we woulda had
> some help workin' this land instead of a half-grown woman we
> gotta carry the load for. And if you was even quarter a man, we
> wouldn't be a bunch of miserable sharecroppers on someone else's
> land—but we is, Ben." (153)

His wife measures Ben's masculine and human worth by his abilities
as a provider—both of babies and of moderately good economic sta-
bility—and finds him seriously lacking. He is not, in Elvira's economically pragmatic perception, "'even quarter a man.'"

He responds to her castigation by abusing alcohol and silently de-
siring to murder her:

> if he drank enough every day he could bear the touch of Elvira's
> body in the bed beside him at night and not have his sleep stolen
> by the image of her lying there with her head caved in or her
> chest ripped apart by shotgun shells. (154)

Ben's murderous impulses are impeded only by "the gram of truth
in her words [that] was heavy enough to weigh his hands down in
his pockets" (153). Apparently, then, he has accepted a purely materialistic conceptualization of manhood to which his situation as deep
South sharecropper denies access. His self-defensive reaction to his
wife's questioning of his masculinity—though suppressed—is, I would
argue, not essentially different in kind from the gang's murderous
exhibitions of phallic power. For if, as Naylor seems to suggest, the
male response to unachievable dreams is violence—and violence, at
least in *The Women of Brewster Place*, directed against women—then
Ben's murder by his surrogate daughter seems not to be an arbitrary
act where the author's explorations of male abuse of women is
concerned.

In her refigurative conflations of *The Bluest Eye*'s primary scenes
of male abuse of Pecola, Naylor depicts the encircling adolescent male
gang as rapists and the (surrogate) father as a protective figure who
asks, when he sees Lorraine—limping and bloodied—coming toward
him: "My God, child, what happened to you?" (172) While, as a narrative event, Lorraine's murder of Ben reflects the utterly chaotic nature of her mental faculties after the rape, it also serves to demonstrate, as part of the expertly wrought symbolic patterns of "The Two,"
the author's precise control of her material. Put simply, Naylor "kills"

Ben because, despite his sensitivity to Lorraine's and his own daughter's circumstances, the urge for violence that is his response to his wife's castigations is of a kind with the reaction of the gang members to their inadequacies. When the text says of Ben's drunken movements near the wall after Lorraine is raped, "Side to side. Side to side. Almost in perfect unison with the sawing pain that kept moving inside of her" (172), it insists that the reader view Ben as part of a continuum of male violence against women of which the actions of the gang are the reprehensible extreme. And though Ben is sensitively sketched by Naylor to a point that his true human failings—his alcoholism, inability to free himself from a restrictive concept of masculinity, and resultant violent urges—are comprehensible, the text fails ultimately to excuse these violent impulses. The manner of Ben's death can, thus, be viewed as a form of (authorial) retribution: Ben dies by having his skull crushed—one of the methods he envisions employing to murder his verbally abusive wife.

In both Naylor's and Morrison's first novels, a sense of societal order is formed as a result of sexually abusive acts. In *The Bluest Eye*, that order is a function of a black community's perceptions that with Pecola's demise it has purged itself of the shadow of blackness. On the other hand, Lorraine's victimization of *The Women of Brewster Place* occasions the development—because of a shared abhorrence regarding the brutal rape—of a sense of community among heretofore largely isolated women. For reasons that will be explored in the following section, however, this achieved woman's community is not depicted as an actual narrative event, but, rather, as the dream of the novel's most prominent character, Mattie Michael.

VII

THE WOMEN *of Brewster Place*'s final story, "The Block Party," presents further evidence of Naylor's command of her material. It is a control that is, ironically, best demonstrated by the apparent failure of the totalizing gestures of this section. In her essay on *Their Eyes Were Watching God*, Barbara Johnson says of the textual unity in narrative forms: "However rich, healthy or lucid fragmentation and division may be, narrative seems to have trouble resting content with it, as though a story could not recognize its own end as anything other than a moment of totalization."[24] Naylor's novel, however, clearly recognizes the richness of its narrative fragmentation, a recognition that is exhibited in the intentional failure of its moment of totalization.

On the surface, "The Block Party" suggests that a new order results from the utter chaos surrounding the brutal rape of Lorraine. It is an order based on the female protagonists' comprehension of their interconnectedness. Ciel's return to the neighborhood, for example, is motivated by a dream that suggests her indistinguishability from Lorraine (whom she has never met). The dream was, according to Ciel:

> "one of those crazy things that get all mixed up in your head. Something about that wall and Ben. *And there was a woman who was supposed to be me*, I guess. She didn't look exactly like me, but *inside I felt it was me.*
> . . . "And she had on a green dress with like black trimming, and there were red designs or red flowers or something on the front." Ciel's eyes began to cloud. *"And something bad had happened to me by the wall—I mean to her—something bad had happened to her.* And Ben was in it somehow." She stared at the wall and shuddered. (179, my emphasis)

Images of Lorraine have entered the unconscious thoughts of all of Brewster's females, causing the dreams of both mothers and daughters to be haunted by the image "of the tall yellow woman in the bloody green and black dress" (175). The protagonists of the individual sections of *The Women of Brewster Place* form, in response to Cora's assertion that a week of rain has failed to wash Lorraine's blood from the wall, a determined and harmonious group working hysterically to tear down the structure. These women:

> flung themselves against the wall, chipping away at it with knives, plastic forks, spiked shoe heels, and even bare hands; the water [from a thunderstorm] pouring under their chins, and plastering their blouses and dresses against their breasts and into the cracks of their hips. The bricks piled up behind them and were snatched and relayed out of Brewster Place past overturned tables, scattered coins, and crushed wads of dollar bills. They came back with chairs and barbeque grills and smashed them into the wall. (186)

Naylor's description of the wall's destruction concludes with a baptizing rain which, much like the symbolically reborn Ciel's tears, serves to demonstrate a sense of harmony between nature and woman, between outside and inside: "Suddenly, the rain exploded around their feet in a fresh downpour, and the cold waters beat on the tops of their heads—almost in perfect unison with the beating of their hearts." (188) As opposed to the text's earlier depiction of harmony between inside and outside—the simultaneity of Ben's drunken movements and Lorraine's throbbing pain (whose phrasing—"Almost in perfect unison"—is repeated in the passage cited above)—the coincidence of rain beat and heartbeat suggests a valuable coalescence of heretofore divided entities. While the coincidence of Ben's movements and Lorraine's pain reflects—as narrative events—the utter chaos of the victim's mind, the harmonious rhythms that follow the destruction of the wall signal an achievement of female unity. Such unity has to do not only with the individual self and her relationship with nature, but also with the development of a community of women.

There is evidence in this section of a conscious refiguration of fe-male-authored precursor texts. Like both *Their Eyes Were Watching God* and *The Bluest Eye*, the female unity described in Naylor's text is intricately related to double-voiced strategies of narration. *The Women of Brewster Place*'s depictions of female unity are elements of the dream of Mattie Michael, the primary agent of female coalescence in the novel. Not only does she act to save Ciel's life, but she serves as a supportive friend for Brewster Place's other females. She provides for Etta Mae Johnson after her ill-fated encounter with Reverend Woods "the light and the love and the comfort" to allow her to transcend her pain (74). Further, she gently chides Cora Lee about her "full load" of children, and, along with Etta Mae, defends Lorraine against Sophie's attacks.

Thus, her dream of female unity seems an imaginative extension of her efforts throughout the text. In this dream, she imbues all of the female protagonists, with the exception of Kiswana Browne,[25] with her desires for unity. Mattie's vision and voice control the final section of the novel and provide the work with a closing hopeful note: the possible coming to fruition of Mattie's dream of a supportive fe-male community. But considering the novel's generally pejorative representation of the products of the female realm of imagination, it is difficult to rest content with such a positive reading of Mattie's dream. Such a reading proves especially difficult if, as textual evidence cited above suggests, Naylor's text does indeed possess a resolute authorial consistency with respect to its symbolic patterns. It seems to me that, like the text's other depictions of the products of the female imagination, Mattie's dream has similarly divisive consequences, not for an individual female, but for the entire novel.

Naylor's failure to represent achieved female community as an actual narrative event adds to the novel's overall narrative disjunctiveness. Instead of serving to unite the text's individual stories, Mattie's dream increases *The Women of Brewster Place*'s sense of disjunction by offering a vision that is directly antithetical to the omniscient narrator's presentation of female unity. In other words, Mattie's dream provides the narrative with an unresolved double voicedness. Because its presentation of female community is not offered as an actual narrative event, Mattie's dream is perhaps most profitably understood as an illusion that serves to perpetuate the text's content and formal disjunctions in much the same way that the self-deceptive dreams of Naylor's characters prolong their personally injurious self-divisions. Neither, then, do the women of Brewster Place or their individual texts ultimately achieve genuine coalescence.

Rather than provide the novel with a concluding sense of unity, Mattie's dream exposes—and even multiplies—the novel's various disjunctions. Without further exploration, Naylor's novel could best be characterized as an unachieved dream of wholeness, as a work that intentionally undercuts its own totalizing moment. But if we return briefly to *The Women of Brewster Place*'s male ancestral text, the generically enigmatic *Cane*, we can, by investigating Naylor's technical indebtedness to Toomer, begin to comprehend the reasons for her novel's various disjunctions.

VIII

IN HER essay "Untroubled Voice: Call and Response to *Cane*," Barbara Bowen argues that despite its unconventional form, Toomer's is a masterfully unified text whose unity is observable only when the literary critic regards it in terms of Afro-American expressive culture. Bowen says:

> *Cane* displays a restlessness with conventional forms. . . . [Toomer] sense[s] that the Anglo-American tradition cannot contain what he has to say . . .
>
> [W]hat distinguishes Toomer's work is that he is as demanding of his form as the Anglo-American novelists are of theirs. Toomer pushes the form of call and response as hard as Joyce pushes the form of the novel. And *Cane*'s most successful moments come when Toomer opens up for us what it means to turn the call-and-response pattern into a literary form.[26]

Bowen's essay seeks to explain, among other things, the problems inherent in attempting to assign to *Cane* a traditional or "conventional" Western generic designation. *Cane* is a work informed by the

expressive principles—particularly call and response—of Black culture. Toomer's work is, if Bowen is correct, a *denigrated* text par excellence, a genuine Black book. In fact, Toomer's own discussion of
his work offers ways in which to connect Bowen's analysis of call and
response in *Cane* to my own discussion of Hurston's employment of
the verbal behavior as narrative strategy in *Their Eyes Were Watching
God.*

Toomer says of the generic diversity and narrative organization of
the text: "*Cane'*s design is a circle [which moves] from simple forms
to complex ones, and back to simpler forms."[27] If, as Bowen persuasively demonstrates, *Cane* represents its author's attempt to turn call
and response into a literary form, then the critic should be able to
observe antiphonal textual interaction occurring both intratextually
and intertextually. Such textual antiphony is perhaps best demonstrated by the texts that conclude *Cane'*s first section, "Portrait in
Georgia" and "Blood-Burning Moon."

In "Blood-Burning Moon," the text's oft-repeated song, the
haunting:

> Red nigger moon. Sinner!
> Blood-burning moon. Sinner!
> Come out that fact'ry door (29),

is the black woman's improvisational riff sung as a protective response to the frightening omen of the full moon. As they are situated
in the text, at the conclusion of each of the story's three sections,
these lyrics operate as an ominous refrain, adding to Toomer's depiction of the inevitability of racial violence in the post-Reconstruction South a foreboding of doom. The narrative provides numerous
other foreshadowings. For example, the story opens with a foreboding
description of the fast-approaching dusk:

> Up from the skeleton stone walls, up from the rotting floor boards
> and the solid hand-hewn beams of oak of the pre-war cotton fac-
> tory, dust came. Up from the dusk the full moon came. Glowing
> like a fired pine-knot, it illumined the great door and soft show-
> ered the Negro shanties aligned along the single street of factory
> town. The full moon in the great door was an omen. (28)

Just as ominous as the full moon proves for the story's characters are
the images of death and fire that foreshadow the racially motivated
lynching of Tom Burwell in the story's conclusion. These images are
themselves effectively prefigured in the text that directly precedes
"Blood-Burning Moon," the poem "Portrait in Georgia." This poem,

which impressionistically describes a white woman's beauty in terms of a lynched, burned black body, reads as follows:

> Hair—braided chestnut,
> coiled like a lyncher's rope,
> Eyes—fagots,
> Lips—old scars, or the first red blisters
> Breath—the last sweet scent of cane,
> And her slim body, white as the ash
> of black flesh after flame. (27)

In terms of an intertextual relation between Toomerian poem and short story, I believe—with Bowen—that "Portrait in Georgia" serves as much as an extra-textual "omen" of the tragedies that unfold in "Blood-Burning Moon" as the moon, the refrain improvised in response to the moon's full and blood-red presence, and the foreboding imagery such as that which appears in the story's opening paragraph serve as intratextual omens. Thus, antecedent imagist poem, improvised folk song and experimental short story—which have been traditionally ascribed varying degrees of artistic sophistication—interact and provide a powerful conceptualization of deep South lynching. These pieces form, as it were, a circle of texts, calling and responding to one another in a clearly Afro-American expressive culturally informed manner. Both poem and story explore lynching's sexually related motivations. The poem does so in reference to a white Southern woman's beauty, a beauty whose alleged inspection has apparently precipitated the lynching of a black man. In the story, on the other hand, the racially motivated violence is a consequence of its black female protagonist's physical desirability to both the easily-provoked Tom Burwell and to the son of a former slaveowner who bemoans the end of America's peculiar institution.

Toomer's multi-generic text can be thickly described in terms of the general cultural world view that informs the call and response pattern. That world view insists, as Geneva Smitherman suggests in a passage cited in chapter 1 of this study:

> The universe is hierarchical in nature. . . . Though the universe is hierarchical, all modes of existence are necessary for the sustenance of its balance and rhythm. . . . Thus we have a paradigm for the way in which "opposites" function. That is, "opposites" constitute interdependent, interacting forces which are necessary for producing a given reality.

In Toomer's text, improvisational vernacular song and "high" literary genre "interact" and provide *Cane* with its black and brilliant "chaotic" wholeness. By employing discursive "opposites" that constitute the range of expressive options available to the Afro-American literary artist (what Toomer himself calls "simple" and "complex" forms) and infusing even the most complex forms with antiphonal potentials, Toomer is able to faithfully and artistically represent the Afro-American folk spirit that had seemed to him "so beautiful" during his brief period of immersion in Afro-American culture.

Toomer's text arises largely out of what was, for him, a startling development in his attempt to resolve double consciousness. In a letter to *The Liberator*, he says:

> I have strived for a spiritual fusion analogous to the fact of racial intermingling. Without denying a single element in me, with no desire to subdue one to the other, I have sought to let them function as complements. I have tried to let them live in harmony. Within the last two or three years, however, my growing need for artistic expression has pulled me deeper and deeper into the Negro group. And as my powers of receptivity increased, I found myself loving it in a way that I could never love the other. A visit to Georgia last fall was the starting point of almost everything of worth that I have done. I heard the folk-songs come from the lips of Negro peasants. I saw the rich dusk beauty that I had heard many false accents about, and of which til then, I was somewhat skeptical. And a deep part of my nature, a part that I had repressed, sprang suddenly to life and responded to them.[28]

This passage does not represent, of course, the final moment of Toomer's attempt to resolve his double consciousness. Ultimately, as critics of his work well know, he again represses the black elements of his "nature" and self which had provided him with the creative impetus to compose *Cane*, easily one of the signal achievements in the Afro-American literary tradition. But *Cane* represented for Toomer not only a celebration of the "very rich and sad and joyous and beautiful" Afro-American folk spirit, but also an attempt to preserve it in the face of what he perceived as its wholesale rejection by Afro-Americans. In an unpublished autobiography, he says:

> But I learned that the Negroes of the town objected to them [Black folk-songs and spirituals]. They called them "shouting." They had victrolas and player-pianos. So, I realized with deep regret, that the spirituals, meeting ridicule, would be certain to die out. With Negroes also the trend was towards the small town and then towards the city—and industry and commerce and machines. The

folk-spirit was walking in to die on the modern desert. That spirit
was so beautiful. Its death was so tragic. Just this seemed to sum
life for me. And this was the feeling I put into "Cane." "Cane"
was a swan-song. It was a song of an end. (xxii)

For Toomer, writing here to express his confusion about "why people have expected me to write a second and a third and a fourth book
like 'Cane' " (xxii), his text documents the death of the Afro-American
folk spirit. According to the author, early-twentieth-century black mi-
gration to cities and increasing contact with the by-products of modernity serve to separate the Afro-American permanently from the
communal principles of his or her culture. *Cane*, then, is Toomer's
lament for the modern Afro-American's cultural disconnectedness.

Hence, the sense of generic "chaos" that his friend Waldo Frank
perceived in Toomer's text[29] could be viewed as the author's means
of providing his work with an apparent unity of form and content.
Cane's apparently chaotic form seems to complement its textual depiction of a people increasingly separated from its soul—from itself.
In his delineation of characters such as: the male suitors of Karintha
and Fern, who prove unable to appreciate their intense spirituality;
Esther, who concocts elaborate fantasies as antidotes for an emotionally barren life; and northern men and women who, because they
lack highly developed sensibilities, cannot establish intimate relationships, Toomer creates an Afro-American panorama of individuals
almost completely isolated from one another by the effects of
modernity.

As we have seen, however, *Cane* does indeed possess a subtle artistic unity. This textual unity is fully discernible only in terms of
Afro-American expressive practices—practices infused with the communal folk spirit whose death Toomer prematurely proclaims in his
autobiographical statement. In fact, Toomer's view of his text notwithstanding, *Cane* does not, finally, suggest the death of the Afro-
American folk spirit but, rather, its remarkably vibrant (expressive)
durability. Just as Toomer's prediction of the demise of the Afro-
American spiritual proves erroneous (ironically, the folk songs that
the author so admired endure largely because they were preserved
by means of "modern" recording devices), so, too, is his assessment
of his text ultimately incorrect.

Darwin Turner offers in his introduction to *Cane* a profitable way
to assess the Toomerian view of his acclaimed work: "No matter what
it may have been for him, *Cane* still sings to readers, not the swan
song of an era that was dying, but the morning hymn of the Renais-

sance that was beginning" (xxv). In its achievement—despite its apparent disjunctiveness—of expressive unity, Toomer's text stands as
a distinguished example of the resilience of an Afro-American folk
spirit that privileges coalescence.

IX

THE WOMEN *of Brewster Place*'s primary inheritance from its male
precursorial text is technical in nature. More specifically, it has to do
with how most provocatively to depict the disunity of Afro-Americans
while, at the same time, acknowledging and faithfully representing
Black cultural impulses that insist on unity. There is, to be sure, sufficient evidence of refiguration of the content of Toomer's text such
as Naylor's employment of the image of a bastard community that I
discussed earlier in the chapter. But perhaps the clearest such example, and one even more illuminating where the unity of Naylor's
text is concerned, is the employment in the novel's initial section,"Mattie Michael,' of *Cane*'s central trope. Upon her arrival in the
walled-in community of Brewster, Mattie smells a scent strongly
reminiscent of the almost-forgotten aromas of her Tennessee
childhood:

> For a moment it smelled like freshly cut sugar cane, and she took
> in short, rapid breaths of air to try to capture the scent again.
> But it was gone. And it couldn't have been anyway. There was
> no sugar cane on Brewster. (8)

Naylor's introduction of cane is accomplished in terms of the memory of her protagonist, as if the author wants to evoke in the reader
her memory of Toomer's text. The scent awakens in Mattie specific
recollections of people and events in her past: "Sugar cane and summer and Papa and Basil and Butch" (8). But what this scene awakens
in the informed reader of Afro-American literature is *Cane*'s central
trope. And while Mattie's conclusion that the scent she smells could
not be cane possesses a clear and literal meaning, it also contains,
for that informed reader, an equally apparent implication having to
do with Toomer's figuration of the cane trope. In the essay "Journey
Toward Black Art: Jean Toomer's *Cane*," Houston Baker argues:
"Throughout Part One there is an evocation of a land of sugar cane
whose ecstacy and pain are rooted in a communal soil."[30] For Baker,
Toomer employs cane as a symbol of Afro-American deep South com-

munal impulses. If Baker is correct, then Mattie's statement suggests that the northern climate that Brewster typifies does not foster such communal inclinations.

When read in the light of such information, Mattie's subsequent efforts can profitably be viewed as her attempt to establish in the urban North the patterns of unity and communalism that had existed when the black American population was located primarily in the agrarian South. And like the failure of the MacTeer sisters' attempts to save Pecola's baby, Mattie's labors are ultimately unsuccessful because the northern environment proves "unyielding" to such efforts. The divisive effects of modernity cannot be undone, even by the strenuous efforts of Mattie, whose rescue of Ciel suggests that she possesses the communal inclinations and incantatory powers of her deep South forebears. *The Women of Brewster Place* evokes and refigures *Cane* in order to demonstrate canonical precedence for its imaginative exploration of the difficulties of (comm)unity in an intrinsically divisive setting. Like Toomer, Naylor seems to believe that the Afro-American folk spirit has met its demise in the urban desert of modernity.

In her *New York Times Book Review* statement, as we have seen, Naylor suggests that readers of *The Bluest Eye* "can see plainly what [narrative] strategies failed." When we are aware of *Cane*'s specific refigurations in Naylor's text, it becomes clear that what the younger female novelist views as faulty about Morrison's novel is the ultimate coalescence of its distinct narrative voices. For Naylor, such coalescence runs contrary not only to the text's myriad depictions of Afro-American division (including Pecola's pain-inspired schizophrenia), but also to her female precursor's clear understanding of the almost indefeasible obstacles to Afro-American unity. Morrison's resolution of her text's double voicedness is, for Naylor, a thematically unwarranted authorial imposition of a totalizing gesture onto a richly fragmented narrative strategy. This unjustified resolution represents, for Naylor, an authorial dream of wholeness which, like Mattie's dream, is not sufficiently grounded in the textual reality that precedes it.

Certainly the "correctness" of Naylor's apparent reading of *The Bluest Eye*'s narrative strategies is not incontestable. What is not debatable, however, is the fact that both authors perceive almost insurmountable obstacles to Afro-American coalescence in the modern North. Of the texts we have examined to this point, only *Their Eyes Were Watching God* can, apparently because of its deep South and timeless setting, present female resolution of division as possible. In the final novel to be treated in this study, Alice Walker's *The Color Purple*, the author delineates a female's (and, in fact, an entire Afro-American community's) achievement of unity. In addition to sharing with Hurston's novel a deep South setting, *The Color Purple* also serves as a provocative delineation of an Afro-American woman's defeat of divisive patriarchal forces that demand women's silence and subservience.

4

The Color Purple and the Achievement Of (Comm)unity

> *The women sang lustily. Their songs were cotton-wads to stop their ears.*
>
> Jean Toomer
> *Cane*

> *Guided by my heritage of a love of beauty and a respect for strength—in search of my mother's garden, I found my own.*
>
> Alice Walker
> "In Search of Our Mother's Gardens"

BIOGRAPHICAL AND critical statements by Alice Walker concerning Jean Toomer's *Cane* and Zora Neale Hurston's *Their Eyes Were Watching God* suggest that it is certainly possible to explore—as I have in chapters of this study devoted to *The Bluest Eye* and *The Women of Brewster Place*—the "parented" status of the award-winning novel *The Color Purple*. Where the male-authored text is concerned, Walker comments in her collection of "womanist prose" *In Search of Our Mothers' Gardens* that Toomer's provocative depiction of Afro-American women has had a significant influence on her. For example, in the collection's much-quoted title essay, Walker begins her account of her successful search for the source of her own artistic talents with a particularly astute reading of the women who are so compellingly sketched in *Cane*. She discusses Toomer's depiction of women who "forced their minds to desert their bodies"[1] in ways that suggest that, for the author, *Cane*'s women are self-dividing predecessors to both Hurston's Janie and *The Color Purple*'s much-abused protagonist Celie.

I believe, however, that such an analysis of Walker's novel would fail to permit a critical focus on what are, for this study, *The Color Purple*'s most significant intertextual dimensions. The reasons for such an approach's explicative failure are suggested by a brief examination of the author's motivations for beginning an essay about black women's creativity with what she views as a male misrepresentation

of women. While Walker is deeply concerned in her work as a whole
with exploring the patriarchal forces which compel women to employ
such self-dividing defensive mechanisms as she believes Toomer observed and recorded, she is primarily concerned here with analyzing
the conditions of an enduring Black female creativity and discussing
her sense of Afro-American woman's artistic community. Consequently,
she suggests that the tragedy of the lives of Toomer's women is not
only that they are the physical and psychological victims of patriarchal attitudes, but also people whose creative impulses are thwarted.
These woman are, for Walker, artists bereft of a medium:

> these grandmothers and mothers of ours were not Saints, but
> Artists; driven to a numb and bleeding madness by the springs
> of creativity in them for which there was no release. They were
> Creators, who lived lives of spiritual waste, because they were so
> rich in spirituality—which is the basis of Art—that the strain of
> enduring their unused and unwanted talent drove them insane.
> Throwing away this spirituality was their pathetic attempt to
> lighten the soul of a weight their work-worn, sexually abused
> bodies could bear. (233)

In other essays, Walker has commented on the "perilous" nature
of her high admiration of Toomer.[2] She believes that *Cane* suggests
the deeply ambivalent nature of its author's attitudes toward women:
both his "sensitivity to women and his ultimate condescension toward them."[3] For Walker, that ambivalence comes into play in his
representation of spiritually wasted women. For despite his sensitivity to the causes of women's degradation, he seems to Walker patently unaware of the many examples of Afro-American women's artistic expression, of women whose artistic sensibilities have not been
thwarted. Thus, while he keenly depicts black women who are utterly
destroyed by racism and sexism, he seems uninformed about examples of women who, like Janie in *Their Eyes Were Watching God*, sur-
vive abuse-inspired self-division and ultimately find outlet for their
creative impulses.

If we accept the Afro-American critic Trudier Harris' characterization of Celie as "a bale of cotton with a vagina" who "gives in to her
environment with a kind of passivity that comes near to provoking
screams in readers,"[4] then the protagonist of *The Color Purple* would
appear to have more in common with the Toomerian women than
surely Walker intended. Further exploration of "In Search of Our
Mothers' Gardens," however, provides material for what I believe is
a more accurate reading of Celie's initial passivity, and insight into

the most significant aspects of *The Color Purple*'s intertextuality. For while Walker's essay begins with discussions of female passivity, it does so in order to suggest the obstacles to a vibrant Afro-American woman's creativity. Subsequent information in "In Search of Our Mothers' Gardens" suggests that where her corpus—and, particularly, *The Color Purple*—is concerned, it is most fruitful to concentrate primarily on *maternal* influences.

Walker offers her view of a cooperative black female artist's generational relationship:

> it is to my mother—and all our mothers who were not famous—
> that I went in search of the secret of what has fed that muzzled
> and often mutilated, but vibrant, creative spirit that the black
> woman has inherited . . .
>
>   And so our mothers and grandmothers have, more often than
> not anonymously, handed on the creative spark, the seed of the
> flower they themselves never hoped to see: or like a sealed letter
> they could not plainly read. (239-40)

Walker, then, is virtually concerned with discovering the dimensions of a "vibrant, creative" Afro-American woman's "spirit" that has survived despite racist and sexist efforts to suppress it and a general devaluation of its products. In searching for "the secret" of its survival—a survival whose patterns are suggested in the fact that her own work evidences her re-telling (her transference and adaptation to a written form) of her mother's orally communicated tales[5]—Walker expands traditional Western notions of art to include such artifacts of "everyday use" as gardens and quilts. What is essential to Walker is an awareness that, despite the inhibiting forces of sexism and racism, the Afro-American female's creative spirit has been expressed and has not, as her reading of Toomer suggests, been completely muted and discarded.

Her notions of a black female's generational transmission of an artistic spirit and her belief that that spirit is evident in creative readings of their "muzzled" and underappreciated folk art forms become significant factors, I believe, in Walker's conception of *The Color Purple*. For the novel conflates these various perceptions in a delineation of a single woman and her expression—her writing—of her life story. It seems to me that Celie's letters serve, in an environment where men endeavor to silence and control women, as the major outlet for her "muzzled" creative spirit.

In a recent study of twentieth-century women writers' narrative strategies entitled *Writing beyond the Ending*, Rachel Blau DuPlessis employs Walker's discussions of a cooperative black woman artists' generational relationship as the basis for a comprehensive reading of female influence. In her discussion of novels that depict the development of female artists from childhood to adulthood (*Kunstlerromane*), DuPlessis suggests that "the daughter becomes an artist to extend, reveal, and elaborate her mother's thwarted talents."[6] She further asserts:

> The younger artist's future project as a creator lies in completing the fragmentary and potential work of the mother; the mother is the daughter's muse, but in more than a passive sense. For the mother is also an artist. She has written, sung, made, or created, but her work, because in unconventional media, is muted and unrecognized. . . . The traditional notion of a muse is a figure who gives access to feeling or knowledge that she herself cannot formulate. In contrast, this maternal muse struggles with her condition to forge a work, usually one unique, unrepeatable work— an event, a gesture, an atmosphere—a work of synthesis and artistry that is consumed or used.
>
> By entering and expressing herself in some more dominant art form . . . , the daughter can make prominent the work both have achieved. Mother and daughter are thus collaborators, coauthors separated by a generation. (93-94)

I have discussed at some length the means by which Hurston's *Their Eyes Were Watching God* is "consumed" and "used" by Morrison and Naylor in their efforts to delineate the black woman's quest for (comm)unity. To observe its refigurations in *The Color Purple*, however, is to observe the attempts of a literary daughter dedicated not only to exploring obstacles to (comm)unity's achievement, but also, in DuPlessis' phrase, to "completing the fragmentary or potential work of the mother." Such a completion, if my reading of Hurston's text is an astute one, involves the figuration of a female protagonist who, like Janie, resolves her self-division and who, unlike Janie, is able thereafter to achieve a sense of communitas within a sympathetic and supportive community.

Further, Walker's attention to the "unrecognized" brilliance of Hurston's novel motivates her intriguing, though not unproblematic, refiguration of the much-maligned narrative strategies of *Their Eyes Were Watching God*. As I discussed in chapter 1, if critics have expressed a common reservation about the aesthetic success of Hurston's novel, it has concerned Hurston's failure to allow Janie, at the close of what is a quest for voice and self, to narrate the novel.

Apparently in response to such criticisms, Walker creates a text that not only contains figurations of (comm)unity, but one which reflects, in large part, the textual control of an abused protagonist/narrator. In a deft adaptation of the epistolary form and a bold criticism of critics, Walker subtly defends the narrative strategies of her precursor's work by insisting that individual textual control is *not* co-extensive with the achievement or representation of a powerful Afro-American female voice. That achievement, *The Color Purple* suggests, is, rather, a function of an adherence to the communal principles of Afro-American expressivity.

II

THE AFRO-AMERICAN critic Richard Barksdale has suggested in a recent interview that the most important aspect of *The Color Purple* is "what Alice Walker is trying to say about the dilemma of the Black woman in the rural South."[7] Like *Their Eyes Were Watching God*, Walker's novel emphatically insists that a major component of that dilemma is a patriarchal attempt to control the female voice and self, to muzzle, that is to say, the female spirit. In fact, male silencing of the female voice inspires Celie's epistolary impulses. Celie's first letter to God is preceded by Pa's manipulative warnings about the benefits of her silence: "You better not never tell nobody but God. It'd kill your mammy."[8] Thus, male silencing of the female voice represents a pretext, if you will, that occasions the subsequent text in much the same way as the primer that implicitly devalues Afro-American life serves as a generative pretext for Morrison's *The Bluest Eye*.

Like *Their Eyes Were Watching God*, the opening pages of *The Color Purple* are replete with figurations of its female protagonist's plight that evoke Afro-American slavery. Such figurations are clearest in their references to black bondage when Celie describes Pa's psychological and physical abuse. In her initial epistolary entry, for example, she says of the beginnings of her victimization:

> He never had a kine word to say to me. Just say You gonna do what your mammy wouldn't. First he put his thing gainst my hip and sort of wiggle it around. Then he grab hold my titties. Then he push his thing inside my pussy. When that hurt, I cry. He start to choke me, saying You better shut up and get used to it. (11)

When children are born to Celie from this apparently incestuous union,
Pa takes them from their mother as though she has no intrinsic right
to them that he need recognize. She imagines her children have met
horrible fates: that the first is murdered, and that the second is "sold
to a man an his wife over Monticello" (13). Celie's belief in the murder and merchandizing of the fruits of her womb and her brutal mistreatment at Pa's hands suggest that the conditions of her life are not
substantively different than those of female slaves whose children—
including those produced by male slaveowner's coercion and rape—
were frequently sold for financial gain.

Later in the text, when Albert asks Pa for permission to marry
Nettie, Pa effectively transforms the suitor's chivalrous antebellum
act into a slave auction-like treatment of his older daughter. After
careful deliberation, Pa says in response to the younger man's re-
quest:

> I can't let you have Nettie. She too young. Don't know nothing
> but what you tell her. Sides, I want her to git some more school-
> ing. Make a schoolteacher out of her. But I can let you have Celie.
> She ought to marry first. She ain't fresh tho, but I spect you know
> that. She spoiled. Twice. But you don't need a fresh woman no
> how. I got a fresh one in there myself and she sick all the time . . .
>
> She ugly, He say. But she ain't no stranger to hard work. And
> she clean. And God done fixed her. You can do everything just
> like you want to and she ain't gonna make you feed it or clothe
> it. (17-18)

Having earlier in the day done "everything just like you want" to
Celie, Pa offers her to a man who is, in Celie's prophetic words, of
"the same shape as Pa" (14). As Barbara Smith says of the young
protagonist's future husband: "The man, whom Celie does not even
know . . . , is of the same sorry ilk as Celie's father. By merely shift-
ing the locale of Celie's hell, Walker shows how little difference there
is between the circumstances of an abused daughter and an abused
wife."[9]

Male treatment of the young Celie as a commodity is further observable in the scene in which Albert accepts Pa's offer of his oldest
daughter. Celie recalls that:

> Pa called me. *Celie,* he say. Like it wasn't nothing. Mr.
> _____ want another look at you.
>   I go stand in the door. The sun shine in my eyes. He's [Mr.
> _____] still up on his horse. He look me up and down.
> Pa rattle his newspaper. Move up, he won't bite, he says.

I go closer to the steps, but not too close cause I'm a little scared of his horse.

Turn round, Pa says.

I turn round. One of my little brothers come up. I think it was Lucious. He fat and playful, all the time munching on something.

He says, What you doing that for?

Pa says, Your sister thinking about marriage . . .

*   *   *   *

She good with children, Pa say, rattling his paper open more. Never heard her say a hard word to nary one of them. Just give 'em everything they ast for, is the only problem.

Mr. _____ say, That cow still coming [as Celie's dowry]?

He say, Her cow. (20)

With no more control over her eventual fate than her enslaved ancestors, Celie will, like her cow, be forced to perform as a beast of burden. In a post-Reconstruction black community in which, where Celie is concerned, black men have assumed the role of slaveowners, she is forced to submit to the virulent inspection of a perspective taskmaster who will prove nearly as vile in his mistreatment of her as Pa.

Celie's naivety is reflected in her belief that the conditions of her new domicile will be less oppressive and will, as a result, present opportunities for escape. Specifically, she plans to use Albert's physical attraction to Nettie as a means to effect her own and her sister's liberation from male tyranny. Celie says:

It took him the whole spring, from March to June, to make up his mind to take me. All I thought about was Nettie. How she could come to me if I marry him and he be so love struck with her I could figure out a way for us to run away. Us both be hitting Nettie's schoolbooks pretty hard, cause us know we got to be smart to git away. (19)

In terms of the narrative tradition of recorded—written—Afro-American responses to slavery and virtual bondage which Walker is clearly and self-consciously echoing here (a tradition which has been astutely discussed by other critics[10] and which includes such works as Richard Wright's *Black Boy* and Frederick Douglass' *Narrative*), what is most striking about Celie's reflection here is the configuration of literacy and freedom. In Douglass' *Narrative*, for example, when the young slave's "kind" master Mr. Auld discovers that his wife has been educating Frederick, he pointedly explains to his wife why it is "unsafe . . . to teach a slave to read":

A nigger should know nothing but to obey his master—to do as he is told to do. Learning will spoil the best nigger in the world. Now. . . . if you teach that nigger . . . how to read, there would be no keeping him. It would forever unfit him to be a slave. He would at once become unmanageable, and of no value to his master.[11]

There is no space here to offer a fully detailed account of literacy's role in Douglass' desire for, if not his actual achievement of, freedom. Briefly, however, Auld's statement generates in the young slave "a new and special revelation"—that literacy represents "the pathway from slavery to freedom" (45).

Celie is as aware of Douglass of the fact that she has "to be smart to git away." Pa's denial to her of access to formal education after he impregnates her and his offering of her as homemaker, field hand, and sexual servant to his ideological double serve to clarify his desire to confine Celie permanently to the role of "nigger." In the essay mentioned earlier, Trudier Harris says of Celie's life with her husband: "Plowing a man's field for twenty years and letting him use her body as a sperm depository leaves Celie so buried away from herself that it is hard to imagine anything stirring her to life—just as it is equally hard to image her being so deadened" (158). Harris' discussion of Celie as "buried away from herself" and "deadened," however, is effectively undermined by the fact that it is Celie who narrates and controls the text of *The Color Purple*. Such a narration—which Harris herself at one point in her essay calls "absolutely wonderful" (156)— would be impossible for someone as emotionally deficient as Harris claims Celie is. Harris attempts to account for what she views as an inconsistency between a "deadened" character and a verbally inspirited narrator by insisting that Walker's narrative strategies are flawed. Specifically, she argues that the novel is marred by a "war between form and content":

> The form of the book, as it relates to the folk speech, the pattern and nuances of Celie's voice, is absolutely wonderful. The clash between Celie's conception and her writing ability, however, is another issue. I can imagine a black woman of Celie's background and education talking to God . . . , but writing letters to God is altogether another matter. Even if we can suspend our disbelief long enough to get beyond that hurdle, we are still confronted with the substance of the book. What Celie records—the degradation, abuse, dehumanization—is not only morally repulsive, but it invites spectator readers to generalize about black

people in the same negative ways that have been going on for
centuries. (156)

Apparently, Harris believes that because the protagonist does not actively struggle against male devaluations in the first half of the novel,
she could not possibly be cognitively energetic enough to have written the letters that make up much of the text of *The Color Purple*.

A more fruitful way of viewing Celie's letters than the primarily
pejorative manner suggested in Harris' essay is offered, if we return
at this point to "In Search of Our Mother's Gardens," by Walker's
discussion of Afro-American women's creativity. As we have seen,
Walker concludes a provocative reading of Toomer's debilitatingly
self-divided women by asserting that the primary problems for such
women result from a lack of an outlet for their creative energies.
Viewed in the light of Walker's comments, Celie's letters constitute,
it seems to me, the otherwise defenseless protagonist's valiant efforts,
in the face of a literal patriarchal silencing of her oral communication
(a silence that effectively cuts her off from participating in the expressive rituals of her people), to prevent an erasure of the creative
spirit.

Such an erasure is, for Walker, a self-protective response to the de-
humanizing mistreatment Celie encounters. These letters represent
her refusal, unlike her young, similarly incestuously abused fictive
forebears in *The Bluest Eye* and *Invisible Man*, to react to such abuse
by retreating into voicelessness or by "throwing away" spirituality.
For Walker, the alternative to the physically and psychologically
abused female's attempt at (artistic) expression is "a numb and
bleeding madness." Celie, however, is able to escape such a fate by
means of her letters. These letters serve as an outlet for her artistic
energies and the manner in which she lightens the burdens of what
she believes is an inescapable condition.

Harris' criticisms of Celie's inability to react forcefully to male mistreatment center, in part, around the critic's belief that the protagonist's response is inconsistent with an Afro-American tradition of vehement response to such abuse. She suggests that, unlike a physically
passive Celie, "Even slave women who found themselves abused frequently found ways of responding to that—by running away, fighting
back, poisoning their masters, or through more subtle defiant acts
such as spitting into the food they cooked for their masters" (157). In
this litany of Afro-American women's responses to oppression and
abuse, Harris, however, fails to mention perhaps the most subtle of
such responses, and the class of reactions with which Celie's actions

have the most in common: the creation of expressive art forms that encode vehement protest against abominably tyrannical people and institutions.

John Blassingame's discussion in *The Slave Community* of the manifold benefits to slaves of the creation of such art forms as folk tales, secular songs, and spirituals provides a most fruitful means of comprehending more fully the tradition out of which Celie's record of her life springs. Blassingame says:

> the mere existence of these cultural forms is proof that the rigors of bondage did not crush the slave's creative energies. Through these means the slave could view himself as an object, hold on to fantasies about his status, engender hope and patience, and at least use rebellious language when contemplating his lot in life. The therapeutic value of this should not be dismissed lightly. Not only did these cultural forms give the slave an area of life independent of his master's control, they also were important psychological devices for repressing anger and projecting aggressions in ways that contributed to mental health, involved little physical threat, and provided some form of recreation. By objectifying the conditions of his life in folk tales, the slave was in a better position to cope with them.[12]

Close attention to Walker's figurations of Celie's plight in terms of slavery suggests that the author endows her character with the subtle artistic powers of the aforementioned folk forms' anonymous creators. Celie's letters are the written equivalent of a black woman's garden or quilt—an outlet for her creative energies and the means by which she maintains a positive sense of self. The virtually enslaved Celie creates out of her life experiences art which, like the cultural forms that Blassingame and Walker discuss, possesses a distinctive therapeutic value and offers her (artistic) control of her existence.

Despite their various merits, however, Celie's early letters do prove problematic from an Afro-American expressive cultural standpoint. Instead of corresponding to the communal inclinations of Afro-American expressivity, these letters represent an individual's attempts at self-help. Unlike the folk forms of which Blassingame speaks, or, for that matter, the "everyday use" art that Walker praises in "In Search of Our Mothers' Gardens," Celie's letters initially evidence little or no concern for the community or expressive interaction with an audience. While I will explore the communicative shortcomings of Celie's letters more fully in the following section, it is interesting to note at this point that instead of arising from communal impulses, her first letters, as Nettie reminds her, result from a communicative disability brought on by shame and extreme degradation: "you said your life made you feel so ashamed you couldn't even talk about it to God, you had to write it, bad as you thought your writing was" (122). Considering the depths of her pain and the violence-bolstered male opposition to her speech, such communicative shortcomings are, I believe, understandable. But the protagonist's achievement of (comm)unity becomes possible only when she—and her letters—evidence less self-interested attitudes vis-à-vis communication.

III

SOME CRITICS have suggested that scrutiny of *The Color Purple*'s form— its epistolarity—will not offer significant critical insight into Walker's novel.[13] Close attention to the novel's provocative adaptation of the epistolary form, however, does permit discernment of the text's most suggestive thematic concern: Celie's achievement of a communal voice.

In a recent study entitled *Epistolarity*, Janet Altman says of the differences between diary and epistolary fiction:

> What distinguishes epistolary narrative from . . . diary novels . . . is the desire for exchange. In epistolary writing the reader is called upon to respond as a writer and to contribute as such to the narrative . . .
>
> To a great extent, this is the epistolary pact—the call for response from a specific reader within the correspondent's world.[14]

If Altman's assertions are correct, then the epistolary narrative form, because of its intrinsic insistence upon active exchange between writer and reader, is a potentially ideal medium through which Afro-American writers can render the quintessential black verbal behavior of call-and-response. For what Altman refers to as "the epistolary pact— the call for response," accurately characterizes the (unspoken) agreement between speaker and audience in Afro-American oral communication, the contours of which I discussed in detail in my chapter on *Their Eyes Were Watching God*.

Walker's text provides evidence which suggests that she is grappling in the form of *The Color Purple* with what is a major aesthetic and philosophical dilemma for Afro-American writers: how to infuse written texts with the antiphonal properties of orally transmitted texts, how, in other words, to suggest that a reading audience can, like the audience of an orally transmitted text, significantly alter the text's communication. Writers have viewed this problem from a variety of conceptual positions. For some, including the novelist Gayl Jones, written and oral literature are completely diverse activities. Jones says:

> for me fiction and storytelling are different. I say I'm a fiction writer if I'm asked, but I really think of myself as a storyteller. When I say "fiction," it evokes a lot of different kinds of abstractions, but when I say "storyteller," it always has its human connections. . . . There is always that kind of relationship between a storyteller and a hearer—the seeing of each other. The hearer has to see/hear the storyteller, but the storyteller has to see/hear the hearer, which the written tradition doesn't usually acknowledge.[15]

Other authors, including Toni Morrison, rather than seeing fiction and storytelling as different activities, openly embrace the challenge of attempting to infuse "literary"—written—genres with the antiphonal properties of oral forms. Morrison says of her *denigration* of the novel:

> There are things that I try to incorporate into my fiction that are directly related to what I regard as the major characteristics of Black art. . . . One of which is the ability to be both print and oral literature: to combine those two aspects so that the stories can be read in silence, of course, but one should be able to hear them as well. It [the Black novel] should try deliberately to make you stand up and make you feel something profoundly in the same way that a Black preacher requires his congregation to speak, to join him in the sermon . . . , to stand up and to weep and to cry and to accede to or change and to modify—to expand on the sermon that is being delivered. . . . [H]aving at my disposal only the letters of the alphabet and some punctuation, I have to provide the place and space so that the reader can participate. Because it is the affective and participatory relationship between the artist or the speaker and the audience that is of primary importance.[16]

Like Jones, Morrison insists that a participatory relationship between teller and hearer is essential in Afro-American textual communication. It is the Afro-American writer's challenge to be simultaneously a fiction writer and a storyteller and, in doing so, to infuse written literary forms with the expressive capabilities of call-and-response.

Where *The Color Purple* is concerned, Celie's first letters hint that

Walker's text will explore the antiphonal potentials of the epistolary form. Celie's first letter, in fact, suggests an intuitive knowledge of the participatory nature of Afro-American expressivity. For her first words to her audience are a call from her Reader's response:

> Dear God,
>   I am fourteen years old. I have always been a good girl. Maybe you can give me a sign letting me know what is happening to me. (11)

Celie does not, as one might expect, ask her Reader to intervene to terminate the sexual abuse which occasions this first letter. Instead, she requests from her Reader an interpretive (and interpretable) response. Specifically, she desires from God an idea of the sexually abusive act's causes (why someone who has "always been a good girl" is being subjected to such mistreatment) and tangible evidence of His analytical conclusions ("a sign") that she will herself have to interpret.

Celie's choice of and perceptions about this addressee, however, significantly complicate the theoretically ideal union between epistolary form and black verbal behavior. For she addresses her letters not to—as Altman suggests is a necessary feature of the epistolary pact—"a specific reader within the correspondent's world," but to a Reader who is, in the young protagonist's conception, both physically and emotionally dissociated from her world. Because of this perception of a dissociated Reader, Celie's letters exhibit, for the most part, no sense of exchange or engagement with her specific Audience. Altman suggests that "epistolary discourse is the language of the 'as if' present. . . . Epistolary language, which is the language of absence, makes [the addressee] present by make-believe" (140). The vast majority of Celie's initial letters, however, demonstrate no sense that she is engaging an imaginatively "present" audience.

Note, for example, her recounting—nominally for her Reader—of her explanation to her mother of her pregnancy:

> She ast me bout the first one Whose it is? I say God's. I don't know no other man or what else to say . . .
>   Finally she ast Where it is?
>   I say God took it. (12)

This passage from Celie's second letter to God reflects neither a sense of remorse on the part of the writer nor a fear of possible negative Audience response because of her blaming her pregnancy on her Reader. This insensitivity results, it would appear, from her lack of a clear awareness during the letter's composition that she is writing both *to* and *about* God.

Celie's lack of engagement with her Reader is even more clearly observable when she records her fantasies about God's efforts to end Sofia's incarceration:

> I think about angels, God coming down by chariot, swinging down real low and carrying ole Sofia home. I see 'em all as clear as day. Angels all in white, white hair and white eyes, look like albinos. God all white too, looking like some stout white man work at the bank. Angels strike they cymbals, one of them blow his horn, God blow out a big breath of fire and suddenly Sofia free. (90-91)

Celie does not conceive of her Reader as an "'as if' present" deity. There is no sense in her discussion of her God's imagined action that she is addressing her letter to this same figure. While God as Actor in the world is, as Altman suggests is the case with an epistolary addressee, "present by make-believe," certainly does not seem "present" as *Reader* in Celie's depiction of a "make-believe" rescue of Sofia. She does not seem aware in this discussion of God that she is in fact also addressing her letter to God. From her first letter in which God is perceived as actively involved in the world, Celie's conception of Him appears to have altered to the point that His presence, instead of being represented by a subtle sign, is envisioned in melodramatic, Cecil B. De Millian terms.

Celie's lack of engagement calls into question my earlier reference to *The Color Purple* as an epistolary novel if we accept Altman's insistence that there is in such novels a degree of exchange between writer and reader. Epistolary instances such as those noted above clearly indicate that many of Celie's letters lack a desire for exchange. At such moments, it appears that Celie's entries are, as a result, the self-interested expression of a muzzled creative spirit. She is writing not in order to elicit a response from a reader but, rather, simply to record the events of her life. In other words, a significant portion of Celie's text resembles a diary novel more than it does an epistolary novel where the internal reader assumes a great deal of importance in the writer's construction of his or her texts. Instead of employing the epistolary novel form as a template for Afro-American call-and-response, Walker constructs a text whose first letters suggest *failures* of communication.

Despite the vernacular resonances of her epistles, then, it is clear that Celie must develop, as does her fictive forebear Janie, a more acute sense of audience if she is to become a truly effective Black storyteller and self-actualized human being. For if discursive power represents the means by which Hurston's protagonist achieves a positive sense of self and her liberation from the constraining texts of others, then *Their Eyes Were Watching God* insists that that power results from Janie's communal orientation both in terms of a shared textual control (the joining of her tongue and Pheoby's) and the fact that her story is told largely for the edification of a skeptical female community. Celie's initial letters, conversely, exhibit very little sense of engagement of an audience or awareness that she is writing to— let alone for—her God as Reader. In a real sense, then, Celie's quest involves the development of an understanding of an audience's essential role in Afro-American textual communication.

Walker provides, in the case of Mary Agnes' (Squeak's) narration of her efforts to end Sofia's incarceration and her first blues composition, a brief, but suggestive, example of a formerly submissive Afro-American woman's acquisition of textual power. Her texts provide concentrated examples that serve to facilitate our comprehension not only of the means by which Celie frees herself from patriarchal subjugation, but also of her mastery of the tropes of Afro-American expressivity.

IV

SQUEAK'S FIRST significant communicative act occurs when she offers an account of her efforts to gain Sofia's liberation from a potentially murderous incarceration for having punched the town's mayor. Her account is immediately interrupted by the self-piteous rantings of her mate Harpo, who says: "My wife beat up, my woman rape. . . . I ought to go back out there with guns, maybe set fire to the place, burn the crackers up" (94). Squeak, however, vociferously objects to his interruption, an objection she states in the following way: "Shut up, Harpo, I'm telling it" (94). After silencing Harpo, she tells of her successful execution of a plan devised by an organized group of males and females (including Albert, Sofia's sister Odessa, and her prize-fighter boyfriend), based on an acute knowledge of the bizarre kinship networks of the South, and designed to trick Squeak's white uncle— the prison warden—into releasing Sofia from jail:

> I say what yall told me to say. Bout Sofia not being punish enough.
> Say she happy in prison, strong girl like her. Her main worry is

just the thought of ever being some white woman maid. That what start the fight, you know, I say. Mayor's wife ask Sofia to be her maid. Sofia say she never going to be no white woman's nothing, let alone maid. (94)

Squeak then describes a sexual assault by the white warden, an act the warden justifies implicitly (it would appear) as compensation for his promise to carry out what he believes is Squeak's malicious wish. And because Squeak is his blood relative, this act requires additional justification on his part:

He took my hat off, say Squeak. Told me to undo my dress. She drop her head, put her face in her hands.
   My God, say Odessa, and he your uncle.
   He say if he was my uncle he wouldn't do it to me. That be a sin. But this just little fornication. Everybody guilty of that. (95)

The warden attempts to excuse himself from involvement in a taboo-breaking act by means of self-serving designative substitution.

There are, however, positive consequences resulting from Squeak's sacrifice in addition to Sofia's eventual release. Acting courageously and in accord with communal wisdom serves as impetus for Squeak's discovery of herself. This self-discovery is first manifested in her insistence that Harpo call her by her given name:

She turn her face up to Harpo. Harpo, she say, do you really love me, or just my color?
   Harpo say, I love you, Squeak. He kneel down and try to put his arms round her waist.
   She stand up. My name Mary Agnes, she say. (95)

Her courageous act inspires in her an acute understanding of the negative consequences of what the critic Kimberly Benston has called "unnaming."[17] Her insistence on being called by her given name suggests a conscious rejection not only of Harpo's pejorative designation "Squeak," but also of a previous self that had essentially earned this unnaming because, in Celie's words, she did "anything Harpo say" (83).

Having helped to secure Sofia's liberation, she sets about re-creating herself. Her re-creation occasions her discovery of previously uncharted singing abilities. Mary Agnes' voice, which, according to Shug, inspires "folks . . . to thinking bout a good screw" (111), serves as her means of further rejecting her own misnaming. After a period of perfecting her talents—a period in which she cuts her musical teeth by singing Shug's songs—Mary Agnes begins to compose her own lyrics. Celie includes in her text the neophyte blues singer's first composition, a song that might have been entitled "Yellow Girl Blues":

> They calls me yellow
> like yellow be my name
> They calls me yellow
> like yellow be my name
> But if yellow is a name
> Why ain't black the same
> Well, if I say Hey black girl
> Lord, she try to ruin my game (97)

Like her recounting of the details of her sexual victimization, Mary Agnes' blues is essentially concerned with the consequences of (un)naming. Just as she rejects the name Harpo employs to refer to her, she additionally rejects malicious designations that characterize her solely in terms of pigmentation. Her lyrics ("But if yellow is a name/Why ain't black the same") effectively question the fitness of such pejorative designations. Further, she equates verbally damaging unnaming and the physically injurious acts of violence of female adversaries who, having themselves been victimized by what they consider a malevolent naming, "try to ruin my game."

Mary Agnes' example suggests in a powerful way the liberating possibilities for the formerly subjugated female of telling her own story, of controlling, that is to say, the representation of the female self. Her ability to articulate the particulars of her victimization provides her with the power to dictate what she is called and, ultimately, to discover what she can be. She is able to create out of her own life an autobiographical blues that clearly signifies on rivals who insist upon characterizing her solely in terms of her skin color, but who violently refuse to allow themselves to be similarly designated. In this briefly delineated example, then, Walker offers a provocative depiction of a female's achievement of a positive sense of self as a result of her participation in a selfless communal act. Mary Agnes develops a profound textual power when she learns to act in accord with communal inclinations.[18] Celie likewise improves her self-esteem by adopting an Afro-American expressive-communal strategy. To begin to analyze textual manifestations of Celie's improved self-confidence is to observe Walker's figuration of the written Afro-American text as a shared communicative act.

V

WE HAVE seen Celie's initially self-oriented perspectives in terms of her textual relationship with her audience. Her self-orientation is also apparent in narrative incidents, particularly her suggestions to her stepson Harpo about how to secure his wife Sofia's obedience:

> I like Sofia, but she don't act like me at all. If she talking when Harpo and Mr. _____ come in the room, she keep right on. If they ast her where something at, she say she don't know. Keep talking.
>   I think bout this when Harpo ast me what he ought to do to make her mind. I don't mention how happy he is now. How three years pass and he still whistle and sing. I think bout how every time I jump when Mr. _____ call me, she look surprise. And like she pity me.
>   Beat her, I say. (42-43)

After several memorable battles with her husband, Sofia confronts a guilt-ridden Celie: "What you say it for? she ast."

> I say it cause I'm a fool, I say. I say it cause I'm jealous of you. I say it cause you do what I can't.
>   What that? she say.
>   Fight, I say. (46)

Celie's admission of malicious intent suggests that her advice is similar to the "tongue storm" (276) of the muck workers who do not believe that Janie's murder of Tea Cake was a self-defensive act. While the enmity between Janie and her attackers is, at best, hastily reconciled, Celie's malicious act leads to an establishment of a sense of sisterhood with Sofia. This sisterhood, which eventually also includes Shug Avery, is most suggestively manifested in their joint participation in what is, for Walker, a quintessential black woman's communal art—quiltmaking: "Me and Sofia work on the quilt. Got it frame up on the porch. Shug Avery donate her old yellow dress for scrap. And I work in a piece every chance I get. It a nice pattern call Sister's Choice" (62).

Celie's relationship with Shug follows a similar pattern. After the ill blues singer's initial exhibitions of hostility toward the wife of her lover Albert, the two women develop first a strong friendship, and then an intense romantic relationship. As was the case in the development of her friendship with Sofia, the termination of antagonism leads to a communal act of creativity. Celie writes that combing Shug's hair evenuates in the creation of song:

> I comb and pat, comb and pat. First she say, hurry up and git finish. Then she melt down a little and lean back gainst my knees. That feel just right, she say. That feel like mama used to do. Or maybe not mama. Maybe grandma. She reach for another cigarette. Start hum a little tune.
>
> What that song? I ast. Sound low down dirty to me. Like what the preacher tell you its sin to hear. Not to mention sing.
>
> She hum a little more. Something come to me, she say. Something I made up. Something you help scratch out my head. (57)

From her friendship and "creative" interactions with these self-confident women, Celie begins to develop not only a higher self-regard, but also a sense of the benefits of community. These women come to represent for Celie "present" audiences to whom she can speak about the burdens of her life and from whom, unlike her absent Reader, she receives immediate and beneficial response. These relationships additionally offer the protagonist information about the benefits of communal art. This information, I believe, serves to alter substantially the nature of Celie's subsequent letters.

It is significant to note that only when the friendship with Shug begins to blossom does Celie offer a full account of her victimization at the hands of both Pa and Albert. This more detailed account demonstrates her epistolary efforts' altered purpose. Earlier Celie, in response to her sister's suggestion that seeing her being abused by Albert and his children is "like seeing you buried," offers an effective description of the object of her letter writing. She tells Nettie: "long as I can spell G-o-d I got somebody along" (26).

Her Addressee, then, serves as a confidant to whom letters are written as a means of easing feelings of mental anguish and otherwise insufferable loneliness. Celie continues to address letters to God even after Shug has effectively replaced God as the protagonist's primary confidant. These letters, however, subsequently assume much different functions; they become, as it were, accounts of oral narration, (written) telling about (oral) telling.

The altered character of Celie's letters is evident, for example, in her description of Pa's initial abuse act, a description which serves to clarify information offered in her first epistolary entry. Shug's question, "How was it [sex] with your children daddy" (108), inspires Celie's explanation of the circumstances of her initial sexual victimization:

The girls had a little separate room . . . , off to itself, connected
to the house by a little plank walk. Nobody ever came in there
but Mama. But one time when mama not at home, he come. Told
em he want me to trim his hair. He bring the scissors and comb
and brush and a stool. When I trim his hair he look at me funny.
He a little nervous too, but I don't know why, till he grab hold
of me and cram me up tween his legs. (108)

She also tells Shug the story that Pa offers to explain to his wife
the presence of hair in the girls' room (a story whose disbelief Celie
had formerly suggested to the Reader killed her mother):

Mama finally ast how come she find his hair in the girls room if
he never go in there like he say. That when he told her I had a
boyfriend. Some boy he say been sneaking out the back door. It
the boy's hair, he say, not his. You know how she love to cut
anybody hair, he say. (109)

While her elaborations of these previously either recounted or briefly
mentioned stories could possibly be viewed as representing Celie's
increased sensitivity to her Reader's needs, a more persuasive explanation is that her textual relationship with her Addressee has assumed a secondary importance to her relationship to Shug. And while
such narrative acts provide her Reader with information that clarifies earlier letters, this information is not intended to help the Reader
to comprehend Celie's history more fully. Rather, it suggests that
temporal distance from the event and her participation in a recip-
rocal and caring relationship with the blues singer enable the pro-
tagonist/narrator to discuss her painful personal history, the particulars of which she had not, before talking about them with Shug,
been able to record in her letters.

Her recording of her storytelling with Shug, then, suggests her substantially altered view of the act of writing. Instead of writing simply
as a means of expressing her "muzzled" creative energies, Celie writes
to record her spiritual and physical connection with Shug, to suggest,
in other words, her achievement of a sense of community with a
"present" audience. The blues singer has, for all intents and purposes,
replaced God as Celie's primary confidante. Celie replaces—in her
communicative acts—an absent, apparently unresponsive Reader with
a "present," obviously responsive audience whose reactions accord
with Black audience behavior that Toni Morrison describes as a willingness "to stand up and to weep and to cry," and an ability to affect,
in substantial ways, the text's communication. One particularly fas-

cinating feature of this audience's and Nettie's function in the text is that they provoke Celie's greater understanding of the inadequacies of her conception of her initial (white male) Reader.

VI

NETTIE'S LETTERS have (to a certain extent, justly) received generally condemnatory evaluations in responses to *The Color Purple*. Trudier Harris suggests, for example, that "Nettie and the letters from Africa were really extraneous to the central concerns of the novel" (157). And Mel Watkins insists in a review of the novel that these letters are "often mere monologues on African history" which, because they lack the vernacular richness of Celie's epistles, "seem lackluster and intrusive."[19] I agree that Nettie's letters fail to command the reader's attention to a degree equal to Celie's compelling letters.

However, to emphasize their flaws at this point would be to minimize their essential importance in Celie's ultimate achievement of (comm)unity. To be sure, Nettie's letters contain, in addition to too frequently banal discussions of African history and a rather stilted prose style, evidence of a clear problem in Walker's conception of *The Color Purple*. For if Nettie is to assume the textual importance that she is given in the second half of the novel, surely the author should not have allowed her virtually to disappear both from the novel's primary setting and, more problematically, from the thoughts of her sister.

Despite these (no doubt major) flaws, however, Nettie's letters do achieve an undeniable importance in the text of *The Color Purple*. If, as I have suggested, one of the central concerns of Walker's novel is male efforts to dominate and silence women, then Nettie's letters prove both in their content and in their manipulation essential factors in the author's delineation. Indeed, it is Albert's inability to secure Nettie's sexual submission that provokes his obstruction of the sister's communication. Nettie writes in her first letter to Celie that as a consequence of Albert's failed attempts to "Drag me back in the woods," he vows that "I'd never hear from you again, and you would never hear from me" (119).

Albert succeeds in obstructing the sisters' communication for decades. His interception of Nettie's letters occasions both Celie's questioning of the benefits of attempted escape (Celie believes Nettie's escape led to her death) and her belief that she is alone in the world. Consequently, the thoughts of fleeing male tyranny that enter Celie's consciousness when she first learns she may become Albert's wife quickly give way to desires for mere survival. Her reaction to her sister-in-law's appeal to her to fight back in response to her husband's and his children's malice is exemplary of her survivalist mentality at this point in her life: "I think about Nettie, dead. She fight, she run away. What good it do? I don't fight, I stay where I'm told. But I'm alive" (29). She is, in her inability to remove herself from the site of male abuse, like Janie who, after finally being able to acknowledge her husband Joe Starks' myriad shortcomings, is nevertheless unable to effect an escape.

Celie's knowledge that her sister Nettie is alive reawakens in her thoughts of escape: "Now I know Nettie alive I begin to strut a little bit. Think, When she comes home us leave here. Her and me and our two children" (138). Additionally, Nettie's letters or, more precisely, Celie's knowledge of her husband's withholding of them, inspire in her almost uncontrollable desires for a murderous revenge:

> All day long [after finding Nettie's letters] I act just like Sofia. I stutter. I mutter to myself. I stumble bout the house crazy for Mr. _____ blood. In my mind, he falling dead every which a way. By the time night come, I can't speak. Every time I open my mouth nothing come out but a little burp. (115)

Nettie's letters, then, serve to reinforce the novel's thematic focus on the consequences of male attempts to control the female voice. An analysis of the effects of Celie's and Shug's incorporation of Nettie's letters into the text of Celie's life, moreover, provides significant information about the protagonist's achievement of a sense of an "'as if' present" epistolary audience.

The blues singer Shug plays a prominent role in the novel in encouraging constructive usage of female creative energies. Not only does she prove extremely supportive of Mary Agnes' efforts to begin a singing career, but she also encourages the protagonist's cathartic full disclosure of the particulars of her earlier sexual victimization. In fact, Shug's efforts contribute, in ways that are essentially important from an Afro-American expressive cultural perspective, to her lover's resolution of her difficulties with an unresponsive (white) Reader.

Nettie's letters are incorporated into the text of *The Color Purple* as a result of the joint efforts of Celie and Shug. It is Shug who discovers that Albert has been hiding Nettie's letters and who, when she and Celie find the "Bunches and bunches" of Nettie's letters hidden in Albert's trunk, offers to "put them in some kind of order for" Celie (118). Celie, on the other hand, introduces these letters into her own text. She places the first letter that she reads into the body of her own letters to God in the following way:

Dear God,
This the letter I been holding in my hand.

Dear Celie,
I know you think I am dead. But I am not. I been writing to you too, over the years, but Albert said you'd never hear from me again and since I never heard from you all this time, I guess he was right. (112)

Subsequent letters from Nettie are not offered as part of Celie's letters to God, but are, rather, given their own space in Celie's text. They become, in other words, a significant part of her sister's record of the story of her life.

Nettie's letters are, when they concern Celie's life and the particulars of her children's removal from their mother, quite compelling. This is nowhere more apparent then when Nettie records Samuel's discussion of his friendship with Pa and his knowledge of the sisters' family history. After listening to Samuel's story of the lynching of their natural father, their mother's resultant insanity, and the stepfather's theft of Celie's children, Nettie says:

Tears had soaked my blouse when Samuel finished telling me all this. I couldn't begin, then, to tell him the truth. But Celie, I can tell you. And I pray with all my heart that you will get this letter, if none of the others.
Pa is not our pa. (162)

This information, which is intended by Nettie to free her sister from the guilt of believed incest, instead immediately provokes a sense of personal chaos and a final loss of faith in her Reader. In her subsequent entry, Celie says:

I feels daze.
My daddy lynch. My mama crazy. All my little half-brothers and sisters no kin to me. My children not my sister and brother.
Pa not pa.
You must be sleep. (163)

For one of the first times since the text's opening letter where she requests from God a sign, the protagonist directly addresses her Reader. But it is an address that chastises this Reader for His absence and inattentiveness to her plight.

Subsequently, Celie addresses her letters to Nettie. She begins her

second letter to Nettie by telling her sister: "I don't write to God no
more, I write to you" (175). Because of Shug's prominent role in her
life and text, Celie explains to the blues singer her reasons for her
change in addressee. As she tells her dual audience (a "present" Shug
and "as if" present Nettie):

> He [God] give me a lynched daddy, a crazy mama, a lowdown
> dog for a step pa and a sister I probably won't ever see again.
> Anyhow, I say, the God I been praying and writing to is a man.
> And act just like all the other men I know. Trifling, forgitful and
> lowdown . . .
>
> All my life I never care what people thought bout nothing I
> did, I say. But deep in my heart I care about God. What he going
> to think. And come to find out, he don't think. Just sit up there
> glorying in being deaf, I reckon. But it ain't easy, trying to do
> without God. Even if you know he ain't there, trying to do with-
> out him is a strain. (175-76)

Celie is involved in what is a fairly typical twentieth-century philosophical dilemma of "trying to do without" God in a situation where
His absence (or believed absence) causes chaos. The remainder of
Walker's text is concerned with Celie's efforts to resolve personal,
familial, and narrative disjunctions.

While Celie does experience a crisis of faith (in her Reader, nonetheless), her feelings of utter chaos are relatively short-lived. Her initial confrontation with chaos occurs when Shug questions her adoption of a traditional conception of God as "big and old and tall and
graybearded and white" (176). Having herself long before rejected a
white-controlled Christianity's conception of God, Shug explains to
Celie the problems inherent in worshipping (and writing to) the "white
folks' white bible" God:

> Ain't no way to read the bible and not think God white, she say.
> Then she sigh. When I found out I thought God was white, and
> a man, I lost interest. You mad cause he don't seem to listen to
> your prayers. Humph! Do the mayor listen to anything colored
> say? (177)

For Shug, Celie's appeal to a white God as Audience cannot help but
fall on deaf ears. She suggests instead that her friend search elsewhere for signs of deity's presence:

> God is inside you and inside everybody else. You come into the
> world with God. But only them that search for it inside find it.

And sometimes it just manifest itself even if you not looking, or
don't know what you looking for. (177)

Shug's discussion of her repudiation of the traditional (white)
Christian God in favor of a non-Christian deity intentionally recalls
a young Janie's discovery of a natural God under a blossoming pear
tree in Hurston's novel. While Janie's initial encounter with God offers comprehension of the original conception of marriage and an or-
gasmic "pain remorseless sweet that left her limp and languid,"[20]
Shug's first such encounter—which also occurs in a natural setting—
produces lasting feelings of unity. She tells Celie:

> My first step from the old white man was trees. Then air. Then
> birds. Then other people. But one day when I was sitting quiet
> and feeling like a motherless child, which I was, it come to me:
> that feeling of being part of everything, not separate at all. I knew
> that if I cut a tree, my arm would bleed. And I laughed and I
> cried and I run all around the house. (178)

Shug's religious awakening, then, leads to her ecstatic discovery of
her connection with the rest of the world. The young Janie's natural
encounter, while it is unquestionably enlightening in some respects,
leaves her with unanswered questions and sets her on a psychological
quest for an ideal bee man who can make her feel complete. For Shug,
on the other hand, her encounter occasions feelings of wholeness that
Janie is capable of only after a lifetime of pain; *The Color Purple's*
blues singer, that is, immediately discovers that she is "part of everything, not separate at all."

Instead of being instructed, as is Janie, by a (natural) God, Celie is
offered the wisdom of her friend Shug who has, in Janie's wonderful
phrase, "been tuh de horizon and back" (284). In Walker's refiguration of Hurston, Celie's "kissin'-friend" (and audience) both encourages the storyteller's communication of her tale and provides valuable instruction without which that communication would be
ultimately impossible. Specifically, Shug argues vehemently against
her friend's acquiescence to debilitating feelings of division and historical chaos in a supposedly godless world. For Shug, Celie's problems with God arise not from God's absence, but from her acceptance
of a white Christian conceptualization that prevents her from searching for divine presence "inside you and inside everybody else."

Shug rejects—and encourages a similar rejection by her friend
Celie—what Gerald Graff condemnatorially calls "the normalization
of alienation," by which he means the widely held current "assump-

tion that alienation is the normal and unalterable condition for human beings."[21] For those who accept this view of a normalized alienation, even history—that is, the retrospective ordering of past human
events into a coherent episodic narrative—fails to provide a sense of
continuity. History itself becomes a disjunctive force:

> If history lacks value, pattern, and rationally intelligible mean-
> ing, then no exertion of the shaping, ordering imagination can
> be anything but a refuge from truth. Alienation from significant
> external reality, from all reality, becomes an inescapable con-
> dition. (60)

In *The Color Purple*, Walker's protagonist also is forced to confront,
in her encounter with the nightmare of her unintelligible family history, the type of chaos that Graff describes. Celie, however, takes an
important first step in rejection of such historical chaos when she and
Shug travel to her childhood home to find the graves of her mother
and natural father. After obtaining from her stepfather information
about the graves' location, she and Shug—in a scene reminiscent of
Walker's search of Hurston's grave:[22]

> look for Ma and Pa. Hope for some scrap of wood that say some-
> thing. But us don't find nothing but weeds and cockleburrs and
> paper flowers fading on some of the graves. Shug pick up a old
> horseshoe somebody horse lose. Us took that old horseshoe and
> us turned round and round together until we were dizzy enough
> to fall out, and where us would have fell us stuck the horseshoe
> in the ground.
>   Shug say, Us each other's people's now, and kiss me. (167)

After striving quite literally to achieve a sense of familial continuity
in a neglected graveyard, Celie begins to come to terms with her past.
Having advanced psychologically to a point where talking about her
personal history proves cathartic, the protagonist—aided by an accurate knowledge of her familial past (including the fact that her ca-
lamitous sexual abuse was not incestuous)—is able to conquer a sense
of chaos. At the close of her journey Celie has, with the able and informed assistance of Nettie and Shug, achieved a unified and unifying
Black perspective and expressive power. She is able to reject her former conception of an absent white male God in favor of a notion of
a natural, present, non-gendered deity. Further, she is able, because
of Nettie's letters from Africa that provide a revised and accurate version of family history, to liberate herself from an oppressive, loveless
marriage and to manifest a profound verbal ability that allows her,
in effect, to signify her way to freedom.

In a scene which recalls Janie's liberation through the power of words, Celie effectively thwarts her husband's attempts to prevent her exit. When he inquires what is wrong with her and insists that she will leave his home only "Over my dead body," Celie responds: "You a lowdown dog is what's wrong, I say. It's time to leave you and enter into the Creation. And your dead body just the welcome mat I need" (180). Having already survived the angst of alienation and achieved, despite its divisive effects, a sense of (comm)unity, Celie is ready to "enter into the Creation" and to experience, just as Janie does after the death of her equally repressive husband Joe Starks, life's joyous possibilities. Nettie's much maligned letters, particularly those which concern family history, prove essential to the resolutions recorded in Celie's later epistles. Quitely clearly, they are the impetus for Celie's triumph over an alienation caused by a nightmarish personal history.

The texts of Celie and Nettie, the dual narrative voices of *The Color Purple*, thus, become unified in much the same manner that the scraps of well-worn cloth are combined into a magnificent quilt—into Afro-American women's art. Like a quilt which represents, in a real sense, the transmutation of tattered raiments of a familial and tribal history into a new and usable present form, so, too, does the text of *The Color Purple*—of a protagonist who is an unparalleled (and commercially successful) seamstress—suggest a reconstruction of a "traditional" history and possibility. The written product of the efforts of Celie and Nettie (and Shug), while it is not aesthetically unflawed like the Sister's Choice quilt that Celie, Sofia, and Shug jointly create, is certainly the function of similar black women's communal artistic impulses and, in a sense, its discursive equivalent. The texts of Celie and Nettie are merged, like a quilt's patches, into a unified whole in *The Color Purple;* the dual narrative voices of the novel suggest not, as they do in Naylor's text, the impossibility of (comm)unity, but, rather, its gratifying achievement.

VII

THE COLOR Purple is devoted to charting the achievement of unity—individual, tribal, and textual—despite the presence of powerfully divisive forces. Unlike *The Women of Brewster Place*, Walker's novel vigorously insists in its final pages on (comm)unity's possibility.

Such insistence is immediately evident in the series of reconciliations that occur between what appear to be irreparably estranged characters. These reconciliations occur because of male characters' "recognition of androgyny"—to use the feminist critic Carolyn Heilbrun's term—their comprehension, in other words, of the erroneousness of sex role stereotyping. Harpo's and Sofia's reestablishment of their relationship, for example, occurs when Sofia observes clear signs of her estranged husband's efforts to care for his ailing father in a manner that he would have previously rejected as "woman's work." Sofia tells Celie about Harpo's attempts to prevent his father's decline (a decline precipitated by an overwhelming guilt about his mistreatment of Celie and/or by his wife's leave-taking curse):

> Harpo went up there [to his father's house] plenty nights to sleep with him. . . . Mr. _____ would be all cram up in the corner of the bed. Eyes clamp on different pieces of furniture, see if they move in his direction. You know how little he is, say Sofia. And how big and stout Harpo is. Well, one night I was walking up to tell Harpo something—and the two of them was just laying there on the bed fast asleep. Harpo holding his daddy in his arms.
>
> After that, I start to feel again for Harpo, Sofia says. And pretty soon us start work on our new house. (201)

Their reunion comes about only when Harpo can openly demonstrate his capacity for tenderness. Their new relationship, while not altogether unproblematic, is made possible by Harpo's new willingness to respect his wife's decisions and not—as he had before—attempt to make her abide by his wishes.

Similarly, Celie's friendship with her formerly abusive husband occurs as a result of his repudiation of patriarchal attitudes. Celie describes the metamorphosis that Albert undergoes in the following way:

> look like he trying to make something out of himself. I don't mean just that he work and he clean up after himself and he appreciate some of the things God was playful enough to make. I mean when you talk to him now he really listen, and one time, out of nowhere in the conversation us was having, he said Celie, I'm satisfied this the first time I ever lived on Earth as a natural man. It feel like a new experience. (230)

Albert's new status as "natural man" is demonstrated in his response to Celie an Shug's romantic love for one another, a response that Celie says "really surprise me cause it so thoughtful and common sense":

> When it come to what folks do together with they bodies, he say, anybody's guess is as good as mine. But when you talk bout love

I don't have to guess. I have love and I have been love. And I thank God he let me gain understanding enough to know love can't be halted just cause some people moan and groan. It don't surprise me you love Shug Avery, he say. I have love Shug Avery all my life. (236-37)

Albert's repudiation of patriarchal authority serves to create possibilities of true communication between him and the protagonist.

What is perhaps most striking about Walker's figuration of Albert's transformation is the fact that the author places in the mouth of a formerly abusive male a refigured version of Janie's comments in *Their Eyes Were Watching God* about people's inability to accommodate love's less socially accepted manifestations. Clearly, Albert's insistence on a malicious community's inability to alter the course of love—"love can't be halted just cause some peoples moan and groan"—intentionally echoes Janie's instruction to Pheoby that she inform the "zigaboos" who condemn her for her relationship with a younger Tea Cake of love's subtle nuances. Janie says to Pheoby at the end of her story:

you must tell 'em that love ain't somethin lak uh grindstone dat's de same thing everywhere and do de same thing tuh everything it touch. Love is lak de sea. It's uh movin' thing, but still and all, it takes its shape from de shore it meets, and it's different with every shore. (284)

Albert's acceptance of (a lesbian) difference demonstrates that at the conclusion of *The Color Purple*, he has been granted the hard-won wisdom of Afro-American literature's most celebrated female character. He overcomes the effects of patriarchy to the extent that, like Janie, he is aware that love is "uh movin' thing"; he comprehends, in other words, the fact that true love is to be cherished, whatever its manifestations.

The instance of totalization that makes *The Color Purple* a fitting place to conclude this study of Afro-American women novelists' delineations of female attempts at (comm)unity is the achievement of an almost utopian society that is discussed in Celie's final epistolary entry. In this letter, which the protagonist addresses to a large audience ("Dear God. Dear stars, dear trees, dear sky, dear peoples. Dear Everything. Dear God" [249]), Celie records Nettie's return to her home along with her husband Samuel, Celie's children Adam and Olivia, and Adam's wife Tashi. What was formerly the site of a determined— if not altogether successful—patriarchal subjugation of females has become the locus of a felicitous and cooperative Black community. Liberation from patriarchal attitudes leads to the psychological rejuvenation of both male and female characters. As Celie says about her children's misconceptions regarding the community's more senior members:

> I see they think me and Nettie and Shug and Albert and Samuel and Harpo and Sofia and Jack and Odessa real old and don't know much what going on. But I don't think us feel old at all. And us so happy. Matter of fact, I think this the youngest us ever felt. (251)

The Color Purple suggests, in its final pages, the possible resolution of separation. Such resolution is represented as attaining—in ways that is true for neither *Their Eyes Were Watching God, The Bluest Eye,* or *The Woman of Brewster Place*—formal, individual, and tribal dimensions. Not only, as is the case with these other novels, do the distinct texts merge to achieve an expressive unity, but unlike these other works, (comm)unity is depicted as an actual narrative event.

Walker has suggested on numerous occasions her personal and artistic indebtedness to the life and texts (especially *Their Eyes Were Watching God*) of Zora Neale Hurston. *The Color Purple* can be profitably viewed as the subsequent writer's atempt to repay Hurston— the Afro-American female precursor par excellence of contemporary black women's literature—for her numerous contributions toward the preservation of the black woman's creative spirit. Certainly, such efforts on Walker's part include her marking of Hurston's grave and her editing of a collection of her literary forebear's writings.[23] But Walker's most significant form of remuneration is her figuration in *The Color Purple* of an Afro-American female's successful search for self-actualization and community that Hurston so powerfully inaugurates in the Afro-American literary tradition in *Their Eyes Were Watching God*. In her figuration of an achieved Afro-American community of equality between men and women, Walker creates a black female storyteller who triumphantly overcomes sexually oppressive conditions and (unlike Janie) is able to become a part of a community whose members appreciate her worth and her laborious efforts. *The Color Purple* serves both as the younger artist's fulfillment of the precursiorial Afro-American woman novelist's dream of female (comm)unity, and as a complex exploration of the liberating potentials of the communally oriented vernacular female voice.

Notes

Introduction

1. Ntozake Shange, *for colored girls who have considered suicide when the rainbow is enuf* (New York: Bantam, 1977), p. 2. Subsequent references to this choreopoem appear in the text in parentheses.

2. Mary Helen Washington, "Introduction," *Invented Lives* (Garden City, NY: Anchor, 1987), p. xx.

3. Alice Walker, *In Search of Our Mothers' Gardens* (San Diego: Harcourt Brace Jovanovich, 1983), p. 240. Subsequent references to this collection appear in the text in parentheses.

4. Barbara Smith, "Towards a Black Feminist Criticism," *The New Feminist Criticism*, Elaine Showalter, ed. (New York: Pantheon, 1985), p. 174. Subsequent references to this essay appear in the text in parentheses.

5. Despite my privileging here of notions of a self-consciously revisionary Afro-American women novelists' tradition, I am aware of Morrison's recent comments about her unfamiliarity with Hurston's corpus before she began her own literary career. Morrison says of attempts by critics to discern in her two first novels, *The Bluest Eye* and *Sula*, evidence of a Hurstonian influence: "many people who are trying to show certain kinds of connections between myself and Zora Neale Hurston are always dismayed and disappointed in me because I hadn't read Zora Neale Hurston except for one little short story before I began to write. . . . In their efforts to establish a tradition, that bothers them a little bit. And I said, 'No, no, you should be happy about that.' Because the fact that I had never read Zora Neale Hurston and wrote *The Bluest Eye* and *Sula* anyway means that the tradition really exists. You know, if I had read her, then you could say that I consciously was following in the footsteps of her, but the fact that I never read her and still there may be whatever they're finding, similarities and dissimilarities, . . . makes the cheese more binding, not less, because it means that the world as perceived by black women at certain times does exist, however they treat it and whatever they select out of it to record, there is that." Gloria Naylor and Toni Morrison, "A Conversation," *Southern Review* (1985), 21(3):589-90)

Morrison's comments offer support for Smith's contentions that the sources of textual affinities between works in the Afro-American women's literary tradition can be a common cultural experience. Such comments, however, differ significantly from Gloria Naylor's and Alice Walker's expressed needs early in their careers for black female precursors. Walker talks about her need for an Afro-American female artistic model (a need that leads to her famous, laudatory discussions of Hurston and her own oratorically skilled mother) in *In Search Of Our Mothers' Gardens*, and Gloria Naylor insists in "A Conversation" that Morrison's own *The*

Bluest Eye "gave me a validity to do something [become a writer] which I had thought was really male terrain" (575). If the connections between Hurston's and Morrison's novels are indeed accidental, or, in Smith's formulations, are experiential and not textual in origin, I hope nonetheless to show in chapter 2 that such connections are, at the very least, significant and evidence of a racially and sexually motivated black female psychic duality for whose aesthetically sophisticated figuration Afro-American expressive culture has provided provocative—and durable—models.

6. Henry Louis Gates, Jr., "The 'Blackness of Blackness': A Critique of the Sign and the Signifying Monkey," *Black Literature and Literary Theory*, Gates, ed. (New York: Methuen, 1984), p. 290. All subsequent references to this essay appear in the text in parentheses.

7. Sandra Gilbert and Susan Gubar, *The Madwoman in the Attic* (New Haven: Yale University Press, 1979), p. 49. Subsequent references to this study appear in the text in parentheses.

8. James Snead, "Repetition as a Figure in Black Culture," *Black Literature and Literary Theory*, p. 66.

9. Harold Bloom, *Poetry and Repression* (New Haven: Yale University Press, 1976), p. 6.

10. Judith Kegan Gardiner, "On Female Identity and Writing by Women," *Writing and Sexual Difference*, Elizabeth Abel, ed. (Chicago: University of Chicago Press, 1982), p. 186. Subsequent page references to this essay appear in the text in parentheses.

11. While I see the textual system with which I am concerned here as primarily cooperative, it also tends toward vehement and corrective revision of works by black men that either ignore or misrepresent the complexity of Afro-American women's lives. For example, as chapter 2 of this study will suggest, Morrison's *The Bluest Eye* can be seen—at least in part—as a feminist revision of the Trueblood episode in Ralph Ellison's *Invisible Man*, a novel which fails to explore in any depth the potential ramifications of incest for the sharecropper's daughter, Matty Lou.

12. Mikhail Bakhtin, "Discourse in the Novel," *The Dialogic Imagination*, Michael Holquist, ed., Caryl Emerson and Michael Holquist, trs. (Austin: University of Texas Press, 1981), pp. 293-94.

13. *The American Heritage Dictionary of the English Language*, William Morris, ed. (Boston: Houghton Mifflin, 1980), p. 352. Subsequent references to this entry appear in the text in parentheses.

14. Toni Morrison, "Rootedness: The Ancestor as Foundation," *Black Women Writers (1950-1980)*, Mari Evans, ed. (New York: Doubleday, 1984), pp. 341-342. Subsequent page references to this statement appear in the text in parentheses.

15. Geneva Smitherman, *Talkin and Testifyin* (Boston: Houghton Mifflin, 1977), p. 30. Subsequent page references to this study appear in the text in parentheses.

16. Raymond Hedin, "The Structuring of Emotion in Black American Fiction," *Novel* (1982), 16(1):49. Subsequent page references to this essay appear in the text in parentheses.

17. Toni Morrison, *The Bluest Eye* (New York: Washington Square Press, 1970), p. 157.

18. W. E. B. Du Bois, *The Souls of Black Folk*, 1903 (New York: Signet, 1969), p. 45.

19. Michel Foucault, "What Is an Author?" *Language, Counter-Memory, Practice*,

Donald Bouchard, ed.; Bouchard and Sherry Simon, trs.,(Ithaca: Cornell University Press, 1977), p. 131. Subsequent page references to this essay appear in the text in parentheses.

20. Zora Neale Hurston, *Their Eyes Were Watching God*, 1937 (Urbana: University of Illinois Press, 1978), p. 17 (my emphasis). All subsequent references to this novel appear in the text in parentheses.

1. "The Inaudible Voice of It All"

1. Barbara Johnson, "Metaphor, Metonymy and Voice in *Their Eyes Were Watching God*," *Black Literature and Literary Theory*, Henry Louis Gates, Jr., ed. (New York: Methuen, 1984), p. 212. All subsequent references to this essay appear in the text in parentheses.

2. Cheryl Wall, "Zora Neale Hurston: Changing Her Own Words," *American Novelists Revisited: Essays in Feminist Criticism*, Fritz Fleischmann, ed. (Boston: G. K. Hall, 1982), p. 384. All subsequent references to this essay appear in the text in parentheses.

3. Missy Dehn Kubitschek, " 'Tuh De Horizon And Back': The Female Quest in *Their Eyes Were Watching God*," *Black American Literature Forum* (1983), 17(3):109. All subsequent references to this essay appear in the text in parentheses.

4. Zora Neale Hurston, *Their Eyes Were Watching God*, 1937 (Urbana: University of Illinois Press, 1978), p. 17. All references to this novel subsequently will appear in the text in parentheses.

5. For examples of descriptions of this scene as Janie's sexual awakening, see Wall, pp. 384-85; Kubitschek, p. 110; and Lloyd Brown, "Zora Neale Hurston and the Nature of Female Perception," *Obsidian* (1978), 4(3):40.

6. Zora Neale Hurston, "Characteristics of Negro Expression," *Negro: An Anthology*, Nancy Cunard, ed., 1934 (London: Negro University Press, 1969), p. 43.

7. Hurston, "Characteristics," p. 39.

8. Maria Tai Wolff, "Listening and Living: Reading and Experience in *Their Eyes Were Watching God*," *Black American Literature Forum* (1982), 16(1):30-32. Subsequent page references to this essay appear in the text in parentheses.

9. Houston A. Baker, Jr., *Blues, Ideology, and Afro-American Literature* (Chicago: University of Chicago Press, 1984), p. 57.

10. Lillie Howard, "Nanny and Janie: Will The Twain Ever Meet?" *Journal of Black Studies* (1982), 12(4):407 and 405.

11. Zora Neale Hurston, "How It Feels To Be Colored Me," *I Love Myself When I Am Laughing*, Alice Walker, ed. (Old Westbury, N.Y.: Feminist Press, 1979), p. 155.

12. For a full discussion of otherworldly redemption as an emphasis in Black religion, see Olin P. Moyd, *Redemption in Black Theology* (Valley Forge, Pa.: Judson Press, 1979).

13. Ralph Ellison, *Invisible Man* (New York: Random House, 1952), p. 499.

14. Ishmael Reed, "Dualism: in ralph ellison's invisible man," *Conjure: Selected Poems, 1963-1970* (Amherst: University of Massachusetts Press, 1972), p. 317.

15. Henry Louis Gates, Jr., " 'The Blackness of Blackness': A Critique of the Sign and the Signifying Monkey," *Black Literature and Literary Theory*, Gates, ed. (New York: Methuen, 1984), p. 317. Subsequent references to this essay appear in the text in parentheses.

16. For a masterful discussion of the difficulties inherent in the distinction in Gates' theoretical framework between "literature" and "social institutions," see Baker, *Blues, Ideology, and Afro-American Literature*, pp. 99-112.

17. Hurston, "How It Feels To Be Colored Me," p. 155.

18. The text tells us of Janie who has just discovered the benefits of self-conscious self-division: "She wasn't petal-open with [Starks]. She was twenty-four and seven years married when she knew. She found that out one day when he slapped her face in the kitchen" (111). When the next chapter begins, Janie is a long-suffering, silent partner in her marriage who can perceive no substantial benefits in escaping her oppression. The text states: "Now and again she thought of a country road at sun-up and considered flight. To where? To what? Then too she considered thirty-five is twice seventeen and nothing was the same at all" (118).

19. Robert Stepto, *From Behind the Veil* (Urbana: University of Illinois Press, 1979), p. 165. Subsequent references to this study appear in the text in parentheses.

20. For critics who either imply or state explicitly that Janie and Tea Cake share equal power in their marriage, see Wendy McCredie, "Authority and Authorization in *Their Eyes Were Watching God*," *Black American Literature Forum* (1982), 16(1):28; Wall, p. 388; and Kubitschek, p. 111.

21. Wendy McCredie, "Authority and Authorization in *Their Eyes Were Watching God*," *Black American Literature Forum* (1982), 16(1):28. Subsequent references to this essay appear in the text in parentheses.

22. Lloyd Brown, "Zora Neale Hurston and the Nature of Female Perception," *Obsidian* (1978), 4(3):44-45. Subsequent references to this essay appear in the text in parentheses.

23. Darwin Turner, *In a Minor Chord* (Carbondale: Southern Illinois Press, 1971), p. 109.

24. Robert Hemenway, *Zora Neale Hurston: A Literary Biography* (Urbana: University of Illinois Press, 1977), p. 233.

25. Deborah McDowell, "New Directions for Black Feminist Criticism," *Black American Literature Forum* (1980), 14(4):153.

26. The narrator of *The Bluest Eye* (New York: Washington Square Press, 1970) says of Pecola's spatial confinement: "She had long given up the idea of running away to see new pictures, new faces, as [her brother] Sammy had so often done. He never took her, and he never thought about his going ahead of time, so it was never planned. It wouldn't have worked anyway. As long as she looked the way she did, as long as she was ugly, she would have to stay with these people [her parents]. Somehow she belonged to them" (39).

27. In *Sula* (New York: Bantam, 1974), Eva's trip (during which she loses a leg) remains a mystery. What she does to earn money and how she actually loses her leg are never explained either by the narrator or by Eva. There are, however, myths which attempt to explain the leg's disappearance, the most compelling of which has Eva sticking her leg onto the tracks of a moving train as a means to collect insurance money with which to support her children (pp. 26-27, 80). Sula's journey, while not as shrouded in mystery as Eva's trip, nonetheless is not documented in the text. It is Sula's presence within her community that is the narrative's focus; all the reader learns of Sula's journey is that it is ultimately unsatisfying: "Nel was one of the reasons she had drifted back to Medallion, that and the boredom she found in Nashville, Detroit, New Orleans, New York, Philadelphia, Macon and San Diego. All those cities held the same people, working the same mouths, sweat-

ing the same sweat. The men who took her to one or another of those places had merged into one large personality: the same language of love, the same entertainments of love, the same cooling of love. Whenever she introduced her private thoughts into their rubbings or goings, they hooded their eyes. They taught her nothing but love tricks, shared nothing but worry, gave nothing but money. She had been looking all along for a friend, and it took her a while to discover that a lover was not a comrade and could never be—for a woman" (104).

28. McDowell says that contextual approaches to black women's literature are necessary to explicate successfully their imaginative power: "Regardless of which theoretical framework Black feminist critics choose, they must have an informed handle on Black literature and Black culture in general . . .

"This footing in Black history and culture serves as a basis for the study of the literature. [Such an approach is t]ermed 'contextual' by theoreticians. . . . I firmly believe that the contextual approach to Black women's literature exposes the conditions under which literature is produced, published, and reviewed. This approach is not only useful but necessary to Black feminist critics" ("New Directions," p. 156).

29. Geneva Smitherman, *Talkin and Testifyin* (Boston: Houghton Mifflin, 1977), p. 104. Subsequent references to this study appear in the text in parentheses.

30. Perhaps the best example of call and response in *Their Eyes Were Watching God* occurs during the surrealistic buzzard's funeral for Matt's mule. When the "audience" or crowd of buzzards has verified that the mule is dead, the "leader" buzzard lands on the carcass and asks:

> " 'What killed this man?' "
> "The chorus answered, 'Bare, bare fat.'
> " 'What killed this man?' "
> " 'Bare, bare fat,' "
> " 'What killed this man?' "
> " 'Bare, bare fat.' "
> " 'Who'll stand his funeral?' "
> " 'We!!!!!' "
> " 'Well, all right now' " (97).

31. John Blassingame, *The Slave Community* (New York: Oxford University Press, 1979), p. 127.

2. "The evil of fulfillment"

1. Toni Morrison, "Behind the Making of *The Black Book*," *Black World*, February 1974, p. 89.

2. Toni Morrison, *The Bluest Eye* (New York: Washington Square Press, 1970), p. 157. All references to Morrison's novel are hereafter marked by page numbers in parentheses in the text.

3. Toni Morrison, "Rootedness: The Ancestor as Foundation," *Black Women Writers (1950-1980)*, Mari Evans, ed. (New York: Doubleday, 1984), p. 343. Subsequent references to this piece appear in the text in parentheses.

4. See Wright's *Native Son* (New York: Harper and Row, 1940) and *Black Boy* (New York: Harper and Row, 1945), and Baldwin's *Go Tell It On The Mountain*

(New York: Dell, 1953) and the title essay of *Notes of a Native Son* (New York: Bantam, 1955), pp. 71-95.

5. See the famous essays "Everybody's Protest Novel" and "Many Thousands Gone" in *Notes of a Native Son*, pp. 9-17 and 18-36 respectively.

6. James Baldwin, "Alas, Poor Richard," *Nobody Knows My Name* (New York: Dial, 1961), p. 197. Subsequent page references to this essay appear in the text in parentheses.

7. "Strong" is Harold Bloom's term for discursively and tropologically competitive poets whose strength suggests itself in a willingness to battle influential precursors. See Bloom's extremely "influential" study *The Anxiety of Influence* (New York: Oxford University Press, 1973) for the critic's initial definitions of poetic strength.

8. Phyllis Klotman, "Dick-and-Jane and the Shirley Temple Sensibility in *The Bluest Eye*," *Black American Literature Forum* (1979), 13(4):123.

9. Raymond Hedin, "The Structuring of Emotion in Black American Fiction," *Novel* (1982), 16(1):123.

10. Robert Stepto, *From Behind the Veil* (Urbana: University of Illinois Press, 1979).

11. *Black Women Writers at Work*, Claudia Tate, ed. (New York: Continuum, 1983), p. 122.

12. Ralph Ellison, "The World and the Jug," *Shadow and Act* (New York: Vintage, 1964), p. 140.

13. Nikki Giovanni, "Nikka-Rosa," *Black Feelings, Black Talk, Black Judgment* (New York: William Morrow, 1970), pp. 58-59.

14. Victor Turner, *Dramas, Fields, and Metaphors* (Ithaca: Cornell University Press, 1974), p. 233. Subsequent references to this study appear in the text in parentheses.

15. See Jacqueline De Weever, "The Inverted World of Toni Morrison's *The Bluest Eye* and *Sula*," *College Language Association Journal* (1979), 22(4):402.

16. Ralph Ellison, *Invisible Man* (New York: Vintage, 1952). Subsequent page references to this novel appear in the text in parentheses.

17. Zora Neale Hurston, *Their Eyes Were Watching God*, 1937 (Urbana: University of Illinois Press, 1978), p. 216. Subsequent references to Hurston's novel will appear in the text in parentheses.

18. Susan Willis, "Eruptions of Funk: Historicizing Toni Morrison," *Black Literature and Literary Theory*, Henry Louis Gates, Jr., ed. (New York: Methuen, 1984), p. 264. Subsequent references to this essay will appear in the text in parentheses.

19. See *Native Son*, pp. 89-91.

20. James Baldwin, "Many Thousands Gone," p. 30. Subsequent references to this essay appear in the text in parentheses.

21. Most significant of the flaws in Ogunyemi's essay is the critic's suggestion that Morrison "has fictionalized those sociological factors discussed in [Calvin] Hernton's *Sex and Racism in America* without first distancing herself enough from that work." In "Order and Disorder in Toni Morrison's *The Bluest Eye*," *Critique* (1977), 19(1):118. This comment implies that Morrison—like the African critic— needs Hernton's text to explain to her the nature of sexism and racism in America. Also see his discussions of Mrs. MacTeer's "hypocrisy" vis-à-vis her permitting Pecola to live in the MacTeer household temporarily, and his view that the family "merely tolerated her."

22. Chikwenye Ogunyemi, "Order and Disorder in Toni Morrison's *The Bluest Eye*," *Critique*, p. 116.

23. Erich Neumann, *Depth Psychology and a New Ethic*, 1949 (New York: Putnam, 1969), p. 50. Subsequent references to this study appear in the text in parentheses.

24. See James Weldon Johnson, *The Autobiography of an Ex-Colored Man, 1912 (New York: Hill and Wang, 1960)* and Nella Larsen, *Passing*, in *Quicksand and Passing*, Deborah McDowell, ed. 1929 (New Brunswick, N.J.: Rutgers University Press, 1986).

25. W. E. B. Du Bois, *The Souls of Black Folk*, 1903 (New York: Signet, 1969), p. 45.

26. See the description of Cholly's interrupted sexual initiation, *The Bluest Eye*, pp. 114-21.

27. Houston A. Baker, Jr., *Blues, Ideology, and Afro-American Literature* (Chicago: University of Chicago Press, 1984), p. 185. Unless otherwise noted, subsequent references to this study will appear in the text in parentheses.

28. Annette Kolodny, "The Map of Rereading," *The New Feminist Criticism*, Elaine Showalter, ed. (New York: Pantheon, 1985), p. 59.

29. Judith Fetterley, *The Resisting Reader* (Bloomington: Indiana University Press, 1978), p. xii. Subsequent references to this study appear in the text in parentheses.

30. See *Blues, Ideology, and Afro-American Literature*, pp. 50-56.

31. Ralph Ellison, "Richard Wright's Blues," *Shadow and Act*, p. 94.

32. "Richard Wright's Blues," p. 94, my emphasis.

33. Clifford Geertz, *The Interpretation of Cultures* (New York: Basic Books, 1973), p. 417.

34. Henry Louis Gates, Jr., "The Blackness of Blackness: A Critique of the Sign and the Signifying Monkey," *Black Literature and Literary Theory*, p. 293.

35. Phyllis Klotman, "Dick-and-Jane and the Shirley Temple Sensibility in *The Bluest Eye*," p. 125.

36. Toni Morrison, *Song of Solomon* (New York: Signet, 1977), pp. 169, 341.

3. Authorial Dreams of Wholeness

1. Clifford Geertz, *Local Knowledge* (New York: Basic Books, 1983), p. 102.

2. It is possible to suggest that the structure and conclusion of *The Women of Brewster Place* refigure and parody most directly Shange's important choreopoem. While *for colored girls* offers the stories of seven spatially divided female characters who suffer in an oppressively patriarchal Afro-America and ultimately concludes with the joyous songs of a unified black female community, Naylor's "novel in seven stories" ends with what is literally a dream of female (comm)unity. But Mattie's dream, as I will discuss at length later in this essay, suggests, unlike the conclusion of Shange's choreopoem, the utter difficulty of achieving female nexus in an American society that is not radically transformed in terms of its debilitating racism and sexism. Read intertextually, Naylor's text offers a bold criticism of the utopian resolution of *for colored girls*.

3. Elaine Showalter, "Feminist Criticism in the Wilderness," *The New Feminist Criticism*, Showalter, ed. (New York: Pantheon, 1985), p. 265. Subsequent references to this essay appear in the text in parentheses.

4. Sandra Gilbert, "What Do Feminist Critics Want?" *The New Feminist Criticism*, p. 32.

5. Gloria Naylor, *The Women of Brewster Place* (New York: Penguin, 1983), p. 1. All subsequent references to this novel appear in the text in parentheses.

6. Jean Toomer, *Cane*, 1923 (New York: Liveright, 1975), p. 39. All references to Toomer's work are hereafter marked by page numbers in the text.

7. "Famous First Words," *New York Times Book Review*, June 2, 1985, p. 52.

8. It would generally be extremely problematic to argue that a literary artist is consciously employing deconstructionist theories either in her own texts or in her interpretations of the works of others. But Naylor did spend two years in New Haven earning an M. A. at Yale, the indisputable hotbed of deconstruction in America, and her comments—and, as I will demonstrate, her first novel—suggest that she absorbed a good deal of its theoretical suppositions.

9. Jonathan Culler, *On Deconstruction* (Ithaca: Cornell University Press, 1982), p. 249. Subsequent references to this study appear in the text in parentheses.

10. Harold Bloom, *A Map of Misreading* (New York: Oxford University Press, 1975), p. 3.

11. Toni Morrison, *The Bluest Eye* (New York: Washington Square Press, 1970), p. 157. Subsequent references to this novel are hereafter marked by page numbers in parentheses in the text.

12. "Famous First Words," p. 52.

13. Donald Gibson, *The Politics of Literary Expression* (Westport, Conn.: Greenwood Press, 1981), p. 4.

14. In an age when so many critics discuss literature's discursive properties and exclude the mimetic qualities of literature from their analyses, Gibson's "social theory of literature" is refreshing. But in disputing theories of literature which insist "that literature has a nature and character exclusively its own" (6), Gibson overlooks intertextual relations between works of expressive art which have as much to do with individual authors' attempts to establish themselves as writers as they do with their efforts to recreate their social realities in an imaginative way. For Gibson, every authorial impulse has a strictly social origin, an assessment which, it seems to me, fails to account fully for revisionary gestures of the sort that the study examines.

15. Jean Strouse, "Black Magic," *Newsweek*, March 30, 1981, p. 56.

16. Toni Morrison, "Behind the Making of *The Black Book*," *Black World*, February 1974, p. 89.

17. Michele Wallace, "Blues for Mr. Spielberg," *Village Voice* (1986), 31(11):24.

18. Anne Barton, Introduction to *A Midsummer Night's Dream*, *The Riverside Shakespeare*, G. Blakemore Evans, textual ed. (Boston: Houghton Mifflin, 1974), p. 219.

19. Judith Branzburg, "Seven Women and a Wall," *Callaloo* (1984), 7(3):118.

20. Zora Neale Hurston, *Their Eyes Were Watching God*, 1937 (Urbana: University of Illinois Press, 1978), p. 9. All subsequent references to this novel appear in the text in parentheses.

21. Lloyd Brown, "Zora Neale Hurston and the Nature of Female Perception," *Obsidian* (1978), 4(3):39-40.

22. Ntozake Shange, *for colored girls who have considered suicide when the rainbow is enuf* (New York: Bantam, 1977), p. 66. Subsequent references to this choreopoem appear in the text in parentheses.

23. For a similar scene of salvific bathing of a symbolically reborn Afro-American female protagonist—a scene with clear intertextual connections to both Shange and Naylor—see Paule Marshall, *Praisesong for the Widow* (New York: Dutton, 1983), pp. 217-24.

24.. Barbara Johnson, "Metaphor, Metonymy and Voice in *Their Eyes Were*

Watching God," Black Literature and Literary Theory, Henry Louis Gates, Jr., ed. (New York: Methuen, 1984), p. 213.

25.. Naylor subtly suggests that Kiswana Browne and, more specifically, Browne's story, do not "belong" in *The Women of Brewster Place*. Not only does her story fail to conform to the general patterns of the novel's other stories, but Kiswana also never succeeds in becoming a part of the female community that Mattie Michael envisions in "The Block Party."

26. Barbara Bowen, "Untroubled Voice: Call and Response in *Cane*," *Black Literature and Literary Theory*, p. 196.

27. Quoted by Charles T. Davis, "Jean Toomer and the South: Region and Race as Elements within a Literary Imagination," *Studies in the Literary Imagination* (1974), 7(2):32.

28. Quoted by Darwin Turner, Introduction to *Cane* (New York: Liveright, 1975), p. xvi. Subsequent references to this introduction appear in the text in parentheses.

29. Waldo Frank, "Foreword" to *Cane* (New York: Boni and Liveright, 1923), p. x.

30. Houston A. Baker, Jr. *Singers of Daybreak* (Washington, D.C.: Howard University Press, 1974), p. 61.

4. *The Color Purple* and the Achievement of (Comm)unity

1. Alice Walker, "In Search of Our Mothers' Gardens," *In Search of Our Mothers' Gardens* (San Diego: Harcourt Brace Jovanovich, 1983), p. 232. Subsequent references to this essay appear in the text in parentheses.

2. In "Zora Neale Hurston: A Cautionary Tale and a Partisan View," Walker writes that "Toomer's *Cane* comes close" in her estimation to *Their Eyes Were Watching God*, but "from what I realize is a more perilous direction" (*In Search of Our Mothers' Gardens*, p. 86), while in the same collection, in a piece entitled "The Divided Life of Jean Toomer," she derides Toomer for his abandonment of blackness (pp. 60-65).

3. "The Divided Life of Jean Toomer," pp. 61-62.

4. Trudier Harris, "On *The Color Purple*, Stereotypes, and Silence," *Black American Literature Forum* (1984), 18(4):155, 158. Subsequent references to this essay appear in the text in parentheses.

5. In "In Search of Our Mothers' Gardens," Walker says: "Only recently did I realize this: that through years of listening to my mother's stories of her life, I have absorbed not only the stories themselves, but something of the manner in which she spoke, something of the urgency that involves the knowledge that her stories—like her life—must be recorded" (p. 230).

6. Rachel Blau DuPlessis, *Writing beyond the Ending* (Bloomington: Indiana University Press, 1985), p. 93. Subsequent references to this study appear in the text in parentheses.

7. Dolan Hubbard, "An Interview with Richard Barksdale," *Black American Literature Forum* (1985), 19(4):144.

8. Alice Walker, *The Color Purple* (New York: Washington Square Press, 1982), p. 11. All subsequent references to this novel appear in the text in parentheses.

9. Barbara Smith, "Sexual Oppression Unmasked," *Callaloo* (1984), 7(4):171.

10. See especially Robert Stepto, *From Behind the Veil* (Urbana: University of Illinois Press, 1979).

11. Frederick Douglass, *Narrative of the Life of Frederick Douglass*, 1845. (New York: Signet, 1968), p. 49. Subsequent references to this narrative appear in the text in parentheses.

12. John Blassingame, *The Slave Community* (New York: Oxford University Press, 1972), p. 129.

13. See, for example, Hubbard's "An Interview with Richard Barksdale," p. 144.

14. Janet Gurkin Altman, *Epistolarity* (Columbus: Ohio State University Press, 1982), p. 89. Subsequent references to this tudy appear in the text in parentheses.

15. Michael Harper, "Gayl Jones: An Interview," *Chants of Saints*, Michael Harper and Robert Stepto, eds. (Urbana: University of Illinois Press, 1979), pp. 355, 374-75.

16. Toni Morrison, "Rootedness: The Ancestor as Foundation," *Black Women Writers (1950-1980)*, Mari Evans, ed. (New York: Doubleday, 1984), p. 341.

17. See Kimberly Benston, "I Yam What I Am: The Topos of (Un)naming in Afro-American Literature," *Black Literature and Literacy Theory*, Henry Louis Gates, Jr., ed. (New York: Methuen, 1984), pp. 151-72.

18. Of course, Mary Agnes' transformation is not without problems, particularly when she takes up with Grady and begins to abuse drugs to the extent that they blunt her creative talents. She does, however, recover from her chemical dependency and becomes, like her mentor Shug, a successful traveling blues woman.

19. Quoted in Trudier Harris, "On *The Color Purple*, Stereotypes, and Silence," p. 157.

20. Zora Neale Hurston, *Their Eyes Were Watching God*, 1937 (Urbana: University of Illinois Press, 1978), p. 24. Subsequent references to this novel appear in text in parentheses.

21. Gerald Graff, *Literature Against Itself* (Chicago: University of Chicago Press, 1979), p. 60. Subsequent references to Graff's study appear in the text in parentheses.

22. See "Looking for Zora," *In Search of our Mothers' Gardens*, pp. 93-116, for Walker's fascinating account of her attempt to find her female precursor's grave.

23. I am referring, of course, to the episode recounted in "Looking for Zora" and to *I Love Myself When I Am Laughing: A Zora Neale Hurston Reader*, Alice Walker, ed. (Old Westbury, N.Y.: Feminist Press, 1979).

Index